W. H. Irwin

City of Kingston

Alphabetical, general, miscellaneous and classified Business Directory

W. H. Irwin

City of Kingston
Alphabetical, general, miscellaneous and classified Business Directory

ISBN/EAN: 9783337146528

Printed in Europe, USA, Canada, Australia, Japan

Cover: Foto ©ninafisch / pixelio.de

More available books at **www.hansebooks.com**

THE CITY OF KINGSTON.

The fifth City in Ontario in population, is situated at the head of the St. Lawrence River and the end of Lake Ontario. It is the principal port for lake navigation in Ontario possessing the largest and finest harbour in the country. It is a station of the Grand Trunk Railway, and the head quarters of the Kingston and Pembroke Railway. The Public Buildings are very beautiful, the City Hall (the finest one in the Province) the Court House, Post Office, Custom House, Queen's University and College, the Churches and a number of business blocks and private residences. At the Western boundary is located the Kingston Penitentiary and about a mile west of it the Kingston Asylum for the Insane; opposite the city is the Royal Canadian Military College, and Garden and Wolfe Islands. Kingston is a military as well as naval city. Here is stationed 'B' Battery and a troop of cavalry, besides a local troop, a battery, and the 14th Prince of Wales' Own Rifles. The principal business streets are Princess, and parts of Wellington, Bagot, Clarence, Ontario, Brock, Market Square, Montreal, Queen etc., all connected by the Kingston Street Railway. There are two Daily Papers published, *The British Whig*, and the *Daily News*, both papers having weekly editions also. The city returns one member for the Dominion Parliament, Mr. Alex. Gunn, and one for the Local House, Mr. James H. Metcalfe. Kingston enjoys the proud position of being the soundest city financially, its merchants being considered the most prudent and safest men to deal with. The Limestone City, as it is sometimes called, is also the cleanest and healthiest city in Ontario, being built on the solid rock. A new Union Station is about to be built which will greatly add to the city's prosperity, and Kingston bids at no distant date to be one of the foremost cities of the Province. Kingston is distant from Toronto 161 miles, Montreal 172, Quebec 344, Ottawa 95, Hamilton 200, London (Ont.) 276, Detroit 386, St. John, N. B., 752, Halifax 828, and Liverpool 2414 miles. Population 15,000 ; with suburbs of Portsmouth, Barriefield and Garden Island, 17.500.

THE DENTAPHONE.

A recent Scientific Invention, by means of which the deaf hear from the teeth. The sound vibrations are conveyed through the bones of the face and head by new channels to the nerves of hearing.

It consists of a thin flexible diaphragm, and weighs but a few ounces, can be folded and carried like a fan; which it resembles.

EXTRACTS FROM THE PRESS.

FROM THE REV. ISAAC ERRETT,
Editor of Christian Standard.

The Dentaphone is all that it claims to be.

February 20th, 1883.

It was found that the deaf, and partially deaf, could readily hear anything spoken in the room in an ordinary tone of voice.

Pittsburg Presbyterian Banner, Pa.

So carefully has the instrument been tested and so reliable is it in its effects that a man totally deaf for 40 years, was enabled by its aid to hear distinctly.

New York Christian Observer.

The efficacy of the Dentaphone is beyond all question, and it has the unqualified endorsement of leading journals in whose offices experiments and tests were conducted.

FRANK LESLIE'S,
Illustrated Weekly Journal,

The folding fan Dentaphone, is without doubt the best known form of apparatus for conveying sound to the auditory nerve.

The Medical and Surgical Reporter, Philadelphia, Pa.

I have no doubt that the Dentaphone will in time supersede every form of that very inconvenient instrument, the ear trumpet, and I believe aurists can make use of it in diagnosis of disease of the ear.

W. A. RATTACK, M.D.,
Prof. Pathology and Surgery, Cincinnati Medical College.

I have been partially deaf for six years. I find the Dentaphone of great value. I unhesitatingly recommend it to those similarly effected.

REV. FATHER J. H. BURWINKEL, Cincinnati, O.

My Daughter has been 22 years deaf. She finds it of great service in church, and values it very highly and hardly knows how she would get along without.

JAMES E. HUTT, Fenwick, Ont.

There are two sizes of this instrument. The ordinary conversational, $12.00. The Concert and Lecture, extra power, $18.00.

Addresss, **JOHN M. CAMPBELL & CO.,**
2 McNab St. South, Hamilton. General Agents.

Miscellaneous Directory.

CITY COUNCIL, 1883.

Charles Livingston, Mayor; William Allen, John Carson, Robert J. Carson. Leonard Clements, William J. Crothers, George Creeggan, James Downing, William Dunn, Charles F. Gildersleeve, William D. Gordon, William Irving, Edward Law, Thomas H. McGuire, John McIntyre, Joseph Quigley, James Redden, Felix Shaw, Edward H. Smythe, John L. Whiting, James Wilson, William Wilson, Aldermen.

CITY OFFICIALS.—Michael Flanagan, Clerk; Frank C. Ireland, Treasurer James Agnew, Solicitor; William S. Gordon, Assessor and Commissioner; William Coverdale, Surveyor and Engineer; Lewis Middleton, Collector; Alexr. Smyth, Clerk of Market and Harbor Master; Andrew Lanigan, Messenger; John Duff, Police Magistrate; E. J. Barker, Registrar; Fred. J. George, Deputy Registrar.

POLICE DEPARTMENT.—Edwin Horsey, Chief; Robert Bell, Sergeant-Major; Robert Carson, Sergeant; Dennis Sullivan, Detective; William Hoyle, William Hinde, Matthew Campbell, Robert Nesbitt, James Nesbitt, Samuel McCormack, Alexander Snodden, Charles Thompson, Philip H. Small, Constables.

FIRE DEPARTMENT.—Edwin Horsey, Chief; P. Devlin, 1st Assistant; David Hall, 2nd Assistant; Matthew Bateson, Foreman; William Little, Assistant Foreman; J. W. Davis, Secretary; W. McCammon, Treasurer.

FIRE ALARM.—No. 1, St. Lawrence Ward; 2, Ontario Ward; 3, St. Paul's Church, cor. Queen and Montreal street; 4, Montreal Road; 5, All Saints' Church, Division street; 6, George Newland's, Princess and Chatham streets; 7, Corner Barrie and Princess streets; 8, Corner Earl and Barrie streets; 9, Queen's College gate, Arch street; 12, corner King and Gordon streets; 13, Dr. Strange's, cor. King and Union streets; 14, Royal Military College; 15, General Hospital; 22, Locomotive Works.

TRUSTEES.

COLLEGIATE INSTITUTE.—James McCammon, M.D., Chairman; M. Sullivan, M.D., E. H. Smythe, LL.D., William Irving, E. J. B. Pense, George A. Kirkpatrick, M.P.

PUBLIC SCHOOLS.—W. Allen, S. Anglin, W. M. Drennan, W. Dunlop, S. H. Fee, R. M. Horsey, W. Irving, N. C. Polson, W. Robinson, R. V. Rogers, H. B. Savage, R. Shaw, G. R. Waldron, J. Wilson, G. R. Waldron, Chairman; S. S. Phippen, Secretary; W. G. Kidd, Inspector.

SEPARATE SCHOOLS.—Rev. P. A. Twohey, Chairman; W. H. Sullivan, Secretary; P. Smith, E. Garvin, B. Nelligan, O. Tierney, J. McMahon, W. Power, A. Handley, W. Leahey, D. Driscoll, M. Flynn, James Campbell.

KINGSTON POST OFFICE.

James Shannon, Postmaster; William Shannon, Assistant Postmaster; John Kelly, Clerk Registered Letter Department; Robert T. Burns, Clerk Money Order Department; William S. Smyth, Clerk General Delivery; John G. Strachan, James P. Pense, James McBride, Charles W. Macdonald, John L. Renton, Robert A. Adair, Frederick C. Voigt, Clerks; A. H. Miller, Superintendent of Letter Carriers; John Collins, Robert Lewers, L. Paladeau, S. A. McCammon, William O'Reilly, Letter Carriers; Henry Dunbar, Messenger.

Positions of Street Letter Boxes.—1, corner Queen and Ontario streets; 2, corner Montreal and Bay streets; 3, corner Bagot and Queen streets; 4, corner of Princess and Bagot streets; 5, Windsor Hotel, Princess street; 6, corner Clergy and Colborne streets; 7, corner Division and Elm streets; 8, corner Barrie and Princess streets; 9, corner Union and Sydenham streets; 10, Barrie street near Queen's College; 11, Drill Shed; 12, cor. King and Beverly streets, Grove Inn; 13, corner King and Barrie streets; 14, corner King and Union streets; 15, Earl and Ontario streets.

Stamp Vendors.—Charles Hentig, Post Office Lobby. A. Maclean, Ontario street. A. A. Simmons, King street. Elizabeth Delaney, Princess street. G. S. Hobart, Princess street. Henry Wade, corner King and Brock streets. J. G. King, Market Square. John Henderson & Co., Princess street. James Moore, Wellington street. N. C. Polson, Princess street. T. McAuley, King street. Wilson Bros., Princess street. W. J. Wilson, Princess street.

Inspector's Department—*(Over Post Office).*—Gilbert Griffin, Inspector; Allan Jones, Assistant Inspector; Jeremiah Meagher, P. H. Macarow, J. E. Hopkirk, J. C. Strange, Staff; F. Scobell, W. D. Abercrombie, John Hoyland, Railway Mail Clerks.

CUSTOM HOUSE.

(Cor. King and Clarence Streets.)

C. Hamilton, Collector; A. Macalister, Surveyor; A. Shaw, Chief Clerk; R. D. Anglin, 2nd Clerk; M. S. Haddigan, 3rd Clerk; W. Neish, 4th Clerk; T. Driver, Appraiser; T. Meagher, J. Kidd, J. Murphy, T. Robinson, J. McMillan, Landing Waiters; G. H. Pidgeon, Messenger and Packer; P. Nugent, Packer in Excise Warehouses.

INLAND REVENUE OFFICE.

(Market Square.)

Fleming Rowland, Collector; James Spearman, Edward Fahey, Archibald Hanley, A. Howie, Thomas Grimason and John O'Donnell, Officers.

CHURCHES.

CHURCH OF ENGLAND.

Cathedral of St. George—(King, cor. Johnson street).—Very Rev. Jas. Lyster, LL.D., Dean; Rev. Henry Wilson, D.D., assistant minister. Hours of service: Sundays, 11 a.m. and 7 p.m.; daily, 11 a.m.

St. James' Church—(Union cor. Arch).—Rev. Francis W. Kirkpatrick, M.A., rector.

St. Paul's Church—(Queen cor. Montreal).—Rev. Wm. B. Carey, M.A rector.

ALL SAINTS'—(320 Division).—Rev. Thomas Bousfield, rector.

PRISON MISSION.—Rev. C. E. Cartwright, M.A.

METHODIST.

(Hours of service, Sundays 11 a.m. and 6:30 p.m.)

QUEEN STREET.—Rev. H. F. Bland, Pastor.

SYDENHAM STREET.—Rev. Leroy Hooker, Pastor.

METHODIST EPISCOPAL—(Brock cor. Montreal).—Rev. J. Wilson, pastor.

PRIMITIVE—(Brock, between Clergy and Barrie.)—Rev. H. Harris, pastor.

CONGREGATIONAL.

FIRST CONGREGATIONAL—(Wellington cor. Johnson).—Rev. S. N. Jackson, pastor.

BETHEL CHURCH—(Johnson cor. Barrie).—Rev. A. L. McPhadyen, pastor.

BAPTIST—(95 Johnson).—Rev. E. Hooper.

PRESBYTERIAN.

BROCK STREET (201).

CHALMERS'—(129 Earl).—Rev. Finlay McCuaig, pastor.

ST. ANDREW'S (corner Princess and Queen).

ROMAN CATHOLIC.

ST. MARY'S CATHEDRAL—(cor. Clergy and Johnson).—Hours of service: Mass every day at 7.30 a.m. Sundays—Low Mass, 8 a.m.; High Mass, 10.30 a.m.; Vespers, 7.30 p.m. Right Rev. James Vincent Cleary, Bishop of Kingston; Rev. Bernard Higgins; Rev. P. A. Twohey, Chancellor; Rev. Thomas Kelly, Secretary; Rev. P. Hartigan.

CATHOLIC APOSTOLIC (287 Queen).

Rev. J. Gilmour, pastor.

SALVATION ARMY meets at their Barracks every evening at 7.30 p.m. Sundays—7 a.m., 11 a.m., 3 p.m., and 7 p.m.

EDUCATIONAL.

QUEEN'S UNIVERSITY AND COLLEGE.

This institution, one of the oldest and most celebrated in Canada, is situated in the west end of the city, the grounds being bounded by Union, Arch, Stuart and Gordon streets. The houses of the Principal and Professors command a fine view of Lake Ontario and the surrounding country. The college buildings are new, handsome and substantial. The Astronomical Observatory of the institution was founded in 1855, and was deeded to the University in 1861. It contains an equatorial by Mr. Alvan Clarke, with an object glass $6\frac{1}{4}$ inches aperture, a small transit by Troughton & Simms, and an astronomical clock constructed by the assistant observer; also the Beaufoy transit, lent by the Royal Astronomical Society, England, a reflecting telescope by Mr. Short, with a speculum of $7\frac{1}{2}$ inches in diameter, and a reflecting telescope. It is in charge of the veteran Professor Williamson, who is as enthusiastic as ever in the pursuit of knowledge in this line of investigation, and practical astronomy will now be taught to those students who may so desire.

The library contains over 17,000 volumes, and receives considerable additions annually. Donations are sent to it from all quarters. The museum is varied and extensive. Its mineralogical and palæontological collections are particularly valuable.

Queen's College was incorporated with the style and privileges of a University by a Royal Charter, dated October 16th, 1841. A complete curriculum of study leads to the degrees in Arts of B.A., B.Sc., D.Sc., and M.A.; in Theology, of B.D.; and in Medicine, of M.D. These degrees are conferred on those who have gone through the required curriculum and passed the prescribed examinations. The Senate, however, is empowered to confer, besides these, the Honorary Degrees of D.D. and LL.D., for literary, scientific or professional distinction.

It is the desire of the Trustees to attain the highest efficiency in all departments of a University course. Large additions are being made to the equipment of the teaching department in the scientific branches. The Physical and Chemical Laboratories will be better furnished, and especial attention will hereafter be given to practical training in these matters so important to the growth and development of our young country. The addition of a new Professor in Theology will make that department more complete than heretofore.

The Session in Arts begins on the first Wednesday of October, and closes on the last Thursday of April; the session in Theology begins on the first Monday of November, and closes at the same time as the Arts session. There are twenty-three scholarships in Arts and seventeen in Theology, ranging in value from $32 to $100, only three of which are below $50. There are nine University prizes, none of which is under $25, and four gold medals.

Chancellor, Sandford Fleming, C.E., C.M.G.; Principal and Vice-Chancellor, Very Rev. George Monro Grant, M.A., D.D.; Vice Principal, Rev. James Williamson, M.A., LL.D.; Registrar, Rev. George Bell, LL.D.

OFFICERS OF INSTRUCTION.—*In Divinity.*—The Principal, Primarius Professor of Divinity; Rev. John B. Mowat, M.A., Professor of Hebrew, Chaldee and Old Testament Exegesis; Rev. Donald Ross, M.A., B.D., Professor of Apologetics and New Testament Criticism; Rev. James Carmichael (King), Lecturer on Church History. *In Arts.*—Rev. J. Williamson, M.A., LL.D., Professor of Astronomy; Rev. John B. Mowat, M.A., Professor of Hebrew; Nathan F. Dupuis, M.A., F.B.S., Edin., Professor of Mathematics; Rev. George D. Ferguson, B.A., Professor of History and English Language and Literature; John Watson, M.A., LL.D., Professor of Logic, Mental and Moral Philosophy and Political Economy; John Fletcher, M.A., Oxon, Professor of Classical Literature; David H. Marshall, M.A., F.R.S.E., Professor of Physics; — Goodwin, Professor of Chemistry and Mineralogy; Rev. Alexander B. Nicholson, B.A., Lecturer on Modern Languages and Assistant to Professor of Classics; Rev. James Fowler, M.A., Lecturer on Natural Science; Rev. R. Campbell, M.A., (Renfrew) Lecturer on Political Economy. *In Medicine.*—Fife Fowler, M.D., L.R.C.S., Edin. (one of the Surgeons to the Kingston Hospital, Professor of Theory and Practice of Medicine, Clinical Medicine and President of the Faculty; Michael Lavell, M.D. (Surgeon to the Penitentiary; Professor of Obstetrics and Gynæcology, and Registrar; Michael Sullivan, M.D., (Surgeon to the Hotel Dieu), Professor of Principles and Practice of Surgery; Alfred S. Oliver, M.D., (Jail Physician and one of the Surgeons to the Kingston Hospital), Professor of Materia Medica, Therapeutics and Pharmacy; Thomas R. Dupuis, M.D., F.R.C.P.S.K., (one of the Surgeons to the Kingston Hospital), Professor of Anatomy; the Professor of Chemistry in Queen's University, Professor of Chemistry and Practical Chemistry; Kenneth N. Fenwick, M.A., M.D., M.R.C.S., Edin., Professor of Institutes of Medicine; Chamberlain A. Irwin, M.D., (Vice-President of Ontario Medical Association), Professor of

CITY OF KINGSTON. 13

Medical Jurisprudence; C. H. Lavell, M.D., L.R.C.P.S.K., Professor of Ophtalmic and Aural Surgery and Practical Anatomy; H. G. Saunders, M.D., M.R.C.S.E., Professor of Sanitary Science; William H. Henderson, M.D., Professor of Histology and Curator of the Museum; John Herald and Edgar Forrester, Associate Demonstrators of Anatomy. *In Law.*—J. Maule Machar. M.A., Lecturer on Roman Law; Byron M. Britton, M.A., Q.C., Lecturer on Criminal Law; R. Vashon Rogers, B.A., Lecturer on Common Law; G. M. Macdonnell, B.A., Lecturer on the Law of Real Property; Richard T. Walkem, Q.C., Lecturer on Equity; John McIntyre, M.A., Q.C., Lecturer on Medical Jurisprudence.

Acting Registrar of University Council, Archibald P. Knight, M.A. Conservatory Board, the Principal, Professor Williamson, M. Flanagan, Esq. Director of Observatory, Professor of Astronomy. Curators of the Library, the Principal, Professors Mowat and Fletcher. Librarian, Rev. George Bell, LL.D. Curator of Museum, Lecturer on Natural Science. Examiner for Matriculation in Medicine, James Fowler, M.A. Examiners in Gælic, Evan MacColl, Esq., R. M. Rose, Esq., Rev. A. B. Nicholson, B.A. Janitor, John Cormack.

ROYAL COLLEGE OF PHYSICIANS AND SURGEONS.

Affiliated with Queen's University:

REGIOPOLIS COLLEGE is expected to be shortly opened.

COLLEGIATE INSTITUTE (11 Clergy).

A. P. Knight, M.A., Rector; D. A. Givens, B.A., English and Modern Language Master; Thomas Gordon, Mathematical Master; Wm. Meek, Short Hand Master; Colin Scott, Drawing Master; Miss M. L. Phillips, First Preceptress.

CONVENT OF THE CONGREGATION DE NOTRE DAME.

(cor. Bagot and Johnson.)

Mother St. Frances, Superioress. Number of pupils, 150. Number of teachers, 10.

ST. MARY OF THE LAKE (King Street West.)

Mother St. Thecla, Superioress.

CHRISTIAN BROTHERS' SCHOOL (89 Clergy street.)

Rev. Bro. Halward, Director; Rev. Brothers Bardomin, Novatian, Lewis, Anthony and Peter, teachers. Registered number of pupils, 420.

MECHANICS' INSTITUTE (cor. Princess and Montreal.)

John McKay, jr., President; N. C. Polson, Vice-President; Wm. Power, Secretary; C. D. Chown, Treasurer; T. H. McGuire, Secretary; A. McMahon, Recording Secretary and Librarian.

MILITARY.

ROYAL SCHOOL OF GUNNERY, "B" BATTERY, C.A.

(Tete du Pont Barracks.)

Commandant and Assistant Inspector of Artillery, Lieut.-Colonel C. E. Montizambert; Capt. and Bt.-Major C. J. Short; Lieut. and Bt.-Major John Fraser, Adjutant; Lieut. and Bt.-Major Y. E. M. Taschereau; Lieut. and Bt.-Captain A. A. Farley; Surgeon-Major H. Neilson.

Attached Officer—Lieut. and acting Quarter-Master W. E. Imlah.

Establishment of "B" Battery, R.S.G.—1 captain, 5 lieutenants, 1 surgeon, 1 sergeant-major, 1 master gunner, 1 laboratory foreman, 1 ordnance armourer, 2 assistant gunnery instructors, 1 trumpet major, 1 riding instructor, 1 pay sergeant, 9 sergeants, 6 corporals, 4 bombadiers, 8 acting bombadiers, 3 trumpeters, 121 gunners, 6 artificers and 16 horses, making a total of 174.

In addition to the above, 10 officers and 20 non-commissioned officers are allowed to join a short course of instruction.

ROYAL MILITARY COLLEGE OF CANADA, KINGSTON.

Commandant, Edward Osborne Hewitt, C.M.G., Colonel R.E.; Professor of Surveying, Military Topography and Reconnaissance, John Ryder Oliver, Lt.-Col. R.A.; Professor of Mathematics, Mechanics and Artillery, Edgar Kensington, Lt.-Col. R.A.; Professor of Fortification, Military Engineering, Geometrical Drawing and Descriptive Geometry, George Robert Walker, Major R.E.; Professor of Military History, Administration and Law, Douglas F. Jones, Major R.A.; Instructor in Mathematics and Artillery, Samuel Gerrard Fairtlough, Major R.A.; Instructor in Fortification, Military Engineering, Geometrical Drawing and Descriptive Geometry, Edward Raban, Captain R.E.; Assistant Instructor in Mathematics, Geometrical Drawing and Descriptive Geometry, Alfred George Godfrey Wurtele, Lieut. C.M.; Assistant Instructor in Surveying, Military Topography, Physics and Chemistry, John Bray Cochrane, Lieut. C.M.; Professor of English and German, Rev. George Ferguson, B.A.; Professor of French and Drawing and Painting, Forshaw Day, Esq., R.C.A.; Professor of French, Arthur Duponth Duval, Esq., M.D.; Professor of Civil Engineering, Robert Carr Harris, Esq., C.E.; Professor of Physics, Chemistry and Geology, Herbert A. Bayne, Esq., M.A., Sh.D.; Medical Officer, John Lewis H. Neilson, M.D., Surgeon-Major "B" Battery, K.S.G.

4TH PROVISIONAL REGIMENT OF CAVALRY.

John Duff, Lieut.-Colonel; S. C. McGill, Adjutant; W. Maxwell Strange, Paymaster; H. M. Duff, Quarter-Master; Amos S. Bristol, Surgeon; M. J. Brown, Assistant Surgeon; James Massie, Veterinary Surgeon.

No. 1 Troop—Arch. Knight, captain; George Purcell, 1st lieutenant; Thos. Todd, 2nd lieutenant. No. 3 Troop—James Wood, captain; Gilbert Wood 1st lieutenant; John McRory, 2nd lieutenant.

KINGSTON FIELD BATTERY.

John Wilmot, captain; Peter Graham Wilmot; Wm. M. Drennan, 1st lieutenant; J. A. Wilmot, Stanley McNab Henderson, 2nd lieutenants; H. J. Saunders, surgeon.

14TH BATTALION PRINCESS OF WALES' OWN RIFLES.

John Kerr, Lieut.-Colonel; Edward Handley Smythe, Major.

Captains—Joseph Wm. Power, James Galloway, jr., Henry Gorden Hubbell, Charles D. Kerr, James Charles MacDougall, Herbert M. Mowat,

1st Lieutenants—Richard Conway Cartwright, James Murray, jr., Lewis W. Shannon, John S. Skinner.

2nd Lieutenants—Alexr. Buntin, John R. Shannon.

Paymaster, Wm. King. Adjutant, William D. Gordon. Quarter-master, Henry J. Spriggs. Surgeon, John Bigham. Assistant Surgeon, William H. Henderson.

MASONIC.

ANCIENT AND ACCEPTED SCOTTISH RITE.

Rose of Sharon Sovereign Chapter of Rose Croix de H.R.D.M.—Ill. Bro. S. G. Fairtlough, 32°, M.W. Sov.; Sov. Pr. John Kingborn, 18°, R. & P. Prelate; Ill. Bro. W. D. Gordon, 32°, Ex. & P. 1st General; Sov. Pr. W. Waddington, jr., 18°, Ex. & P. 2nd General; Sov. Pr. Philip Bajus, 18°, Ex. & P. Raphael; Sov. Pr. R. A. McMahon, 18°, Ex. & P.G.M.; Sov. Pr. F. Rowland, 18°, Ex. & P. Reg.; Sov. Pr. R. V. Matthews, 18°, Ex. & P. Treas.; Sov. Pr. E. S. Boyden, 18°, Ex. & P. Herald; Sov. Pr. S. Oberndorffer, 18°, Ex. & P.D. of C.; Sov. Pr. H. Birtles, 18°, Ex. & P.C. of G.; Sov. Pr. E. Ball, 18°, Guard.

Meets first Wednesday of each month.

Kingston Lodge of Perfection, No. 7.—Ill. Bro. W. D. Gordon, 32°, I.P.G.M.; Bro. John Kingborn, 18°, Ex. S.G.W.; Ill. Bro. S. G. Fairtlough, 32°, Ex. J.G.W.; Bro. W. Waddington, jr., 18°, Ex. G. Secretary; Bro. Philip Bajus, 18°, Ex. G. Treasurer; Bro. E. S. Boyden, 18°, Ex. G. Orator; Bro. R. V. Matthews, 18°, Ex. G. Almoner; Bro. R. A. McMahon, 18°, Ex. G.M. of Cer.; Bro. H. J. Wilkinson, 18°, R.G. Expert; Bro. Geo. Thompson, 18°, R.G. Asst. Expert; Bro. James Adams, 14°, V.E. Capt. of Host; Bro. E. Ball, 18°, G. Tyler.

Meets second Friday of each month.

Cataraqui Chapter, No. 12.—Ex. Comp. W. Waddington, Z.; Ex. Comp. A. Shaw, H.; Ex. Comp. C. Porter, J.; Comp. W. S. Smyth, E.; Comp. R. V. Mathews, S.N.; V. Ex. Comp. H. Dumble, Treas.; Ex. Comp. R. Bunt, P.S.; Comp. J. Hewton, J.S.

Meets second Monday in February, March, April, May, August and November.

Knights Templar, Hugh de Payen's Encampment.—Fleming Rowland, E.C.; G. W. Andrews, P.E.C.; R. V. Mathews, C.; W. D. Gordon, R.; John Kear, T.; Rev. J. Gallagher, P.; W. Scobell, M.; Major Fairtlough, C.G.; E. Ball, E.

Meets first Friday in February, May, August and November.

Ancient Frontenac, Royal Arch Chapter, No. 1.—Ex. Comp. W. M. Bailie, I.P.Z.; Ex. Comp. W. D. Gordon, Z.; Comp. H. J. Wilkinson, H.; Comp. James Adams, J.; Comp. G. W. Andrews, S.E.; Comp. W. M. Bailie, S N.; Comp. Geo. Thompson, Treas.; Comp. A. LeRichieux, P.S.; Comp. R. M. Horsey, S.S.; Comp. J. A. Irwin, J. A. Irwin, J.S.

Meets third Tuesday in February, May, August, and second Tuesday in November. Annual meeting third Thursday in November.

Kingston Masonic Benefit Association.—R.W. Bro. G. M. Wilkinson, President; V. W. Bro. G. S. Oldrieve, Vice-President; R. W. Bro. John Kerr, Treasurer; R.W. Bro. G. W. Andrews, Secretary.

Ancient St. John's Lodge, No. 3.—H. J. Saunders, W.M.; G. W. Gaden, I.P.M.; H. J. Wilkinson, S.W.; J. Yule, J.W.; E. R. Welch, Treas.; J. Sutherland, Secretary.

Meets first Thursday of each month.

Cataraqui Lodge, No. 92, A.F. & A.M., G.R.C.—Abraham Shaw, W.M.; W. Waddington, I.P.M.; J. R. Smeaton, S.W.; W. S. Smythe, J.W.; James Shannon, Treas.; D. Callaghan, Secretary.

Meets second Wednesday of each month.

MINDEN LODGE, A.F. & A.M, No. 253, G.R.C.—Wor. Bro. W. D. Gordon W.M.; Wor. Bro. J. McEwen, I.P.M.; Wor. Bro. W. M. Drennan, S.W.; Wor. W. Newlands, J.W.; R. W. Bro. G. M. Wilkinson, Treas.; R. W. Bro. D. A. Givens, Sec,; Rev. Bro. R. J. Craig, Chaplain.

Meets every first Monday.

ODD FELLOWS.

KINGSTON UNIFORMED ENCAMPMENT, No. 3.—W. J. Burns, Chief Captain; A. C. McMahon, Subordinate Captain; B. H. Carnovsky, Junior Captain; Wm. Healey, Conductor; George Lee, Warden; Wm. Adams, High Priest; Wm. Dunn, Standard Bearer; J. B. McIver, Scribe; R. S. Mowatt, Treasurer; E. Chatterton, Right General Guide; J. Anderson, Left General Guide; L. Milks, First Guardian; George Wilkinson, Second Guardian; F. Sharp, S. Marshall, J. Dillon and J. Saunders, Chiefs of Sections.

No. 10 Cataraqui meets Tuesday.

No. 59 Kingston meets Friday.

A.O.U.W.

LIMESTONE LODGE, No. 91.—W. B. Little, Master; T. Driver, Recorder.
Meets second and fourth Thursdays in each month in Wilkinson's Building, corner Princess and Montreal streets.

LOYAL ORANGE ASSOCIATION.

No. 6 meets second Wednesday in each month. James Marshall, W.M.; W. J. Morrison, Secretary.

No. 291 meets second Friday in each month. Samuel Thornton, W.M.; George Leslie, Secretary.

No. 316 meets first Tuesday in each month. James Laturney, W.M.; M. Moran, Secretary.

No. 325 meets first Thursday. Wm. Pugh, W.M.; John Lovick, Secretary.

No. 352 meets first Friday. Wm. Makins, W.M.; James Dennison, Secy.

No. 577 meets second Monday. Thomas Lemmon, W.M.; Henry Stoddard, Secretary.

No. 1, DERRY LODGE 'PRENTICE BOYS.—W. J. Moore, W.M.; James Perry, Secretary.

No. 16, TRUE BLUES.—J. Dennison, W.M.; J. W. Marshall, Secretary. Meets last Monday in each month.

ROYAL SCARLET CHAPTER.—Marshal Fair, W.M.C.; James Laturney, Com. S. Meets on the 14th of each month.

ROYAL BLACK KNIGHTS OF CANADA, No. 2.—Sir Kt. James Marshall, W.M.; Sir Kt. Francis Morrison, Reg. Meets second Thursday.

I.O.G.T.

BETHEL LODGE meets on Mondays over Wade's drug store.

JUVENILE TEMPLE meets on Fridays at the Mission, cor. Montreal and Princess streets.

SONS OF TEMPERANCE, No. 2 ST. LAWRENCE DIVISION.—W. M. McRossie, W.P.; W. Monteith, Sec.; G. W. Andrews, D.G.W.P.

CITY OF KINGSTON.

NATIONAL SOCIETIES.

ST. GEORGE'S SOCIETY.—E. H. Smythe, LL.D., President; Samuel Thornton, 1st Vice-President; Charles F. Smith, 2nd Vice-President; Edwin Rose, Treasurer; Alfred LeRicheux, Secretary; W. H. Godwin, T. C. Tillinghast, J. A. B. Smith, Henry Hitchins, W. Hinds, T. Palmer, J. Dolphin, Rev. Thomas Bousfield, Dr. H. J. Saunders, Committee of Management; H. J. Saunders, M.D., H. Evans, M.D., Physicians; Revs. C. E. Cartwright, M.A.; R. V. Rogers, M.A., Thomas Bousfield and F. Prime, Chaplains; W. Hinds, Marshal.

ST. ANDREW'S SOCIETY—(Established 1843).—John McMillan, President; James Craig, 1st Vice-President; Alexander Milne, 2nd Vice-President; Robt. Thomson, Secretary-Treasurer; Rev. Dr. Smith and Rev. F. McQuaig, Chaplains; J. Murray and S. Maxwell, Auditors; N. McNeil, Standard Bearer; Dr. Strange, Physician; Evan McColl, Bard; W. G. Craig, J. Richmond, N. C. Polson, W. R. McRae, G. Fleck, D. Gibson, J. Carruthers, W. McRossie and E. Law.

ST. PATRICK'S SOCIETY.—T. H. McGuire, President.

CATHOLIC SOCIETIES.

CONFRATERNITY OF THE HOLY FAMILY.—Men's branch meets first Sunday in each month. Women's first Friday in each month.

ST. VINCENT DE PAUL SOCIETY (purely charitable) meets every Sunday afternoon in St. Mary's vestry at 4 o'clock. John A. McMahon, President; P. Daley, Vice-President; A. Hanley, Secretary; P. Smith, Treas.; Rev. P. A. Twohey, Chaplain.

CHILDREN OF ST. MARY.—Miss R. A. Fahey, President.

CATHOLIC MUTUAL BENEFIT ASSOCIATION.—Wm. Leahey, President; P. Daley, 1st Vice-President; Michael Maloney, 2nd Vice-President; John G. Buggee, Rec. Sec.; Michael Brennan, Cor. Sec; George W. Weber, Fin. Sec.; Wm. Shanahan, Treas.; Dennis Sullivan, Senior Chancellor; Wm. Sullivan, Junior Chancellor; Robert McCauley, Marshal; Robert Nolan, Guard.

LAW.

FRONTENAC LAW AND LIBRARY ASSOCIATION.—Dr. Henderson, Q.C., President; R. V. Rogers, B.A., Treasurer; J. L. Whiting, B.A., Secretary; B. M. Britton, Q.C., Hon. G. A. Kirkpatrick, Q.C., E. H. Smythe, LL.D., R. T. Walkem, Q.C., James Agnew, Trustees.

BANKS.

BANK OF BRITISH NORTH AMERICA (City Hall).—Duncan Robertson, Manager; Richard Butt, Accountant; J. D. Petrie, Teller; P. Gabbett, Clerk; R. Stafford, Messenger.

FEDERAL BANK OF CANADA (cor. Wellington and Clarence streets).—T. Y. Greet, Manager; W. J. Burns, accountant; R. E. Kent, Teller; James Calder, H. de M. Harvey, Fred. Strange, Pen Ridout, T. X. Rogers, Clerks.

MERCHANTS' BANK OF CANADA (cor. King and Wellington).—G. E. Hague, Manager; A. J. Ferguson, Accountant; W. G. Hinds, Teller; T. E. Merrett, Ledger Keeper; L. R. J. Grier, Discount Clerk; C. H. Goold, Clerk.

BANK OF MONTREAL (cor. King and Wellington).—R. M. Moore, Manager; John M. Greata, Accountant; C. L. Benedict, Teller; P. C. R. Wonham, Bookkeeper; A. R. Moore and G. S. Oliver, Clerks.

RAILWAYS.

KINGSTON & PEMBROKE (Offices, Ontario street)—C. F. Gildersleeve, President; John D. Flower, Vice-President; George Osborne, Secretary-Treasurer; B. W. Folger, Superintendent; J. H. Taylor, Assistant Superintendent; T. W. Walsh, Chief Engineer; George A. Kirkpatrick, Solicitor.

GRAND TRUNK RAILWAY.—Robert Thompson, Freight Agent; John Trenaman, Passenger Agent.

MISCELLANEOUS.

KINGSTON HOSPITAL.—Governors *ex officio* : C. Livingston, Mayor of Kingston; D. J. Walker, Warden of Frontenac; C. V. Price, County Judge; William Ferguson, Sheriff of Frontenac. The Eleven Life Governors: Sir John A. Macdonald, Hon. R. J. Cartwright, John Fraser, Dr. O. S. Strange, E. Chown, Wm. Ford, Dr. M. Sullivan, B. M. Britton, W. B. Robertson, E. J. B. Pense, John Duff. Subscription Governors: Hon. A. Campbell, John Carruthers, D. D. Calvin, Ira A. Breck. Officers: O. S. Strange, Chairman of the Board of Governors; Dr. F. Fowler, Dr. A. S. Oliver, Dr. T. R. Dupuis, Dr. K. N. Fenwick, officers; J. E. Clark, Secretary; Louis Buttner, Steward.

HOTEL DIEU (Brock street).—Sister Monica Brady, Superioress. Average number of patients, 35; number received during the last year, 450.
The Hotel Dieu Female Orphan Asylum is in connection.

HOUSE OF PROVIDENCE (Montreal street).—Sister Mary John, Superioress.

PROTESTANT ORPHANS' HOME (Union street, opposite Drill Shed).—Andrew Miller, Manager; Mrs. E. H. Miller, Matron.

KINGSTON PENITENTIARY.—John Creighton, Warden; William Sullivan, Deputy Warden; M. Lavell, M.D., Surgeon; S. W. Scobell, Accountant; Rev. C. E. Cartwright, Protestant Chaplain; Rev. A. P. Twohey, R.C. Chaplain; Mary Leahy, Matron; Robert R. Creighton, Clerk; P. O'Donnell, Storekeeper; James Weir, Steward.

ASYLUM FOR THE INSANE.—W. G. Metcalf, Medical Superintendent; C. K. Clark, Assistant Medical Superintendent; Wm. Anglin, Bursar; Allan McLean, Steward; Mary Aitken, Matron.

STAGE ROUTES.

BATTERSEA STAGE.—William Arthur, proprietor. Leaves Albion Hotel, corner of Montreal and Queen streets, Tuesday, Thursday and Saturday, and Battersea stage, John Holder, proprietor, Monday, Wednesday and Friday, from Windsor Hotel, at 4 p.m.—to Hickey's Corners, distant from Kingston, 7 miles, 15c.; to Sunbury, 11 miles, 20c.; to Battersea, 16 miles, 25c.

KINGSTON AND GANANOQUE STAGE.—A. B. Carnegie, proprietor. Leaves American Hotel every Tuesday, Thursday and Saturday at 4 p.m. in winter season.

NEWBORO STAGE.—West Preston, proprietor. Leaves St. Lawrence Hotel, cor. King and Queen, daily, at 7 a.m.; arrives at 3 p.m. Fare, $1.50.

INVERARY STAGE.—J. Stoness, proprietor. Leaves Queen's Hotel, Brock street, Tuesday, Thursday and Saturday at 4 p.m.—to Glenburnie, 6 miles, 15c.; to Inverary, 11 miles, 25c.; to Lapum, 16 miles, 50c.

SYDENHAM STAGE.—Leaves Queen's Hotel Brock street, Tuesdays, Thursdays and Saturdays.

NAPANEE STAGE.—H. Finkle, proprietor. Leaves the Albion Hotel, daily, at 3:45 p.m., summer; 3 p.m., winter. Odessa, 12 miles, 25c.; Napanee, 24 miles, 50c.

PICTON STAGE.—William Ellsworth, proprietor. Leaves British American Hotel during winter season, daily, at 7.30 a.m.—to Collinsby, 6 miles, 15c.; to Millhaven, 18 miles. 50c.; to Bath, 20 miles, 50c.; to Adolphustown, 30 miles, $1; to Stone Mills, 35 miles, $1.50; to Picton, 36 miles, $2.

NEWBURGH STAGE.—Henry Finkle & Son, proprietors. Leaves Albion Hotel, Montreal, cor. Queen, daily, at 4 p.m.—to Cataraqui, 3 miles, 10c.; to Westbrook, 5 miles, 15c.; to Odessa, 12 miles, 25c.; to Smith's Corners, 15 miles, 30c.; to Brick School House, 19 miles, 40c.; to Clark's Mills, 22 miles, 50c.; to Newburgh, 24 miles, 50c.

G. M. WEBER & Co.,

MANUFACTURERS

OF THE

BEST PIANO MADE IN CANADA

AT THEIR FACTORY,

42 Princess Street, Kingston.

Every Piano guaranteed for Five years.

Intending Purchasers should call and examine the Pianos, and see the testimonials before buying inferior instruments at higher prices.

ALPHABETICAL DIRECTORY

OF THE

CITY OF KINGSTON.

Abbott George, Gordon.
Abbott Thomas, painter, 382 Division
Abernethy Arch., manager G. Offord, 245 Earl
Abernethy James, laborer, 245 Earl
Abernethy Wm., turner, 178 Ordnance
Abery Edward, laborer, Gordon
Abraham Edwin, 628 Princess
Ada William, salesman, York
Ada Wm., mariner, Clergy
Adair Mrs Margaret, William
Adair Robt. A, Clerk P.O., Barrie
ADAMS EDWARD, (Davidson, Doran & Co.,) 162 King
Adams James, hotel-keeper, 233 King
Adams Wm., boots & shoes, 63 Brock, h 318 Gordon
Agger Charles, shoemaker, 86 York
Agnew Alex., moulder, 307 Earl
AGNEW JAMES, barrister, city solicitor, city hall, h Barrie
Agnew John, co. school inspector, 187 William
Agnew Robert, moulder, 307 Earl
Ahern John, laborer, 98 Ontario
Ahern John, laborer, n s John
Ainslie David J., carpenter, 174 Barrie
Albertson John, spinner cotton co
Albertson Mrs Mary, laundress, 76 Ordnance
Albertson Mrs Mary J., 123 Montreal

ALBION HOTEL, Patrick McLaughlin, proprietor, cor Montreal & Queen
Alderdice Hugh, painter, Princess
Alexander Mrs Jane, 306 Brock
Alexander Julius, brewer, foot Wellington
Alexander Thomas, storeman, King w
ALL SAINTS' CHURCH, (EPISCOPAL), w s Division, between Elm & York
Allen Mrs Agnes, Clergy
Allen Miss Ann, Johnson
Allen Benjamin, carpenter, 29 Charles
Allen Charles, laborer, loco. works
Allen Mrs Elizabeth, 206 Montreal
Allen George, laborer, Wellington
Allen J. A., 500 King
Allen J., laborer, 264 Wellington
Allen John, pianomaker, 189 Pine
Allen Robert W., bill poster, 898 Montreal
Allen Theo., mariner, Barrie
Allen Wilfred, salesman, 183 Clergy
Allen Wm., tinsmith, 197 Wellington
Allen Wm., boots & shoes, 82 Brock
Allen Wm., tinsmith, cor Division & Main
Allinson, Wm., clerk, Albert, cor Nelson
Allwell George, laborer, 41 Bondhead

CITY OF KINGSTON. 21

Alsen Alex., driver, Sydenham
AMERICAN EXPRESS CO'Y., J. S. Patch, agent, cor King & Market Sq
Amey Miss, dressmaker, 106 Princess
Anchinvole G., laborer, 41 Colborne
Anderson Charles, laborer, 88 Bondhead
Anderson Chas. W.W., clerk, 7 Sixth
Anderson Daniel jr., laborer, Sydenham
Anderson David, laborer, 115 Bay
Anderson David, laborer, Sydenham
Anderson James W., Princess
Anderson John, stovemounter Victoria Foundry
Anderson John H., tailor, 22 York
Anderson Joseph, driver, Wellington
Anderson Michael, 178 Bagot
Anderson Thomas, inside porter Windsor Hotel
Anderson Wm., laborer, 37 King w
ANDREWS G. W., merchant tailor, 190 Wellington, h Garratt
Anglin Mrs C., merchandise, 177 Wellington
Anglin R. D., clerk customs, 144 Union
ANGLIN SAMUEL, (W. B. & S. Anglin), 85 Barrack
Anglin Wm., bursar asylum for the insane, 56 Earl
ANGLIN W. B. (W. B. & S. Anglin), 'Union
ANGLIN W. B. & S., sawing & planing mill, Wellington n
Anglo-American Hotel, cor Ontario & Johnson
Angrove John, blacksmith, locomotive works
Angrove Samuel, patternmaker, 71 Gore
Anis Ansel, carpenter, 47 Ordnance
ANIS W. A., merchant tailor, 86 Princess
ANTHONY REV. BRO., teacher Christian Brothers school
Appleton John, blacksmith, cor York & Division
Armstrong Mrs Catherine, 260 Sydenham
ARMSTRONG D. F., boots & shoes, 141 Princess, h 165 King w
Armstrong Frank, photographer, 260 Sydenham
Armstrong Mrs I., 304 Brock
Armstrong Mrs Jane, 213 Earl
Armstrong John, moulder, 213 Earl
Arneil Wm., caretaker, Wellington
Arneil Samuel, sailor, 20 Young's Lane
Arneil Samuel jr., fitter, 20 Young's Lane
Arneil Thomas, carpenter, 324 Division
Arneil Wm., blacksmith, locomotive works
Arneil W. J., watchmaker, 337 Princess
Arnold John, engineer, 25 King e
Arnold Mrs Mary, Wellington
Arratta Michael, mechanic, 83 Johnson
Arthurs James, cabinetmaker, Hamilton's Lane
Ashley C. R., salesman, 173 Sydenham
Ashley John, caretaker court house
Ashley Walter, moulder, 173 Sydenham
Asselstine Henry, carpenter, 302 Johnson
Asselstine Isaac, carpenter, 298 Johnson

Asselstine Isaac, blacksmith, Earl
Asselstine John, carpenter, 286 Gordon
Asselstine John, contractor, 168 Division
Asselstine Mrs M., 222 Alfred
Asselstine Peter, carpenter, 90 Division
Asselstine W. H., salesman, 222 Alfred
Atkinson Thos., mason, e s Collingwood
Aubin Mrs Mary Jane, 83 Johnson
Augustus W., sailor, 163 Division
Austin James, shoemaker, 102 Rideau
Austin Seymour, carpenter, Nelson
Babcock James, laborer, 124 Queen
Babington Mrs Mary, Princess
Bailey Alex., driver Shedden Co.
BAILEY B. & Co., broom-makers, 362 Barrie
BAILEY BENJAMIN, (Bailey Bros.,) h 216 Queen
Bailey E. B., com. traveller, 309 Queen
Bailey Mrs Mary, Ontario
Bailey S., laborer, 105 Colborne
BAILEY WILLIAM, (Bailey Bros.,) h 120 Colborne
Bailie Bros. (Isaac & H. M.,) printers, 190 Wellington, h cor William & Barrie
Bailie Charles, laborer, Chatham
Bailie Hugh, shoemaker, 210 Montreal
Bailie Wm., printer, 83 Brock, h Barrie
Baillie Wm. M., book-keeper, 53 Earl
Bain Herbert, Brock
Baird Alex., salesman, 212 Queen
Baird James H., salesman, 16 Upper Bagot
Baird John, fitter, 16 Upper Bagot
Baird Robert jr., carpenter, 16 Upper Bagot
Baird Robert sr., 16 Upper Bagot
Baird Wm., salesman, 16 Upper Bagot
Bajus Alfred, brewer, 63 Rideau
Bajus John, cellerman, Wellington
Bajus Peter, brewer, Wellington
Bajus Philip sr., shoemaker, 129 Montreal
BAJUS PHILIP, prop'r. Kingston Brewery, 290 Wellington
Bajus William, brewer, 57 Rideau
Baker John, farmer, 269 Division
Baker John F., clerk A. Gunn & Co
Baker Mrs Mary, Earl
Baker Wm., propr. Canteen, R. S. G.
Baldock James G., keeper K. P., Centre
Ball Edward, clerk, 139 Ordnance
Ballman H., speculator, bds St. Lawrence House
Bamford Alex., book-keeper, Wellington
BANK BRITISH NORTH AMERICA, Duncan Robertson, manager, city hall
BANK OF MONTREAL, R. M. Moore, manager, cor King & William
Banington J., Ordnance armourer B Battery, R.S.G.
BAPTIST CHURCH, n s Johnson, bet Wellington & Bagot
Barber Chas. F., carpenter, 286 Alfred
Barber Thomas, carpenter, Arch
Barchand John, carpenter, Johnson
Barclay James, blacksmith, Ontario
BARDOMIN REV. BRO., teacher Christian Brothers school
Barlow William, plasterer, 107 Barrie

Barlow Thomas, engineer, Union
Barney Benjamin, second-hand dealer, 89 Princess
Barnes Mrs Elizabeth, Deacon
Barnes Charles, Union
Barnes ———, bds St. Lawrence House
Barnes Sandy, blacksmith, Ontario
Barr Robert, telegraph repairer, 84 Clarence
Barrigan James, laborer, 176 Clergy
Barron George, engineer, Union
Barron W. J., salesman, Union
Barrow Mrs Mary, 440 King w
Barry Francis, gardener, Regent
Barry John, clerk, 204 Bagot
Barry John, moulder, Loco. works
Barry P. J., salesman, 204 Bagot
Barry Robt., coppersmith, 18 Division
Bartley Mrs Mary, Princess
Bastow Jeremiah, 182 Clergy
Bastow J. G., plumber, 349 King e
Bassam Wm. laborer, 93 Alfred
Bassam Wm. E., shipper, 63 Alfred
Bates B., Ordnance
Bates Mrs Elizabeth, 329 King w
Bates Henry C., clerk, 329 King w
Bates J. J. (Webster, Bates & Co.,) h Princess
Bates Peter, Princess
Bates Samuel, carpenter, York
Bateson Mrs Ann, William
Bateson Mathew, driver, William
Bateson Henry, blacksmith, 326 Division
Baugh G., corporal B Battery, Fort Henry
BAWDEN JOSEPH (Bawden & Machar), h West
BAWDEN & MACHAR (Joseph Bawden, John Maule Machar,) barristers, 343 King e

Baxter Miss Jane, Sydenham
BAYNE HERBERT A., M.A, Ph.D., R. M. C.
Beal Mrs, boarding, 170 Wellington
Beamish Mrs B., North
Beard Harry, teacher, 290 Queen
Beard Mrs Margaret, 84 Simcoe
Beattie Mrs Agnes, Joseph
Beattie Charles, Bagot
Beauchamp John, machinist, 15 Deacon
Beaupre Edward, mariner, 276 Wellington
Beaupre Peter, sailor, 310 Queen
Beaupre Remi, hotel, Market Sq
Beauro Peter, carter, Johnson
Becker Mrs Mary E., 152 Sydenham
Bedsel John, blacksmith, Victoria foundry
Begg Alex., carter, 97 Queen
Begg George, baker, 50 William
Begg James, packer, Queen
Begg W., salesman, Queen
Begg Mrs Mary Ann, William
Behan John, laborer, 131 Montreal
Behan John jr., clerk, 131 Montreal
Behan John Joseph, salesman, cor Patrick & George
Belanger Henry, painter, 264 Sydenham
Belanger Hiliare, painter, 264 Sydenham
Bell Mrs Annie, Princess
BELL REV. GEORGE, LL.D., Registrar Queen's College
Bell John, baker, 25 Ellice
Bell Joseph, tinsmith, Arch
Bell Robert, sergeant-major police, 176 Gordon
Bell, W. P., photographer, cor Princess & Montreal, h 235 Colborne
Belton Mrs Mary, Johnson

Bendle John, moulder, Johnson
Benedict C. L., teller Bank of Montreal
Bennett Alex., baker, cor Princess & Barrie
Bennett Mrs Caroline, 78 York
Bennett George, carter, e s Nelson
Bennett James, laborer, 158 York
Bennett James, shoemaker, Elm
Bennett John, laborer, Bondhead
Bennett Thomas, laborer, Wellington
Bennett Wm., machinist, 342 Division
Bennett Wm., carter, e s Nelson
Benson Mrs Mary Jane, 89 Barrack
Benton Edward, laborer, Locomotive works
Bermingham Cornelius, (J. Harty & Co.,) h cor Sydenham & Colborne
Bermingham James, clerk, Johnson
Berry Herman, hotel, King w
Berry Fred., laborer, Kingston foundry
Bertolini Fenix, sausage maker, Brock, h 88 Wellington
BETHEL CHURCH, (Congregational), n s Johnson, bet Division and Gordon
Bevan Mrs Catherine, Union
Bews James, mason, cor Durham & Park
Bibby Herbert, salesman, 209 Brock
Bibby Fred., mariner, 20 Place d'Armes
Bibby Fred. A., livery, 209 Brock
Biddle Charles, teamster, 429 Division
Biglow Mrs Mary, 147 Colborne
Billman T., sergeant B Battery, R. S. G.

Bindle John, patternmaker, Kingston foundry
Birch Enoch, laborer, Patrick
Birch George, carpenter, Gordon
Birch John, laborer, s s Charles
BIRCH SAMUEL (McKelvey & Birch), h 136 Bagot
Bird Bernard, steward, 63 John
Bird Langley, laborer, 59 Ontario
Birkett John, book-keeper, Maitland
Birtles Henry, engineer, 411 King
Bissell T., mariner, bds St. Lawrence hotel
BISONETTE, G. H., (Bowes & Bisonette,) h cor Arch & Deacon
Bisonette Mrs Lucy, Sydenham
Black James, carpenter, 141 Alfred
Black John, mariner, 56 Magdalen
Blake Mrs Ellen, 25 Ontario
Blake Geo. C., bricklayer, Ann
Blakey Alfred, butcher, Williamsville
BLAND REV. H. F., pastor Queen Street Methodist Church, Colborne
Bloomsley James, forger, Locomo. works
Boakes James W., brakeman, Bay
Bohannan W. G., plater, Ordnance
Bolton Richard, laborer, Johnson
Boon John, teamster, Chatham
Bone John, laborer, Victoria foundry
Bonny George, blacksmith, Alfred
Booth E. A., mariner, 7 Colborne
Booth F. G., gardener, Victoria
Booth George, machinist, Locomo. works
Booth Mrs Mary, dressmaker, 7 Colborne
Bosley G., corporal B Battery, west ditch tower

BOSTON HAT STORE, George Mills & Co., proprietors, 206 Wellington
Boswell P., stove mounter, Victoria foundry
Bower Wm., stove mounter, Victoria foundry
Bourdo Batiste, laborer, 813 Montreal
BOUSFIELD REV. THOMAS, rector All Saints' Church, 322 Brock
Bourne John C., pedlar, 51 Balaclava
Bowen Mrs Mary, 421 King
Bower John, Barrie
BOWES & BISONETTE, (R. James Bowes, G. H. Bisonette), dry goods, 204 Princess
BOWES R. JAMES, (Bowes & Bisonette), h 251 Division
Bowes Timothy, shoemaker, 234 Ontario
Bowie James, machinist, Locomo. works
Boyd James, baker, 289 Princess
Boyd John, mariner, 357 Brock
Boyd Richard, hackman, 157 Montreal
Boyd Thomas, butcher, 65 Plum
Boyd William, farmer, 65 Queen
BOYDEN EDWARD, (Richmond & Boyden), h 3 Vaugh Terrace
Boyle Mrs Bridget, 42 York
Brabant John, barkeeper, 176 Wellington
Braddon John, mariner, Ontario
Bradford John, spinner, Hosiery Co
Bradley Patrick, watchman, 95 Earl
Brady James P., timekeeper, Loco. works
Brady John, laborer, 60 North
Brady John, Park
Brady John, laborer, 80 Rideau
Brady Mrs Margaret, 120 Bay
BRADY SISTER MONICA, Superioress Hotel Dieu, 227 Brock
BRAME HENRY, cabinet maker and undertaker, 251 Princess
Bramley Ralph, laborer, Locomo. works
Branch Joseph, blacksmith, Loco. works
Brand George, cabinetmaker, 216 Queen
Brand George jr., cabinetmaker, 216 Queen
Brand Henry, plumber, 216 Queen
Braniff, Hugh, laborer, 267 Earl
Branagan John, grocer, 224 Montreal
Branigan Mrs E., fancy goods, 360 Princess
Branigan Dennis, salesman, 360 Princess
Breck Ira A., 315 Union
Breck Luther, 158 Earl
Breden John, 102 Beverly
Breedon H. M., William
Brennan Michael, constable, 27 Division
Brennan M., clerk, Union
Brewster William, carter, 2 North
Brick James, salesman, Ordnance
Brickwood James H., saloon, 176 Wellington
Brickwood Philip, 247 Victoria
BRIGGS THOS., manager Frontenac Loan and Investment Society, 169 King w
BRITISH AMERICAN HOTEL, Arch. McFaul, propr., cor King & Clarence
BRITTON B. M., (Britton & Whiting,) h 3 Sydenham
Britton E. H., law student, 3 Sydenham
BRITTON & WHITING, (B. M. Britton, Q.C., John L. Whiting, B.A.,) barristers, 69 Clarence

BROCK PRESBYTERIAN CHURCH, Brock, bet Montreal & Sydenham
Brokenshire Mrs E, Ontario
Brokenshire John, pump manufactory, 74 Ontario, h 160 King e
Brokenshire John jr., pump-maker, 160 King e
Brooks Albert, fitter, Alfred
Brooks Thomas, carpenter, 61 Collingwood
Brooks William, tinsmith, 273 Brock
Brophy Mrs Margaret, 59 Wellington
Brophy Wm., salesman, Earl
Brouse Harry, driver, Locomotive works
Brown Andrew, book-keeper, Clergy
Brown Charles, laborer, Johnson
Brown David, moulder, King
BROWN GEORGE, (J. W. Brown Co.,) 352 Princess
Brown H., restaurant, city hall
Brown James, Stuart
Brown John, laborer, 89 King w
BROWN J. W., (J. W. Brown & Co.,) h 824 Barrie
BROWN J. W. & Co., (J. W., Geo., and S. G.,) carriage manufacturers, 308 Barrie
BROWN S. G., (J. W. Brown & Co.,) h 352 Princess
Brown Wm., helper, res Portsmouth
BROWNE JAS., (James Browne & Co.,) h 138 Gordon
BROWNE JAS. & Co., wholesale grocers and wine merchants, Ontario
BROWNE PATRICK, (James Browne & Co.,) h 138 Gordon
Brownley Henry, machinist, Ordnance
Brownley Mrs Henry, Bagot
Brownley Thomas, fitter, 142 Ordnance
Brownlow Wm., machinist, Ordnance
Bruyiere John, millwright, Bondhead
Bryant Francis, blacksmith, Kingston foundry
Bryant Fred., moulder, Victoria foundry
Bryant Fred., mason, Adelaide
Bryant George, blacksmith, Sixth
Bryant John, stone dealer, Division
Bryant R., moulder, 265 Division
Bryant Robert, carpenter, 278 Queen
Bryant Wm., painter, hd Division
Bryden George, clerk, bds Waggoner House
Bryson James, keeper K. P., 210 Gordon
Burke Anthony, laborer, Locomotive works
Burk Mrs Jane, 389 Ontario
Burk Richard, engineer, fire hall
Burk Steven, laborer, 67 Bay
Burk Mrs Sarah, 58 Rideau
Burke Thomas, carpenter, 48 Place d'Armes
Burns Mrs Ellen, 295 Johnson
Burns Henry, engineer, Elm
Burns Michael, laborer, Wade's Lane
Burns John, laborer, 217 Barrack
Burns John, carpenter, 42 John
Burns Patrick, watchman, 298 Montreal
Burns Patrick, baker, 41 Ordnance
Burns R. E., salesman, 282 Johnson
Burns Robert, laborer, Bagot
Burns Robert, carpenter, car works
Burns Simon, Earl
Buggeo John, hotel, Market Sq
Bulger James, laborer, 96 Ontario

CITY OF KINGSTON. 27

Bulger Patrick, laborer, Kingston foundry
Bull Geo., blacksmith, Loco. works
Bulch John, mariner, bds St. Lawrence Hotel
Buncker James, blacksmith, William
Bunt John, blacksmith, 281 Wellington
Bunt Richard, blacksmith, 281 Wellington
Bunt Richard jr., foreman blacksmith, Montreal
Bunt Wm., blacksmith, Arch
Burgess James, carpenter, 129 Colborne
Burgess John, carpenter, 292 Victoria
Burnhart George, painter, bds St. Lawrence Hotel
Burns Robt. J., carpenter, s s John
Burns Robt. T., clerk money order dept. P.O., 282 Johnson
Burns W. J., accountant Federal Bank
Burns W. J., salesman, John
Burrows, Wm., collector canal office and inspector of gas, Clarence, h 162 Earl
BURTON J. V. B., foreman Victoria foundry, 57 Queen
Bush Mrs Sarah, cor James and Cherry
Bushell John, mariner, 374 King e
Bushell Philip, laborer, 79 Elm
Bushey D. M., carpenter, York
Bushey Francis, carpenter, 487 Alfred
Bushey Robert, carpenter, 400 Division
Bushfield John, blacksmith, Johnson
Busker, Frank, bds St. Lawrence Hotel
Busso Mrs Agnes, 76 York
Busso Wm., salesman, 76 York
Butt Richard, accountant bank B. N. A., Earl
BUTTNER LOUIS, steward Kingston Hospital
Byers David, 283 Earl
Byrns John, Sydenham
Cagie Napoleon, upholsterer, bds Queen's Hotel
Caldback James, teamster, Colborne
Caldback James, carder, cor Second and Alfred
Caldback John H., salesman, bds Colborne
Calder James, clerk, Federal Bank
CALDWELL & SON, lumber merchants, cor Ontario & Place de Armes
Callaghan Daniel, accountant, 168 Sydenham
Callaghan David, salesman, 46 Colborne
Callaghan James, cabinet maker, 46 Colborne
Callaghan James, carpenter, Johnson
Callaghan James, jr., tuner, Johnson
Callaghan Thomas, engineer, Sydenham
Callaghan William, finisher, Johnson
Calvert William, bar tender, New Burnett House
Cambridge Hervey, laborer, Wellington
Cambridge Thomas, laborer, Wellington
Cameron Mrs. Marion, Maitland
Cameron Sam., mariner, Victoria
Cameron William, carpenter, 147 Pine
Campbell Alexr., grocer, Montreal
Campbell Daniel, driver Shedden Company, Bagot

Campbell Geo. S., outside porter, Windsor Hotel
Campbell James, wood dealer, foot Brock
Campbell James, mason, 158 Pine
Campbell John, carpenter, 481 Albert
Campbell John, book-keeper, Ontario
Campbell John, King w
Campbell John, moulder, Locomotive Works
Campbell Matthew, policeman, 49 Beverley.
Campbell Michael, grinder, Montreal
Campbell Peter, laborer, 87 Barrie
Campbell R & M., grocers, 294 Princess
Campbell Robert, carter, Gordon
Campbell Miss Sarah, 206 William
Campbell Thomas, carpenter, Princess
Campbell William, plasterer, Pine
Campion C., salesman, Princess
Campion Richard, painter, Locomotive Works
Campion Wm., laborer, Earl
CANADIAN EXPRESS CO., J. S. Patch, agent, cor. King & Market Square
CANADIAN LOCOMOTIVE & ENGINE CO., (limited), Wm. Harty, managing director; H. Tandy, superintendent; Jos. W. Pyke, secretary; G. A Newman, asst. secretary, Ontario
Canal Office, Wm. Burrows, collector, Clarence
Canfield, W. A., manager King Hosiery Co., Arch
Cannem Henry, laborer, 422 Division
Cannon Geo., clerk, 188 Division
Cannon G F., salesman, 188 Division
Cannon William, merchant tailor, 273 Princess
Cannon Wm., clerk, 273 Princess
Capes Duncan, drover, Princess
Carey John, moulder, 307 Brock
Carey Joseph, pensioner, William
CAREY REV. W. B., M.A., rector St. Paul's Church, 213 Queen
CAREY & SON (Wm. & Thomas) music dealers, 159 Princess, h Rideau (*see advt. inside front*)
Card Mrs. Harriet, Princess
Carlton Mrs. Julia, King
Carlton Wm., moulder, Kingston Foundry
Carmichael W. D., com. traveller, Wellington
Carnegie Wm., trader, Johnson
Carnovsky B. H., piano maker, 680 Princess
Carnovsky Robert, 680 Princess
Carnovsky T., baker, 680 Princess
Carr Alexr., machinist, Rideau
Carr James, machinist, Rideau
Carron George, mariner, Gore
Carroll Mrs. Ann, Earl
Carroll Mrs. C., 81 Ontario
Carroll James, moulder, Kingston Foundry
Carroll John, blacksmith, Locomotive Works
Carroll Patrick, 294 Ontario
Carroll Patrick, engineer, Barrie
Carroll Robert, Davidson, Doran & Co., h 10 Stuart
Carroll Timothy, tailor, Rideau
Carroll William, laborer, Brock
CARRUTHERS BROS. (J. B. & W. C.) financial agents, 44 Clarence
CARRUTHERS J. B. (Carruthers Bros.) h West
Carruthers George, grocer, 252 Princess
Carruthers John, cor. Sydenham & Earl

CARRUTHERS W.C. (Carruthers Bros.) h 89 Sydenham
Carruthers Wm., 259 Princess
Carscallen T. B., grocer, cor. Princess & Barrie
Carson & Co. (W. H. & John), grocers, 322 Princess
Carson Charles, fitter, cor. King & Barrack
Carson Robert, wholesale grocer, 330 Princess, h Brock
Carson Robert, police sergeant, 220 Gordon
Carson Mrs. S., 103 Wellington
Carson Wm., messenger, Kingston Hospital
Carter Daniel, laborer, Locomotive Works
Carter Robert, 110 Bagot
Carter Thos., grocer, 647 Princess
Carter T. C., printer, 647 Princess
Cartmill Nathaniel, machinist, 203 Alfred
Cartwright Hon. Sir Richard, 13 King w
Cartwright R. C., medical student, 13 King w
Casey Mrs. Ellen, Bagot
Cassidy Donald, mariner, bds St. Lawrence House
Cassidy John, carver, n s John
Cassidy Mrs. Margaret, Wellington
Cassidy Mrs. Nancy, 153 Alfred
Cassidy Mrs. Sarah, 51 John
Cassidy William, farmer, bds St. Lawrence House
Cassidy William H., carpenter, 153 Alfred
Castle Jno., wood worker, Princess
Castle Joseph, laborer, Locomotive Works
Caswell John, carriage maker, Princess
Caswell Thos. A., carriage maker, Princess
Cathala A., laborer, Kingston Foundry
Cathala August, watchman new Burnett House
CATHOLIC APOSTOLIC CHURCH, 287 Queen
Caulfield, Thomas, mariner, 206 Bagot
Cavanagh Henry, painter, Car Works
Caverly Nathaniel, blacksmith, York
Chadwick Allan, shipper, Court House
Chadwick Harvey, carter, bds 273 Princess
Chadwick Wm. M. (Greenwood & Chadwick), h 341 Barrie
Chalkey Robert, moulder, 88 York
Chalkley Robert, laborer, 253 Division
CHALMERS' CHURCH (Presbyterian) Earl, bet Bagot and Sydenham
Chamberlin Benjamin, carpenter, 244 Colborne
Chambers Rev. Thomas, 20 William
Chambers Wm., student-at-law, 202 William
Chance Ellis, 159 Brock
Chance W. H., barber, Wellington
Chapman Elisha, laborer, 266 Sydenham
Chapman H. E., laborer, Chatham
Chapman Sydney, contractor, 59 Colborne
Chapman W. J., carpenter, 124 Colborne
Charles Edwin, carpenter, Gore
Charles J. A., book-keeper, 192 Sydenham
Charlton Robert, foreman Locomotive Works, 161 Bagot
Chatterton Edward (Chatterton & McLeod) h 281 Princess

Chatterton & McLeod, carpenters, 277 Princess
Chestnut James, 238 Victoria
Chesley James, gardener, Kingston Hospital
Childs Henry, superintendent Kingston Car Works
Choran D., blacksmith, Car Works
Chown A. F., clerk, 252 Bagot
Chown Albert P., druggist, 124 Princess, h 46 Brock
CHOWN ARTHUR, hardware, 252 Bagot, h 297 Queen
CHOWN & CUNNINGHAM (Edwin Chown, Henry Cunningham and Chas. D. Chown, founders) 248 Bagot, foundry cor. King & Queen
CHOWN CHAS. D., (Chown & Cunningham), h William
CHOWN EDWIN (Chown & Cunningham), 185 Brock
Chown Oliver, clerk, Bagot
Chown Robert, moulder, Johnson
CHRISTIAN BROTHERS' School (Rev. Bro. Halward, director) 89 Clergy
Chrisley Edward, hostler, 77 Colborne
Chrisley William, porter, 333 Princess
Christmas Henry, butcher, res Williamsville
Christmas Thos. J., laborer, King
Christmas Wm., mariner, King nr Queen
CHRONICLE & NEWS (weekly), Lewis W. Shannon, prop., 67 Princess
Chrystor Robert, book-binder, Bagot
Cicolari Alexr., 113 Wellington
CITY HOTEL (Arch. McFaul, prop.,) 129 Princess
Clancy Frank, clerk, 113 Ontario
Clancy Thos., laborer, 113 Ontario

Clancy Miss Jane, Brock
Clancy Michael, laborer, 133 Bagot
Clapham Wm., laborer, King
Clark Alfred J., tel. operator, Park
Clark Charles H., eating house, Bagot
Clark Edmund, boiler maker, Second
Clark Edmund, jr., driller, Locomotive Works
Clark Edward, accountant, 48 Clergy
Clark Fred., machinist, 54 Bay
Clark H. C., salesman, 48 Clergy
Clark James, currier, Tannery
Clark J. E., book-keeper, 48 Clergy
Clark J. H., dentist, 190 Wellington
Clark Joseph, machinist, Arch
Clark Mrs. Mary, laundress, 148 Division
Clark Mrs. Mary Ann, 17 Bondhead
Clark Pat., butcher, 847 Princess
Clark P. B., com. traveller, 186 Queen
Clark Peter, laborer, 474 Montreal
Clark Robert, mason, 19 Agnew's Lane
Clark Thomas, clerk, 86 Queen
Clark Wm., moulder, cor. First & Alfred
Clark William, laborer, 255 Johnson
Clark William J., laborer, Park
Claxton Matthew, tinsmith, 27 Charles
Clay Henry, baker, Barrack
Clayton Daniel, carpenter, 59 Ontario
Clayton Martin, carpenter, 187 Bagot
Cleary Mrs. Catharine, Park
CLEARY VERY REV. JAMES VINCENT, Bishop of Kingston, the Palace, 225 Johnson

Cleary Owen, book-keeper, 272 Sydenham
CLEMENTS LEONARD, L.D.S., dentist, 140 Wellington (see card)
Clenington Thomas, laborer, Locomotive Works
Clerihew Geo., book-keeper, Earl
Cliff John, broker, 132 Clarence
Cliff Mrs. Mary, 132 Clarence
Clifford George, laborer, 131 Colborne
Clint P., grocer, foot Johnson
Clock Enis, laborer, Colborne
Close William, boiler maker, 268 Queen
Close William, moulder, Locomotive Works
Cloud John, machinist, bds 103 Brock
Clugston Robert, mason, Brock
Cockade Mrs., Main
Cockburn Jas., cabman, 148 Pine
Cockburn John, steam fitter, 275 Ontario
Cockburn Wm., blacksmith, 277 Ontario
Cochrane Edward, piano maker, Ontario
Cochrane Mrs. Christina, Johnson
Cochrane James, mariner, Gordon
COCHRANE LIEUT. JOHN BRAY, C.M., R.M. College
Cochrane William, laborer, Barrie
Cochrane William, tanner, 41 Barrack
C.O.D. STORE, hats, caps, gents' furnishings, 206 Princess
Coffey, Fred., laborer, King w
Coffey Thomas, caretaker, Bagot
Coffey William, maltster, 57 Herchmer
Coggan Albert, carpenter, Rideau
Coggan Jesse, carpenter, James
Coleman Dennis, pensioner, Victoria
Colfer Miss Ann, 179 Clarence
Collins Mrs. Caroline, 337 Princess
Collins Dewitt, fireman, Rideau
Collins John, letter carrier, 6 George w
Collins Mrs. Margaret, Sydenham
Collins Pat., carter, 192 Barrack
Collins Thomas, laborer, 438 Division
Comeo Joseph, mariner, Ontario
Compord Thos., laborer, Locomotive Works
Conlan Mrs. Ann, William
Conlan John, tailor, William
Conley Henry, clerk, Barrie
Conley Patrick, storeman, York
Conley Thomas, merchant tailor, 86 Brock, h 45 Gore
Conley William, stone cutter, 368 Division
Connelly Patrick, mariner, 163 York
Connelly John, mariner, 168 York
Connelly Patrick, laborer, 163 York
Connolly James, laborer, Bondhead nr Bay
Connolly John, blacksmith, Locomotive Works
Connor James, piano maker, 354 Brock
Connors Wm., machinist, Locomotive Works
Conroy Michael, grocer, Market Square, h 27 Ellice
Conroy Patrick, 27 Ellice
CONVENT OF THE CONGREGATION OF NOTRE DAME, 203 Bagot
Conway Frank, freight and passenger agent K. & P. RR., bds new Burnett House
Conway James, storeman, 91 Wellington
COOK REV. CHARLES, Baptist, 93 Johnson

KINGSTON TIN WORKS.

JAMES REID,

MANUFACTURER OF

TINWARE, MILK CANS, &C.

SPECIAL AT   'OBBING.

Office ar   ı Streets,

T.C.   ST

"British   Street.

For Genuine Goods, First Class Fit, Superior Workmanship, combined with Moderate Prices, we excel over all competitors in this city.

T. C. TILLINGHAST, THE TAILOR,

KINGSTON.

Coombs William, turner, Locomotive Works
Coon Edward, contractor, 95 Queen
Cooney Patrick, pensioner, 346 Johnson
Cooper Mrs. C., Young's Lane
Cooper Chas., switchman, Park
Cooper Ebenezer, clerk, Princess
Cooper J. G., accountant, 298 Gordon
Cooper Joseph, laborer, bds St. Lawrence Hotel
Cooper Thomas, gardener, Earl
Cope Fred., laborer, Sydenham
Copeland Wm., 198 Sydenham
Copley James, carder, Charles
Corbett C. F., clerk G. T. R., Barrie
Corbett C. H., gaoler, Court House
CORBETT JOHN, hardware, cor. Princess and Wellington, h 123 George
Corbett William, tinsmith, 413 Princess
Cormack John, janitor Queen's College
Cornford Thos., laborer, 24 Elm
Cornelius Mrs. E., boarding, 47 Princess
Cornelius John, sailor, 47 Princess
Corrigan Daniel, trader, 58 Bondhead
Corrigan John, laborer, 111 Ontario
Corrigan M. P., salesman, 99 Bondhead
Corrigan Patrick, laborer, 99 Bondhead
Corrigan Richard, carriage maker, 271 Division
Corrigan Thomas, laborer, 106 Ontario
Corrigan William, mariner, West
Cosby Charles S., shoemaker, 113 Brock
Costello Alex., moulder, North
Costello Mrs M., 21 Barrack
Costello Samuel, laborer, North
Costello Samuel, moulder, Locomotive Works
Cotters John, laborer, Car Works
Couper Daniel, salesman, res Williamsville
Couper Ebenezer, salesman, bds 772 Princess
Couper John, carpenter, cor Chatham and Second
Coughlin James, driver Shedden Co
Coushart David, fitter, William
COUSINEAU F. X. & CO., dry goods, 80 Princess
COVERDALE WILLIAM, city engineer, 321 King w
Coward Mrs. E. J., Brock
Coward John, moulder, Princess
Coward Mark, salesman, Brock
Coward Wm., baker, 20 Beverly
Cowie Thomas, mason, 23 John
Cowley William, carpenter, Locomotive Works
Cowmen Richard, carder, 298 Montreal
Cox John, laborer, Park
Coxworthy Mrs. M., 475 Princess
Coy Miss Sarah, 101 Queen
Coyle James, printer, Alma
Coyles James, salesman, 25 Balaclava
Coyle James, sr., laborer, 25 Balaclava
Coyne Louis, second hand dealer, 45 Princess
Craig Adam, laborer, Locomotive Works
Craig Andrew, King
Craig Arthur W., Alfred
Craig James, 437 King w
Craig James, finisher, Alfred
Craig James, coppersmith, Locomotive Works

Craig James A., boiler maker, Barrack
Craig Robert, weaver, 29 King w
Craig Thomas, gardener, Regent
CRAIG WM. G. (A. Gunn & Co.) h 57 West
Craig Mrs. Mary G., Arch
Crawford George, Princess
Crawford David, gardener, 238 Earl
Crawford James, grocer, 182 Princess, h 124 Division
Crawford J. J., cutter, Wellington
Crawford John, gardener, 26 Hamilton's Lane
Crawford John, machinist, King
Crawford Mrs. Mary, Union
Crawford Robert, coal dealer, foot Queen, h 98 Clergy
Crawford Robert, painter, Earl
Crawford William, carpenter, 108 Barrack
Cridiford John, barber, cor King and Clarence
CREDIT VALLEY RR., V. G. Hooper, agent, 42 Clarence
Creeggan Geo., Main, cor Pickard
Creeggan J. G., clerk, Division
Creeggan John, clerk, cor Main and Pickard
Creelan Edward, blacksmith, Locomotive Works
Creeley Alphonse, cooper, (P. Bajus)
Creighton George, printer, George
Crillin Edw., boiler maker, James
Crillin Wm., laborer, Hamilton's Lane
Crook James R., mariner, Alfred
Crothers Hutchinson (H. & W. J. Crothers), Queen
Crothers H. & W. J. (Hutchinson and William John), bakers and confectioners, 207 Wellington
Crothers William J. (H. & W. J. Crothers), Rideau
Crowe Henry, laborer, 129 Alfred
Crowe Henry, jr., laborer, 129 Alfred
Crowley Chas., hotel, Market Sq
Crowley Charles W., tobacconist, 41 Princess
Crowley James, machinist, Car Works
Crowley John, grocer, Rideau
Crowley Peter, laborer, Centre
Crowter William, painter, 115 Ordnance
Crozier David, piano maker, bds Waggoner House
Crozier James, printer, bds cor Brock and Bagot
Crozier Robert, pressman, bds Waggoner House
Curley John, sailor, 69 Bay
CRUMLEY EDWARD (Spence & Crumley), h 48 Union
Crumley Henry, salesman, 48 Union
Crumley Hugh, carpenter, 48 Union
Crumley John, laborer, 49 Main
Cruse Thomas, 322 Gordon
Cruse William H., shoemaker, 60 Elm
Crysler C. B., inspector weights and measures, Clarence, h 69 Union
Crystle William, porter City Hotel
Cuddiford Edward J., stonecutter, 682 Montreal
Cudmore Daniel, 59 William
Cudmore Jno., laborer, 59 William
Cullen Patrick, laborer, Park
Cullen Patrick, sr., laborer, cor John and Thomas
Cullen William, oiler, George
Cullen Wm., laborer, n s Charles
Cummings Michael, laborer, 374 Brock
Cunningham Miss Agnes, 21 King w

Cunningham David, cabman, 180 Bagot
Cunningham David, jr., printer, 180 Bagot
Cunningham David, builder, Arch
CUNNINGHAM HENRY (Chown & Cunningham), h 169 Earl
Cunningham Mrs. Jane, Barrie
CUNNINGHAM JOHN, dealer in sewing machines, 348 King e
Cunningham John, salesman, 348 King
Cunningham John, laborer, Car Works
Cunningham Robert, 216 Division
Cunningham Samuel, carpenter, 18 Deacon
Cunningham Thos., clerk, Bagot
Cunningham William, 118 Barrie
Cunningham William, blacksmith, Young's Lane
Curley Mrs. Mary, n s John
Curragh James, finisher, Kingston Foundry
Curran Robt., boiler maker, King w
Curtis C. L., M.D., 136 Wellington
Curtis Mrs. Lucy, 228 Wellington
Curtis Patrick, boots and shoes, 109 Brock
Cushion Thos., laborer, 28 Alma
CUSTOM HOUSE, cor King and Clarence
Dacey Martin and John, shoemakers, Ontario
Dacey Martin, shoemaker, 191 Ontario
DAILY & WEEKLY BRITISH WHIG (E. J. B. Pense, prop.,) 386 and 440 King e
DAILY NEWS (Lewis W. Shannon, prop.,) 67 Princess
Daley James, printer, 16 Place de Armes
Daley James, agent, Division
Daley John, sailor, 16 Place de Armes
Daley Joseph, stone cutter, 94 Bay
Daley Mrs., 16 Place de Armes
Daley Patrick, stone cutter, bds St. Lawrence Hotel
Daley Pat., printer, 121 Ordnance
Daley Thomas, grocer, 16 Place de Armes
Daley William, grocer, Princess
DALTON W. B. (J. Muckleston & Co.,) h 186 Johnson
Darragh John, clerk, 194 Alfred
Darragh Geo., carpenter, Montreal
Daunt Joseph (Kelly, McKay & Daunt), h Gordon
Davey George, carpenter, Beverly
Davey John, carpenter, Sydenham
Davey Stuart, carpenter, Johnson
David M., broker, 265 Princess
David Sam., laborer, 82 Colborne
David Wm., broker, 241 Princess
DAVIDSON, DORAN & CO., proprietors Kingston Foundry, 87 Ontario
DAVIDSON GEORGE (Davidson, Doran & Co.,) h 32 Ontario
Davidson John, laborer, 30 York
Davidson John, jr., butcher, 80 York
Davidson Mrs. Mary A., Barrie
Davidson Thomas, keeper K.P., 49 Pembroke
Davison John W., carpenter, Princess
Davis Mrs. Ellen, 148 Ordnance
Davis Francis, carpenter, Car Works
Davis George, laborer, Kingston Foundry
Davis James, shoemaker, 100 Barrack
Davis James, boots and shoes, 269 Princess
Davis James, engineer, 42 Wellington
Davis John, carpenter, Locomotive Works

Davis R. F. (Sheldon & Davis), h 32 King e
Davis Richard, laborer, Locomotive Works
Davis Robt., ship builder, Ontario
Davis Steward, carpenter, Locomotive Works
Davis Wm., carpenter, Car Works
Davin Wm., laborer, Loco. Works
Dawson A., maltster, King w
Dawson Alex. A., clerk, Second
Dawson A. A., druggist, 248 Colborne
Dawson Eaton, spinner, Cotton Co
Dawson Edward, finisher, 279 Division
Dawson Francis, laborer, 282 Montreal
DAY FORSHAW, R.C.A., R.M. Coll., 179 Division
Day Mrs. Harriet, 161 Park
Deary Patrick, stove mounter, Victoria Foundry
Dechron Adolphus, blacksmith, James
Decks William A., blacksmith, 205 Brock
Decks W. W., salesman, bds 205 Brock
Deel Charles, plumber, 141 Wellington
Dehaney Francis, teamster, 25 Ontario
Dehaney Wm., pensioner, Bagot
DeLacey Miss Nellie, dressmaker, 314 Princess
Delaney Mrs. E., dry goods, 288 Princess
Delaney Pat., machinist, Thomas
Delaney William, carpenter, Car Works
Delaney Wm., machinist, Barrie
Demphy James, packer, 96 York
Dempsey Miss Mary, Johnson
Dempsey Samuel, grocer, 265 Princess

Denn Wm., caretaker, Sydenham
Dennee Averisto, butcher, Montreal
Dennis Mrs. Frances, grocer, cor Princess and Clergy
Dennismore John, laborer, John
Dennison Jas., laborer, 367 Brock
Dennison James, jr., boat builder, 367 Brock
Dennison Mrs. Mary, laundress, 73 Ordnance
Denny James, blacksmith, Locomotive Works
Densmore Charles, laborer, Car Works
Derowin Louis, carpenter, Ontario
Derry Miss Eliza, 28 Ontario
Derry Hugh, mason, Second
Derry James, boiler maker, 50 William
Derry P., mason, 240 Colborne
Derry Patrick, grocer, Second
Derry Thomas, boiler maker, 86 Colborne
Derry William, mason, s s Pine
Derry William H., engineer, 256 King e
DesRochers Joseph, machinist, Earl
Devan Maurice, carpenter, 16 Colborne
DEVANA JOHN, grocer, cor King and Princess
Devine Jas., carter, 9 Upper Bagot
Devlin Pat., cabman, 85 Barrack
Devlin Peter, cabman, Montreal
Devlin Terrence, laborer, Locomotive Works
DICK D. J (W. J. Dick & Son) h 187 Clergy
Dick James, salesman, 995 Alfred
DICK W. J. & SON (W. J. & D. J.,) boots and shoes, trunks, valises, etc., 168 Princess
DICK W. J. (W. J. Dick & Son), h 293 Alfred

CITY OF KINGSTON. 37

Dickinson Robert, tinsmith, 229 Gordon
Dickinson Robert J., salesman, 229 Gordon
Dickson James, blacksmith, Locomotive Works
Dickson Jno., mariner, 80 Barrack
Dickson John, shoemaker, 245 Ontario
Dickson John R., M.D., 176 Johnson
Dillon J. E., salesman, Brock
Dillon Joseph, boots and shoes, 111 Princess
Dine George, blacksmith, Locomotive Works
Dine Mark, rivetter, Loco. Works
Dine Philbert, blacksmith, Loco. Works
Divis A., cooper, 130 Ontario
Dix Samuel, machinist, Locomotive Works
Dixon Knapp, spinner, Hosiery Co
Dodd Geo., blacksmith, 5 O'Kill
Dodd John, blacksmith, 10 George
Dodd John, jr., engineer, 10 George
Dodd Jos., blacksmith, Car Works
Dodd Thomas, moulder, Kingston Foundry
Dolan Martin, harness maker, 219 Princess
Dolan Michael, harness maker, 219 Princess
Dolphin John, machinist, 21 Gordon
DOMINION IRON LADDER CO., 390 Princess
DOMINION SALVAGE AND WRECKING CO., (John Donnelly, wreck master,) 196 Ontario
Donald Mrs. Jane, 772 Montreal
Donnelly David, laborer, Earl
Donnelly Felix J., boiler maker, 223 Gordon
Donnelly James, clerk, 54 Bondhead
DONNELLY JOHN, wreck master Dominion Salvage and Wrecking Co., Ontario, h 212 Wellington
Donnelly Joseph, 52 Gordon
Donnelly M., stove mounter, Victoria Foundry
Donnelly S., finisher, Kingston Foundry
Donoghue Mrs. Ann, 223 Wellington
Donoghue Charles, grocer, 301 Ontario
Donoghue Daniel, grocer, 301 Ontario
Donoghue James, grocer, 301 Ontario
Donoghue John, wharfman, Barrack
Donoghue John, engineer, cor King and Queen
Donoghue Mrs. M., Johnson
Donoghue Michael, carpenter, O'Kill
Donoghue Michael, laborer, 162 Bagot
Donoghue Timothy, 409 King
Donoghue Fred., laborer, O'Kill
Donovan Mrs. Catharine, Brock
Doolan Jeremiah, laborer, 92 Rideau
Doolan Jno., laborer, 80 Magdalen
Doolan Timothy, hotel, 320 King
Doran Mrs. Ann, 115 Queen
Doran B. & Co., dry goods and millinery. 126 Princess
Doran Bridget (B. Doran & Co.,) h 42 Barrie
Doran Daniel, Johnson
DORAN MICHAEL (Davidson, Doran & Co.,) h 81 Ontario
Doran Wm., painter, 257 King c
Dougherty Charles, book-keeper, bds City Hotel

Dougherty Edward, butcher, 856 Princess
Dougherty John, laborer, 149 Bagot
Dougherty John, laborer, Elm
Dougherty William, laborer, Elm
Douglas H. J., bailiff, 322 King e
Douglas James A., piano finisher, 322 King e
Douglas Robert, mason, Centre
Douglas Robert, moulder, Locomotive Works
Douglas William, mason, Park
Dovey James, shoemaker, 109 Ordnance
Downes Jas., laborer, Wellington
Downey Timothy, shoemaker, 210 Bagot
Downing James, Alice
Downing William, carpenter, 165 King w
Downs James, blacksmith, Barrie
Dowsley William, saddler, Locomotive Works
Doyle Edward, carpenter, Park
Doyle Hugh, grocer, cor Barrie and Brock
Doyle Jeremiah, grocer, 717 Princess
Doyle James, blacksmith, bds McGrath House
Doyle Miss Johanna, John
Doyle John, tanner, bds Waggoner House
Doyle John, blacksmith, Locomotive Works
Doyle Mrs. M. A., 76 Wellington
Doyle Michael, bar tender, cor Clarence and Wellington
Doyle Patrick, laborer, 102 Rideau
Doyle Wm., butcher, 726 Princess
DRENNAN W. M., manufacturer and dealer in furniture, 75-77 Princess, h Earl
Driscoll Dennis, mason, cor Gore and Wellington
Driscoll Patrick, foreman Locomotive Works
Driver John, salesman, 128 Queen
Driver Thos., appraiser Customs, 161 Queen
Driver William, clerk, 128 Queen
Drury Mrs. Mary, Princess
Duff Edward, laborer, 40 York
Duff John, magistrate, 450 Princess
Duffy James, laborer, Montreal, nr Charles
Duffy Timothy, laborer, Rideau
Duffy Wm., moulder, 113 William
Duigman Michael, sailor, 107 Ordnance
Dumble Henry, cor Brock and Wellington
Dumphey Edward, painter, 258 Queen
Dumphey Martin, painter, 258 Queen
Dumphy Jas., steward, 258 Queen
Dumphy James, jr., packer, 258 Queen
Dunbar Andrew, prop. Queen's Hotel, 127 Brock
DUNBAR & CO. (John Dunbar & Alex. G. Flett,) merchant tailors and clothiers, 100 Princess
Dunbar Henry, messenger Post Office, res Post Office
DUNBAR JOHN (Dunbar & Co.,) h Vaughn Terrace
Duncan, Alexander, carpenter, Car Works
Dunlop A. W., book-keeper, Rideau
Dungan Edward, machinist, bds Ontario
Dunlop James, 96 Rideau
Dunlop James M., grocer, 20 Princess
Dunlop John, 87 Colborne
Dunlop John W., 13 Maitland
Dunlop Miss Mary, 13 Maitland

CITY OF KINGSTON. 39

Dunlop Robert, tailor, 29 John
Dunlop William, cutter, 56 Union
Dunn John, laborer, 50 O'Kill
Dunn Mrs. Julian, grocer, 222 Wellington
Dunn Pat., cigar maker, 120 Bay
Dunn William, stoves and tinware, 229-231 Princess
Dunnett William, foreman Shedden Co
Dupuis Thos. R., M.D., cor Montreal and Brock
Dupuis Nathan F., M.A., F.R.C.S., prof. Queen's College
Dupuy Mrs. Sophia, 164 Barrie
DUVAL ARTHUR DUPONTH, M.D., R. M. College
Duxbury R. W., foreman carder, Hosiery Co
Dwyer E. J., salesman, 42 Barrie
Dwyer Jno., porter Burnett House
Dwyer Michael, laborer, Loco. Works
Dyde Sam, book-keeper, William
Dyer Hobart, com. traveller, William
Dykes James, painter, 95 Pine
Eacutt Isaac, mechanic, Park
Earley John, bar tender, cor Ontario and Clarence
Earley John, laborer, cor Ontario and Clarence
Early T. J., salesman, cor Ontario and Clarence
Easton Robert, driver Shedden Co
Eaves Dan., carter, 147 Ordnance
Eaves Jas, cabman, 32 Bondhead
Eaves Mark, laborer, 149 Ordnance
Eaves Wm., painter, 150 Colborne
Edwards Mrs. Alice, dressmaker, 170 Brock
Edwards Richard, clerk, 117 Ordnance
Edgar David, fireman, Ford & Sons

Edgar D., moulder, Car Works
Egan Daniel, porter, Wellington
Egan Michael, laborer, 67 Queen
Egan John, moulder, Victoria Foundry
Eggleton Charles, salesman, Bondhead
Eggleston Jas., laborer, 65 Bondhead
Elder Chas., carpenter, bds Island House
Eilbeck & Murray (R. J. Eilbeck and James Murray, jr.,) agents, foot Princess
Eilbeck R. J. (Eilbeck & Murray), foot Princess
ELKINGTON FRANCIS, County Clerk, 282 Victoria
Elliott Anthorn, groom, 236 Wellington
Elliott George, trader, 45 Main
Elliott James, laborer, Redan
Elliott Mrs. Jane, 21 Balaclava
Elliott J. G., reporter *Whig*, bds Burnett House
Elliott Matthew, tinsmith, 368 Division
Elliott Robert, carpenter, 368 Division
Elmer A., barber, 74 Princess
Elmer Jos., barber, 161 Princess
Elmer R. H., barber, 161 Princess
Elmer Thos., baker, 209 Montreal
Elmer Thomas, moulder, Earl
Elmer Thomas, prop. saloon, 201 Princess, h Montreal
Elmer Wm., moulder, Victoria Foundry
Elsimere Alex., guard K.P., Gordon
Emmett Maitland, engineer, bds Waggoner House
Empey Fred., saloon, King
England Thos., gardener, Regent
English Anthony, boarding, 71 Clarence

JAMES REID,

FURNITURE MANUFACTURER, UNDERTAKER AND EMBALMER,

Rooms 254 & 256 Princess Street, Kingston.

OUR SERVICES CAN BE HAD AT ANY HOUR DAY OR NIGHT.

Three First Class Hearses.

All kinds of Upholstering and Repairing promptly attended to.

WADDINGTON BROS.

WHOLESALE AND RETAIL DEALERS IN

BEEF, MUTTON, PORK, SMOKED TONGUES,

Bologna and Other Sausages, Hams, Lard, &c.

We make a specialty of VENISON, which, in season, we have always on hand

KING STREET, MARKET SQUARE, KINGSTON.

A. SIMMONDS,

DEALER IN

Old and New Books, Stationer, &c.

OLD BOOKS BOUGHT.

228 PRINCESS STREET, KINGSTON, ONT.

English David, farmer, Princess
English Mrs. Mary Ann, Agnew's Lane
Ennis Andrew, laborer, 11 Rideau
Ennis James, 11 Rideau
Ennis John, mariner, 11 Rideau
Ennis John, spinner, Cottton Co
Enright Michael, driver, Chatham
Enright Thos., laborer, Ordnance
Erskin John, laborer, Loco. Works
Esford John, laborer, Loco. Works
Evans Benjamin, gardener, Johnston
Evans James, keeper K.P., 287 King w
Evans John, machinist, Loco. Works
Evans Richard, 25 Chatham
Evard Robert, book-keeper, Queen
Everitt Miss Harriett, 231 Bagot
Eward F. W., blacksmith, 240 Division
Eward Fred, blacksmith, 240 Division
Fahey Edward, exciseman, 58 Bagot
Fahey M., merchant tailor, 344 King e
Fahey Mrs. M., confectioner, 68 Princess
Fahey Martin, 35 Wellington
Fair Jas., constable, 251 Division
Fair W. J., book-keeper, 45 Gore
Fairburn Wm., laborer, Park
FAIRTLOUGH MAJOR SAM'L GERRAD, R.A., R.M.C.
Fallon Dominic, saloon keeper, Princess
Fallon James, laborer, Young's Lane
Fallon Michael, carter, s s Charles
Fallon Patrick, carter, Rideau
Fanning John, laborer, 83 Johnson
Fanning Patrick, laborer, 34 Alma
Fannon John, clerk, 83 Johnson

Farebrother John, carpenter, 390 Princess
FARLEY LIEUT. & BT. CAPT. C.A., "B" Battery, Tete du Pont Barracks
Farley J., teamster, Car Works
Farley Thomas, moulder, 146 Queen
Farmer John, salesman, Bowes & Bisonette
Farrell Alex., 295 Alfred
Farrell Mrs. M., 295 Alfred
Farrell Martin, 524 Princess
FARRELL THOMAS, grocer, Market Square, Brock
Farrelly John, carter, 307 Johnson
Farrelly Thomas, fitter, Loco. Works
Farrell Wm., twister, Cotton Co.
Farrington James, 18 Wellington
Feddie Phillip, blacksmith, Loco. Works
FEDERAL BANK, T. Y. Greet, manager, cor. Wellington & Clarence.
FEE SAMUEL H., M.D., 405 Princess
Fee Wm., cattle dealer, 265 Princess
Felix Alex., mariner, Ontario
Felix Alex., fitter, Loco. Works
Fell D. J., saloon keeper, 143 Princess
Fenwick George S., (Fenwick, Hendry & Co.) h cor. Centre & King
Fenwick George W., e s Nelson
Fenwick Hendry & Co., (G. S. Fenwick, Mrs. M. Hendry, M. G. Sutherland) wholesale grocers, 267-9 Ontario.
FENWICK K. N., M.D., physician, surgeon &c., 141 King e
Fenwick Thos. M., M.D., 420 King e

Ferguson Mrs. Agnes, 72 Ellice
FERGUSON A. J., accountant Merchants' Bank, 102 Bagot
Ferguson Arch. M., student at law, Earl
Ferguson Daniel, mechanic, Montreal
FERGUSON REV. GEORGE D., professor, Queen's College
Ferguson Wm., sheriff, 179 King e
Ferns Mrs. C., fancy goods, 116 Princess
Ferrier George, machinist, 99 Chatham
Ferris Mrs. Mary, 387 King w
Ferris Robert, carpenter, bds 340 Princess
Ferrington Chas. W., mariner, Second
Field Charles, gardener, 154 Gordon
Fielding John, laborer, Cotton Co.
Fields Arthur, barber, 49 Princess
Fillion E. M., driver, Sydenham
Filtz George, carpenter, 140 Bagot
Filtz Philip, piano maker, Johnson
Finn Wm., planer, Loco. Works
FIRE INSURANCE ASSOCIATION of London, Eng., Thos. Mills agent, 91 Clarence
FIRST CONGREGATIONAL CHURCH, 128 Wellington
Fisher John, trader, 51 Barrack
Fisher John, laborer, Barrie
Fitzgibbon Henry, moulder, Loco. Works
Fitzgerald Mrs. Catherine, 98 Ontario
Fitzgerald Jas., engineer, Beverly
Fitzgerald Thomas, head waiter, Windsor Hotel
Fitzgerald Wm., fitter, Loco. Works
Fitzgivens Patrick, laborer, King
Fitzpatrick Mrs. Mary, laundress, 127 Division

Flanery James, 11 Arch
Flanagan Andrew, Princess
FLANAGAN MICHAEL, city clerk, 110 Bagot
Flanagan Michael E., gardener, bds 110 Bagot
Flanagan Patrick, laborer, Rideau
Flanagan Patrick, engineer, Earl
Flanagan Thomas, cabman, 109 William
Flemming John, cabman, Park
Flemming Thos., cabman, Park
Flemming Wm., laborer, Loco. Works
FLETCHER JOHN, M.A., professor Queen's College
Fletcher John, Bagot
FLETT ALEX, (Dunbar & Co.) h 74 Colborne
Fleury Thomas, laborer, Earl
Flint Charles, laborer, King nr Queen
Flood Anthony, hotel keeper, bds St. Lawrence House
Flood James, laborer, 244 Ontario
Flyn Francis, moulder, 31 Union
Flynn Michael, moulder, 81 Union
Flynn Michael, tinsmith, Barrie
Flynn William, tinsmith, Loco. Works
Foden John, machinist, 114 Ordnance
Foley Michael, carter, Earl
Folger Bros, B.W. & M.H., bankers, cor. Ontario & Clarence
Folger B.W. (Folger Bros.), h cor Earl and King
Folger F. A., (Folger Bros.) h Clergy
Folger & Hanley, general ticket agents, foot Brock
Folger M. H. (Folger Bros.), foot Emily
Follest W. B., carter, w s Nelson
Ford Edward, tanner, Ford & Sons

Ford R. M. (Ford & Sons) h cor. Johnson and Barrie
Ford & Sons (Wm. G. & R. M.) props. Cataraqui Tannery) 312 King e
Ford William G. (Ford & Sons) h 196 Queen
Forder Thomas Geo., machinist, 144 Colborne
Forrest Jas., salesman, 35 Union
Forrest Wm., carpenter, 35 Union
Forrester Edgar, prof. Queen's College
Forrester Gus, bar tender, City Hotel
Forsyth Andrew, machinist, Loco. Works
Forsyth George, trader, cor. Nelson & Princess
Forsythe George, fitter, Loco. Works
Forsyth James M., 46 Wellington
Forsyth J. B., agricultural implements agent, Montreal, h cor. Colborne & Clergy
Forsythe Mrs. Margaret, 834 Princess
Forsyth Robert, farmer, 263 Division
Foster John, embalmer, bds Albion Hotel
Foster John, book-keeper, bds Windsor Hotel
Foster Wm., machinist, Bagot
Fountain James, whitewasher, 179 Sydenham
Fowler Fife, M.D., L.R.C.S., 251 Brock
Fowler Henry C., student at law, 251 Brock
Fowler Rev. James, M.A., professor Queen's College, Union cor Gordon
Fowler W. G., mason, 323 Johnson
Fowler Mrs. Mary, King w
Franklin Charles D., Gordon
Franklin Joseph A., flour and feed, 213 Princess, h Union
FRALICK F. J., clerk, Burnett House
FRALICK J. W., prop. Burnett House, Ontario
FRALICK W. G., clerk, Burnett House
Francis Carrett, laborer, e s Beverly
Francis Jno., shoemaker, Princess
Francis Lewis, ladder manufacturer, 7 Simcoe
FRASER DONALD, private banker, 842 King, h 95 Union
FRASER LIEUT. & BT. MAJOR JOHN, Adjutant " B " Battery, Tete du Pont Barracks
Fraser John, clerk, e s College
Fraser J., manufacturer, Princess
Fraser Samuel, mariner, 97 Queen
Frazer Mrs. Catharine, 188 King e
Frazer Roderick, mariner, 109 Barrack
Free Frank, moulder, Loco. Works
Free John, clerk, 82 Queen
Free Robert, mason, 153 Division
Freeman R., telephone agent, Burnett House
Friendship Chas., gardener, John
Friendship George, blacksmith, Division
Friendship Thos., gardener, John
Froiland H. M., M.D., 183 Wellington
Froiland J. D., gold and silver smith, 183 Wellington
Frizell Robert, shoemaker, Sydenham
FRONTENAC LOAN AND INVESTMENT SOCIETY, Thos. Briggs, manager, 49 Clarence
Frost Edward, laborer, 5 York
Fuller Fred., clerk, William
Funnell David, engineer, 72 Bond. head

Funnell David, 728 Montreal
Funnell R. K., piano maker, Barrie
Furlong Thos., laborer, 48 Ordnance
Furzell Alex., blacksmith, Loco. Works
Garbett P., clerk, Bank B.N.A.
Gaden G. W., book-keeper, 321 Gordon
Gage John, blacksmith, Loco. Works
Gage Robert, architect, Montreal, h Alfred
Gage Robert, blacksmith, Car Works
Gahagan John, mariner, 274 Wellington
Gallagher Emanuel, laborer, 229 Wellington
Gallagher Francis, piano maker, 91 Rideau
Gallagher P., sergeant "B" Battery, R.S.G.
Gallagher Thomas, mariner, 84 Charles
Gallagher Thomas, saloon keeper, Montreal
Gallagher Wm., laborer, Thomas
Gallagher Wm., cabman, Johnson
Gallivan James, engineer, 76 Earl
Gallivan James, moulder, 76 Earl
Gallivan, John, helper, McEwen & Son
Gallivan John, engineer, 285 Alfred
GALLOWAY JAMES, hatter and furrier, 84 Princess
GALLOWAY JAMES, jr., cor Johnson and Division
Ganeau Francis, mariner, n s John
Garbutt D. J., grocer, 352 Princess
Garbett William, porter G.T.R., Bagot
Gardiner David B., 149 Earl
Gardiner James, butcher, 188 Ordnance

Gardiner Jas., mariner, 59 Charles
Gardiner John A., bailiff, 459 Princess
GARDINER J. O. & Co., biscuit and confectionery manuf'rs, cor Division & Earl, (*See adv p 3*)
Gardiner J. O., (J. O. Gardiner & Co.) h 311 Queen
Gardiner R. & J., dry goods, 102 Princess
Gardiner Robt., (R. & J. Gardiner) h 151 Earl
Gardiner Thos., salesman, 151 Earl
GARRETT RICHARD WM., B.A., M.D., 201 Wellington
Garrigan & Co. James & Wm. J., boot makers, 51 Princess
Garrigan James (Garrigan & Co.) h King e
Garrigan W. J., (Garrigan & Co.) h Clarence
Garde Mrs. M., Barrie
Garvin Edward, laborer, 76 Ordnance
Garvin Edward, gardener, 141 Montreal
Gaskin Capt. John, 253 Ontraio
Gaskin Thomas, engineer, 214 Barrie
Gates Joseph, farmer, Pine
Gaudien Charles, clerk. Windsor Hotel
Gaudreau Z., grocer, cor Ontario and Union
Gaudry Arthur, Second
Gautt William, salesman, Princess
Gavine Wm., rope maker, Victoria
Gay Robert, carpenter, 109 Union
Gaw Samuel, 109 Union
Gawley Mrs. Sarah, Clergy
Geale John, law student, Princess
Geary Edward, shoemaker, 82 Barrie
Geary George, laborer, 82 Barrie
Gee Mrs. Mary, hotel, 242 Ontario

CITY OF RINGSTON. 45

Goodfrey —, law student, Macdonnell & Mudie
George Chas., salesman, William
GEORGE JOSEPH, manufacturer organs and pianos, 110-14 Gore, h 28 Wellington
Gerald Geo., mariner, 25 Barrack
Gerard Edward, engineer, Bagot
German Henry, tailor, Barrack
Gibbon John, laborer, Locomotive Works
Gibson David, grocer, 345-847 Princess
Gibson James, 118 Union
Gibson Walter, tinsmith, Loco. Works
Gibson Wm. H., driver, Princess
Gilbert Mrs. Jane, 194 Barrie
Gilbert John, clerk, 194 Barrie
Gilchrist David, tinsmith, 309 Earl
Gilchrist John, laborer, 309 Earl
GILDERSLEEVE C. F., steamboat proprietor, 40 Clarence, h 45 King e
GILDERSLEEVE J. P., general insurance and steamship agent, issuer of marriage licenses, and notary public, 42 Clarence, h 166 King e
Gildersleeve Miss L., 268 King e
Gill Mrs. Catherine, 214 William
Gillespie James, sawmiller, bds 47 Princess
Gillie Jas., engineer, 285 Earl
Gilmartin Louis, clerk, cor Queen & Bagot
Gilmour Alex., carpenter, 23 Ontario
Gilmour Andrew J., tinsmith, 29 James
Gilmour Robert, saddler, Park
Gilmour Samuel, pedlar, Johnson
Gilmour Wallace, (Linton & Gilmour) h Montreal
Gilmour Wm., laborer, Princess
Giroux Mrs. Hannah, Nelson
Givens Chas., laborer, Beverly
Givens Mrs. Susan, Montreal
Givens D. A., B.A., master Collegiate Institute
Givens Capt. Wm., mariner, 133 Division
Glasgow Robert, currier, 358 Montreal
Glazier Ezekiel, carpenter, 25 Place de Armes
Gleeson Mrs. Ann, George
Gleeson James, ice dealer, King w
Glidden John, laborer, 133 Queen
Glidden Wm., license inspector, 457 Princess
Glen Andrew, machinist, Loco. Works
Glynn Mrs. Margaret, 260 Johnson
Godwin Wm. H., teacher, n s Pine
Goodearl Arch., machinist, Loco. Works
Goodearl C., mariner, 157 Bagot
Goodearl Humphrey, cabinet maker, Wellington
Goodearl J. A., clerk G.T.R., 116 Johnston
Goodearl Jno., mariner, 157 Bagot
Goodell Chauncey, laborer, Earl
Goodell Mrs. P., Earl
Goodfellow D. K., clerk G.T.R., 240 Gordon
Goodfellow Mrs Susan, Arch
Goodman Michael, laborer, Loco. Works
Goodwin John, laborer, Barrack
Goold C. H., clerk Merchants' Bank, Earl
Gordon Thos., master Collegiate Institute, 200 Queen
Gordon Wm., sergeant "B" Battery, R.S.G.
Gordon Wm. D., insurance agent, 13 Montreal, h 186 Queen
GORDON WM. S., city assessor, 847 Brock

Gorham Mrs. E. L., fancy goods, 355 King
Gorman Daniel, mariner, s s John
Gorman Patrick, carpenter, 576 Montreal
Gorman Robert, helper, Locomotive Works
Gorman Patrick, machinist, bds Waggoner House
Gorman Samuel, laborer, Agnew's Lane
Gormley James, cabman, 57 Bay
Gough John, carpenter, 15 Colborne
Gould Arthur J., Union
Gould Chas., mariner, 204 Bagot
Gould Chas., engineer, 204 Bagot
Gould Col. James K., Union
Gould Jos., tinsmith, 170 Queen
Gourdier Lucas, caner, 135 Ordnance
Gow Walter, laborer, 316 Montreal
Gowdey James, butcher, 258 Princess
Gowan John, mariner, 127 Montreal
Goyette Charles, engineer, Rideau
Grady Michael, Earl
Graham Mrs. Ann, 184 Bagot
Graham Charles, laborer, Loco. Works
Graham Chris J., grocer, Earl
Graham James, carpenter, 145 Ordnance
Graham John, hotel, Market Sq
Graham Mrs. Phœbe, Chatham
Graham Thomas, laborer, 132 Queen
Graham Thomas, hide buyer, Dufferin
Graham Thos., painter, Patrick
Graham Wm., laborer, 12 Ellice
Grallvin Daniel, laborer, 5 Bay
Granger Marshall, 64 Charles
Gralton John, laborer, Wellington nr Princess
GRAND TRUNK FREIGHT OFFICES, Robert Thomson agent, cor Ontario & William
Grant Alex. C., painter, 439 Princess
Grant D. B., carpenter, Ontario
GRANT VERY REV. GEORGE MONRO, principal & vice chancellor Queen's College
Grant John, carpenter, bds cor Queen & Wellington
Grant Mrs., Young's Lane
Grant Thomas, helper, Barrie
Grant Thomas, laborer, Car Works
Gravelle Joseph, carpenter, Bagot
Gravelle Oliver, w s College
Gravelle Oliver, salesman, College
Graves Sydney, driver, Victoria
Gray Ezra, laborer, Bondhead
Gray George, laborer, 268 Sydenham
Gray Israel, laborer, wks P. Bajus
Gray James, saloon keeper, Montreal
Gray John, laborer, John
Gray John jr., mason, w s Albert
Gray Mrs., silver plater, 316 Barrie
Gray Samuel, driver, 272 Sydenham
Gray Samuel, salesman, 277 Sydenham
Gray W., teamster, Montreal
Gray Wm., laborer, Stephen
Graysdell Samuel, bottler, Chatham
Greata John M., accountant Bank Montreal
Greaza Chas., clerk, 146 Ordnance
Greaves George, laborer, Chatham
Greaves John, moulder, 373 Division
Greaves Reuben, gardener, Macdonnell
Greaves S., shoemaker, Princess

Greaves T., blacksmith, Chatham
Greaves W. D., carriage trimmer, hd Princess
Green Charles, laborer, Sydenham
Green Jas., spinner, Cotton Works
Green John, butcher, cor Earl & Bagot
Green Roger, laborer, Johnson
Greensville Wm., Nelson
Greenwood & Chadwick, (Joseph Greenwood, Wm. M. Chadwick) marble dealers, 243 Princess
Greenwood John A., confectioner, 286 Princess
Greenwood Joseph, (Greenwood & Chadwick) h 622 Princess
Greer Roger, carpenter, Loco. Works
GREET T. Y., manager Federal Bank, h 98 Barrie
Grier L. R. J., discount clerk Merchants' Bank, Maitland
Griffin Mrs. C. A., fruit & provisions, 290 Ontario
GRIFFIN GILBERT, post office inspector, Post Office, h King w
Griffith Edward, porter G.T.R., Ontario
Griffith Samuel, agent, Johnson
Grigor Charles, fancy goods, 119 Princess
Grimason Mrs. Eliza, hotel keeper, 340 Princess
Grimason James, laborer, 340 Princess
Grimason Thomas, inland revenue officer, 340 Princess
GRIMSHAW HENRY, prop. St. Lawrence House, cor King and Queen
Grimshaw S. A., joiner, 284 Division
Grogan John, laborer, 309 Johnson
Groves Joseph, laborer, 79 Rideau
Guardefee Chas, laborer, Ontario
Guild John, grocer, 73-5 Bay

GUNN A. & CO., (Alex. Gunn, Samuel Harper, Wm. G. Craig) wholesale grocers, 125-7 Ontario
GUNN ALEX., M.P., (A. Gunn & Co.) h 196 Johnson
Gunn Daniel laborer, 197 Nelson
Gunn Mrs. Mary, 75 Ordnance
Gunn Walter, laborer, Boudhead
Gunn W. A., bds Burnett House
Gurnsey Braiden, carpenter, 300 Queen
Guy Mrs. Catharine, 88 Colborne
Guy Mrs. Caroline, Barrie
Guy Z., book-keeper, Second
HAAZ BROS. (Anthorn & Otto,) vinegar manufacturers, 130-2 Ontario
Hackett John, trader, 158 Ontario
Hackett Johnston, boots & shoes, 355 Princess
Hackett Jos., mariner, Wellington
Hadden Alfred, driller, Loco. Works
Hadden George, blacksmith, York
Haddigan M. J., clerk customs, 25 Johnson
Haffner, John, butcher, 240 Princess
Hazart Joseph, sailor, cor Ontario & Clarence
Hagarty Daniel, grocer, 152 Ontario
Hagerty David, hotel keeper, 104 William
Hagerty D. J., clerk, cor William & Bagot
Hagerty Michael, moulder, Loco. Works
Hagerman Mrs. Ann, Wellington
HAGUE G. E., manager Merchants' Bank, h cor William & King
Haight Charles, tinsmith, Gordon
HAINES & LOCKETT (John J. Haines, T. G. Lockett) boots & shoes, 184 Princess

JAMES LATURNEY,
Carriage and Sleigh Manufacturer,

392 Princess Street, above Barrie.

EVERY STYLE OF CARRIAGE OR SLEIGH MADE TO ORDER.

Wood Work of every Description made to Order and kept on hand.

REPAIRS IN EVERY BRANCH PROMPTLY ATTENDED TO.

I also Manufacture the Celebrated

Iron Ladders for Buildings
— ALSO —
FIRE ESCAPES.

Every person travelling should have one of those Escapes. They are made of iron and can be carried in your trunk, and are light, safe and reliable.
All orders by mail promptly attended to.

HARDWARE HOUSE
Opposite Windsor Hotel, Princess Street.

CALL AND SEE A FINE ASSORTMENT OF

FARMERS' UTENSILS,

CARPENTERS' TOOLS,

& PAINTERS' SUPPLIES,

BEST QUALITIES.

Barbed Wire and Cut Nails a Specialty.

LEADS, OILS, VARNISHES, BRUSHES, &c.

ALL GOODS CHEAP FOR CASH.

T. G. Rudd.

Hales Wm., currier, (Ford & Sons)
Hales Wm., grocer, Sydenham
Haley Mrs. Cathrine, 236 Ontario
Haley Thomas, laborer, Johnson
Hall David, plumber, Ontario
Hall John, stoker, Fire Hall
Hall Mrs. Mary, 13 Bondhead
Hall Rev. Thos., congregationalist, 447 Princess
Hall Thos., moulder, Car Works
Hall Wm., carter, 29 Barrack
Hallett Charles, moulder, 29 Young's Lane
Halligan J. & Co., grocers, 33 Brock
Halligan John, (J. Halligan & Co.) h 185 William
Halligan Richard, laborer, 274 Montreal
Halligan Mrs., 151 Wellington
Halpin James, blacksmith, Loco. Works
Hallowell Henry, laborer, Loco. Works
Halt Samuel, laborer, Charles
HALWARD REV. BRO., director Christian Brother's School, 89 Clergy
Hamann O., sergeant "B" Battery, R.S.G.
HAMER JOHN, hardware, 55 Princess
HAMILTON C., collector customs, Custom House
Hamilton Claud, clerk, Sydenham
Hamilton Edward, tailor, 45 Arch
Hamilton James, mason, 248 Earl
Hamilton James, machinist, Loco. Works
Hamilton J., moulder, Car Works
Hamilton Samuel, blacksmith, 125 Union
Hamilton Robert, painter, 14 Agnew's Lane
Hammond Patrick, mariner, Brock
Hanko Alfred, helper, Locomotive Works
Hanley Arch., inland revenue, York
Hanley James, clerk, 172 Ontario
Hanley John, cabman, 16 Agnew's Lane
Hanley J. P., clerk G.T.R., cor Earl and Wellington
Hanley Thos. (Folger & Hanley), h cor Earl and Wellington
Hanley Thomas A., operator, 76 Wellington
Hanlon John, laborer, George
Hannay William, watchman, Wellington
Hanscomb William, laborer, 825 Johnson
Hansen Chris., laborer, Locomotive Works
Hansen Louis, fishmonger, 90 Wellington
Hanson Thos., laborer, Wellington
HARBACK H. A., ale and porter bottler, 69 Princess
HARDY J. C. (Hardy & Murray), h 191 Clergy
Hardy Joseph, engineer, n s Collingwood
HARDY & MURRAY (J. C. Hardy and W. J. Murray), dry goods, 176 Princess
Harkess John, superintendent House of Industry, 356 Montreal
Harkness S., butcher, 299 Princess
Harkness William, butcher, 214 Wellington
Harkness William, butcher, 850 Princess
Harley Thomas, carpenter, Car Works
Harmer Daniel, boots and shoes, 107 Princess
Harmer James, engineer, Ontario
Harmer Wm., carpenter, Montreal
Harper Mrs. E. H., 249 Johnson

HARPER SAMUEL (A. Gunn & Co.) h Emily
Harper Samuel, upholsterer, Car Works
Harper Samuel H., 124 George
Harris Alex., salesman, 87 Wellington
Harris A. S., train despatcher, 196 Colborne
Harris David, rope maker, 76 Durham
Harris Mrs E., 76 Durham
Harris Rev. Henry, Johnson
Harris H. J., 22 Bondhead
Harris John, laborer, Johnson
Harris R. C., Alfred
HARRIS ROBERT CARR, C.E., Royal Military College
Harrison Henry, shoemaker, Bagot
Harrison Thos., bricklayer, 150 Rideau
Harrold Alex., carpenter, 227 Earl
Harrold James, carpenter, Bagot
Harrold William, carpenter, 184 Gordon
Hart Patrick, laborer, 91 Earl
Hartery James, laborer, 55 Arch
Hartley Mrs. A., Barrack
HARTIGAN REV. P. (Roman Catholic,) 223 Johnson
Harty Mrs. Ellen, Johnson
Harty Jas. & Co., varnish manufacturers, 182 Ontario
HARTY WM., managing director Can. Loco. & Engine Works, h Johnson
Harvey Mrs. Ann, Earl
Harvey H. de M., clerk, Federal Bank
Harvey Wm. C., clerk, Earl
Harwood Mrs. Susan, 101 Johnson
Haslett Wm., engineer, 31 Division
Hatch C. H., agent Richelieu & Ontario Navigation Co., foot Johnson, h 6 Bondhead
Hatch Wm., tanner, 216 Rideau
Hates Harry C., clerk, 5 Hates Terrace, King w
Hatton William, mariner, Earl
Hansen John, blacksmith, Loco. Works
Hawkin Edward, shoemaker, 320 Barrie
HAWLEY T. B., manager Stroud Bros., h 109 Princess
Hawkins Mrs. Jane, music teacher, 127 Colborne
Hay David, helper, McEwen & Son
Hay Wm., tailor, bds 103 Brock
Hayden Henry, warehouseman, 31 King w
Hayward Thomas, salesman, Earl
Hayward Wm., blacksmith, 301 Johnson
Haywad, Wm., Earl
Harlett Wm. J., boiler maker, 476 Brock
Head Sanger, harness maker, 255 Division
Healey Thos., shoemaker, Deacon
Healey Wm., shoemaker, Wellington
Heenan James, moulder, Loco. Works
Henderson Charles. W. W., salesman, cor Colborne & Clergy
Henderson George, engineer, 70 Bondhead
HENDERSON HENRY, photographer, 90 Princess
Henderson John, carpenter, 59 Collingwood
Henderson Jas. A., barrister, 51 Clarence, h cor Wellington & Johnson
HENDERSON JOHN & CO. (Wm. Middleton, Mrs. John Henderson,) booksellers, news dealers & stationers, 88 Princess
HENDERSON MRS. JOHN (John Henderson & Co.,) h Gordon

CITY OF KINGSTON.

Henderson J. R., salesman, 117 Earl
Henderson J. S., grocer & wine merchant, 57 Brock, h 185 Queen
Henderson Mrs. Jane, Gordon
Henderson P. R., secy.-treasurer Kingston Cotton Co., Earl
Henderson William H., M.D., cor Montreal and Brock
Hendry J. A. (J. A. Hendry & Bro.) h 106 Bagot
Hendry J. A. & Bro., wholesale grocers, cor Ontario & Clarence
Hendry John, salesman, 122 Johnson
Hendry Mrs. M. (Fenwick, Hendry & Co.) 267 Ontario
Hendry Robert, jr., com. traveller, 122 Johnson
Hendry W. D., clerk, 110 Bagot
Henley Miss M., fancy goods, 181 Wellington
Hensley Mrs. Mary, George
Hentig Charles, stamp distributor, 558 Princess
Herald John, professor Queen's College
Herald John, jr., medical student, Gordon
Hermiston Mrs. E., 62 Wellington
Hermiston James, printer
Hero Geo., laborer, Loco. Works
Herrimen Mrs. Mary, 92 Bay
Hersey Thos. A., carpenter, 101 Chatham
Hess George, blacksmith, Wade's Lane
Hess George, jr., Wade's Lane
Hewlett C. H., sergeant "B" Battery, R.S.G.
HEWITT COL. EDWARD OSBORNE, C. E., commandant R.M.C., 11 Emily
Hewitt George, machinist, Union
Hewitt Thomas Plumber, Earl

Hewson John, engineer, Barrie
Hewton J. sec. & treas. Kingston Hosiery Co., 100 Barrie
Hewton Miss Martha, Earl
Hewton Robt., keep. K.P., King w
Hickey C. A., dry goods, 114 Princess
Hickey Daniel C., M.D., Barrie
Hickey John, salesman, 114 Princess
Hickey J. Z., chief clerk freight depot, G.T.R., 21 King w
Hickey M. & Co., millinery, 164 Princess
Hicks Benjamin, bds Windsor Hotel
HIGGINS REV. BERNARD (Roman Catholic), 225 Johnson
Higgins John, tailor, 12 John
Hight Mrs. M., Agnew's Lane
Hill Edward C., salesman, 103 Wellington
Hillyard Robert, salesman, bds 58 Earl
Hilton Thomas, saddler, Locomotive Works
Hinds David, gardener, Johnson
Hinds John, laborer, w s Victoria
Hinds Mrs. Mary A., 141 King e
Hinds Wm., policeman, res Williamsville
Hinds W. G., teller Merchants' Bank, 141 King e
Hines Wm., laborer, Johnson
Hinton Edward, laborer, Agnew's Lane
Hinton Richard, blacksmith, bds Waggoner House
Hipkiss Thomas, laborer, s s John
Hipson Joseph, boiler maker, 130 Division
Hiram William, carpenter, Loco. Works
Hiscock Edgar, turner, Loco. Works
Hiscock Joseph, steward, Bagot

Hislop Mrs. Mary, Wellington
HITCHEN HARRY, supt. dept. Immigration & Crown Lands, cor Ontario & William
Hoag John, switchman, 708 Montreal
HOBART G. S., druggist and depositor Kingston auxiliary British & Foreign Society, 155 Princess, h cor Brock & Clergy
Hodges William F., carpenter, 112 York
HODGINS GEO. S., draughtsman Canadian Engine and Locomotive Works, h King
Hodgson Thomas, stonecutter, Barrie, h 76 Arch
Hogan Dennis, tailor, bds Albion Hotel
Hogan James, hotel, 310 Ontario
Hogan Jas., mariner, 310 Ontario
Hogan, Mrs. Jane, milliner, 154 Ordnance
Hogan Jos., laborer, 310 Ontario
Hogan Morris, moulder, Kingston Foundry
Hogan Patrick, shoemaker, 51 Colborne
Hogan Patrick, mariner, Dufferin
Hogan Wm., laborer, 23 Bondhead
Hogle Charles, salesman, Brock
Holden James, stonecutter, bds St. Lawrence Hotel
Holden Robt., blacksmith, 234 Bagot
Holder Mrs. Benjamin, cor Queen and Montreal
Holder Robt. photographer, cor Montreal & Queen
Holland E. & Co., millinery, 907 Wellington
Holland G. A., engineer, 4 Rideau
Holland Martin, tanner, 4 Rideau
Holland Wm., laborer, 54 Cherry
Hollowell Henry, laborer, 262 Johnson

Holman Sam'l, laborer, 181 Queen
Holman Samuel, jr., painter, 181 Queen
Holmes John, 277 Montreal
Holroyd Jno, carpenter Car Works
HOOKER REV LEROY, pastor Sydenham St. Methodist Church, 181 William
Hooper Cavalier, com. traveller, Clarence
HOOPER REV. E., pastor Baptist Church, 93 Johnson
Hooper Mrs. H. J., 160 Sydenham
HOOPER V. G., general ticket agent, 42 Clarence, h 114 Clarence
Hope John, gardener, Wade's Lane
Hopeson Wm., baker, 87 Victoria
Hopkirk J. C., post office clerk, Wellington
Hopper George, harness maker, bds 919 Princess
Hoppins Abiram, agent H. B. Rathbun & Son, Bagot
Horan John, laborer, 52 Magdalen
Horan Michael, laborer, s s John
Horn Alex. (Oldrieve & Horn), h 270 Gordon
Hornibrook Francis, blacksmith, 19 Colborne
Horneybrook John, laborer, 19 Colborne
Horsey Edward, M.D., Union
HORSEY EDWIN, chief of police and fireman, 151 Brock
HORSEY R. M., hardware, 189 Princess, h 164 Queen
Horton W. C., fish dealer, 62 Brock
HOTEL DIEU, Sister Monica Brady superioress, 227 Brock
Houghton Mrs. Ann, Alfred
Houghton Isaac, gardener, Centre
Houlder George, carpenter, 166 York

HOUSE OF PROVIDENCE, Sister Mary John, superioress, Montreal
Houston Mrs Martha, 62 Adelaide
Houston Thos., driver,(R.McFaul)
Howard J., serg., instructor, "B" Battery.
Howie A., inland revenue officer, 224 Gordon
Howland James, salesman, 142 Division
Howland Thos., cab driver, 142 Division
Howland Thos., cabman, Brock
Howland Thos., jr., clerk, Brock
Hoyle Earnest, waiter, St Lawrence Hotel
Hoyle Wm., policeman, Cunningham.
Hubbard Henry, carpenter,Rideau
Hudder T., loom fixer, Montreal
Hugg Chas. carpenter, 67 Bondhead
Hughes Chas., laborer, Rideau
Hughes Mrs. M., Earl
Hughson Albert, machinist, McEwen & Son
Hugo Nicholas, 44 Livingston
Hull Edward, agent, Centre
Hull Ewd., blacksmith, Loco. Works
Hull Thos., moulder, Brock
Hunt Miss Bridget, 381 Brock
Hunt John, laborer, 22 Earl
Hunter Mrs. E., 110 Barrack
Hunter George, carpenter, 108 Barrack
Hunter Henry, carpenter, 16 Alma
Hunter Jas., machinist, 330 Division
Hunter John W., planer, Loco. Works
Hunter Peter, pressman, 146 Barrack
Hunter Robert, engineer, 843 Montreal

Hurley Jno. J., mariner, Queen
Hurst Jas., carter, c s Beverly
Hurst John, laborer, William
Hurst Wm., mason, Beverly
Huson John, planer, Loco Works
Hussey Robt., bds St. Lawrence Hotel
HUTCHESON JAMES E., auctioneer, 86 Brock
Hutcheson E. J., clerk, 86 Brock
Hutcheson Wm., salesman, cor Earl & Bagot
Hutcheson Mrs Mary, cor Earl & Bagot
Huton Dickson, tinsmith, Gordon
Hyatt D., laborer, Frontenac
Hyland David, Alfred
Hyland E. J., tinsmith, 497 King, h 77 Gore
Ilett John, salesman, 2 Sydenham
Illsey Charles, Union
IMMIGRATION AND CROWN LANDS DEPT., R McPherson, agent, Harry Hitchen, supt., cor Ontario & William
Inglis John, accountant, 152 Bagot
INLAND REVENUE OFFICE, Market Square
Ireland Chas. F., 36 Alice
Ireland Mrs. Eliza, 36 Alice
Ireland K. M., clerk, 36 Alice
Irving Wm., builder, 44 Clergy
Irving Wm., manager Kingston Car Works
Irwin Alex., cooper, 39 Barrack
IRWIN CHAMBERLAIN, M.D., cor King & William
Irwin Francis, 328 Queen
IRWIN F. W., manager Singer Manufacturing Co., 238 Princess
Irwin John, mariner, 41 Rideau
Irwin Robt. salesman, 47 Earl
Irwin Thos. turner, Loco. Works
Irwin Wm., laborer, 41 Rideau
Irwin Wm., machinist, 47 Earl

Isidore John, cutter, Kingston Hosiery Co.
Jack Hugh, 61 Union
Jackson Charles, blacksmith, Loco. Works
JACKSON JOHN M., manufacturing upholsterer & dealer in furniture, 113 Brock (See p 2)
JACKSON REV. S. N., Congregationalist, 84 Gore
Jackson Wm., foreman News, 279 King w
Jacquith Isaac, carpenter, Union
James Mrs. Bridget, 181 Queen
James Daniel, shoemaker, 190 Colborne
James M., hotel, 350 Princess
James Martin, carpenter, Car Works
James Thos, butcher, 316 Princess
Jamieson David, plumber, 42 Johnson
Jamieson George, painter, 38 York
Jamieson Joseph, plumber, 42 Johnson
Jamieson Thomas, plumber, 42 Johnson
Jarrell George, mariner, 27 Barrack
Jarvis Jas. T., salesman, bds cor Colborne & Barrie
Jarvis Wm., laborer, 214 Earl
Jeffries Francis, baggageman, Park
Jeffers Mrs Margaret, Gordon
Jenkins Edward, stove mounter, Victoria Foundry
Jenkins John, blacksmith, 177 George
Jenkins John C., blacksmith, 157 George
Jenkins Samuel, carpenter 390 Princess
Jenkins Walter, blacksmith, 162 George
Jenman George, mariner, 238 Bagot
Jennings C. W., book-keeper, 56 William
Jennings Charles, book-keeper, 48 Rideau
Jerrett Wm., laborer, George
Johnson George, carpenter, 258 Johnson
Johnson James, laborer, Montreal
Johnson James B., (Johnson & Peters), h 49 Earl
Johnson Hugh, laborer, 43 York
Johnson John, blacksmith, Loco. Works
Johnson Joseph, blacksmith, Loco. Works
Johnson Joseph S., machinist, 51 Earl
Johnson Mrs. M., Earl
Johnson Mrs. Mary, 181 Colborne
Johnson N. B., Alfred, cor Johnson
Johnson & Peters, (James B. Johnson, Thos. Peters), barbers 155 Wellington
Johnson Wm., engineer, 415 King
JOHNSTON ALBERT C., watchmaker, 192 Wellington, h cor Earl & Clergy
Johnston Fred, salesman, 185 Earl
Johnston Gilbert, engineer, 225 Bagot
Johnston John, laborer, 191 Ordnance
Jones Allan, asst. Post Office inspector, 13 Maitland
Jones Mrs. Ann, Hamilton's Lane
Jones Chas., tinsmith, bds Albion Hotel
Jones Mrs. Catharine, 74 Barrack
Jones David, carpenter, 204 Montreal
JONES MAJOR DOUGLAS F., R.A., R.M.C., 305 King w
Jones Edwin, painter, 250 Division

JONES HUGH F., foreman job dept., *Whig* Office, h Brock nr Division
Jones James, baker, Sydenham
Jones J. H., barber, 50 Clarence
Jones Mrs. Margaret, 801 Princess
Jones Mrs. Sarah, 304 Queen
Jones Thos., barber, 29 Division
Jones Thos., gardener, 133 Division
Jones W. I., fancy goods, 280 Princess
Jones Wm., butcher, Centre, cor Princess
Jones William, blacksmith, Loco. Works
Jones Wm., broker, n s Plum
Jordon Henry, fitter, Loco. Works
Jordon James, machinist, Loco. Works
Joyce John, painter, Elm
Joyce Thos., painter, 258 Division
Kane Dennis, carriage maker, 217 Wellington
Kane James, blacksmith, 217 Wellington
Kane John, bds McGrath House
Kane Mrs. Mary, 67 Colborne
Karch Joseph A., grocer, 365 Earl
Karr J. S., agent, bds Albion Hotel
Kavanagh Jas., salesman, 21 Arch
Kavanagh John, flour & feed, Market Square
Kavanagh John, carpenter, Sydenham
Kean John, fitter, Loco. Works
Kearney Mrs. Catharine, Johnson
KEARNS JAMES, agent Great North-West Telegraph Co., 34 Clarence, bds 8 Clergy
Kearns Patrick, driver, Barrie
Kearns Robt., mechanic, George
Keaton Mrs. Bridget, 128 Division
Keaton Chas., printer, 65 Bay
Keegan Bernard, moulder, s s Charles
Keeley Robert, jeweller, bds Burnett House
Keeley W. J., jeweller, 75 Wellington
Keen George, carpenter 23 Ellice
Keenan James, smelter, foot Orchard
Keenan Michael, laborer, 50 Bondhead
Keenan T. J., salesman, 262 Montreal
Keeting Patrick, laborer, 150 Rideau
Kehoe John, laborer, Johnson
Keikey Wm., laborer, e s Beverly
Kelly Daniel, 317 Brock
Kelly Isaac, carpenter, 37 Earl
Kelly John, clerk reg. letter dept., P.O., 172 Johnson
Kelly John, laborer, 99 King w
KELLY, MACKAY & DAUNT, (John McKay, Joseph Daunt,) brewers, King w
Kelly Mrs. Mary, 18 Johnson
Kelly Mrs. Mary, 234 Earl
Kelly Martin, mariner, 234 Earl
Kelly P., boiler maker, 94 William
Kelly Sam'l, machinist, 117 King w
KELLY REV. THOS., Roman Catholic, 225 Johnson
Kelly Thos., driller, 234 Earl
Kelly Wm., laborer, 15 York
Kelo Mrs. Margaret, Gore
Kelby William, blacksmith, Loco. Works
Kelso Ephraim, carter, 236 Earl
Kelson Jas., baker, Barrie
Kemp Andrew, 309 Barrie
Kemp Wm., wood worker, 160 Clergy
Kemp Edw., clerk, 160 Clergy
Kemp Geo. J., bookkeeper, 160 Clergy
Kemp W. J., carpenter, 160 Clergy

Kendall Robert, blacksmith, Loco. Works
Kendall William, laborer, Loco. Works
Kenny James, harness maker, Wellington
Kennedy Mrs. C., 107 Queen
Kennedy Henry C., clerk, Johnson
Kennedy M., engineer, Rideau
Kennedy Joseph, mariner, O'Kill
Kennedy Owen, hotel, 228 Ontario
Kennedy Peter, cutter, 110 Barrie
Kennedy Robert, carpenter, 96 Barrie
Kennedy Samuel, carpenter, Dufferin
Kennedy Thos., machinist, Loco. Works
Kennedy Wm., mariner, 65 Arch
Kenny Walter, wood worker, bds Odessa House
KENSINGTON LT.-COL. R. A., Royal Military College
Kent Noel, 161 King e
Kent R. E., teller Federal Bank
KENT RYBERT, director and treasurer Canadian Express Co., cor King and Brock, h 85 King e
Keon Geo., laborer, Loco. Works
Kerley W., sergt.-instructor "B" Battery, R.S.G.
KERR JOHN, manager Kingston Gas Light Co., 79 Queen, h 155 Earl
KERR CHARLES D., bookkeeper Kingston Gas Light Co., 155 Earl
Kerr John, mechanic, Park
Kettlewell Charles, laborer, Loco. Works
Keyes J. G., clerk, 188 Colborne
Keyes Robert, grocer, 303 Earl
Keyes Wm., carpenter, 164 Clergy
Kidd J., landing waiter Customs, 254 Sydenham
Kidd Robert, laborer, Stephen
Kilcauley Patrick, engineer, Bagot
Kilcauley J., printer, Bagot
Killeen Patk., jr., laborer, Thomas
Kilpatrick James, 332 Montreal
Kilpatrick Samuel, stone cutter, Sydenham, h 249 Division
Kinchler Thos., laborer, Johnson
King Mrs. Ann, 162 Ordnance
King D. G., printer, Gore
King George, painter, 11 York
King Horace, fitter, Loco. Works
King Jas., saloon keeper, Rideau
King James, storekeeper, 100 Barrack
King John, carpenter, 11 York
King John, laborer, Patrick
King Joseph, shoemaker, 464 Montreal
King Joseph George, druggist, cor King and Market Square, h Princess
King Robert, pattern maker, Earl
King Thomas, laborer, Victoria
King W., architect, bds Burnett House
King Wm., carpenter, King nr Barrack
King Wm., District Paymaster, 82 Montreal
Kinghorn Jas., trader, e s Victoria
Kinghorn John, man. McMillan, King e
Kinghorn John M., clerk, King e
KINGSTON AUXILIARY BRITISH & FOREIGN BIBLE SOCIETY, G. S. Hobart, depositor, cor Princess & Bagot
KINGSTON BOTTLING WORKS, W. Pipe, prop., 285 Princess
KINGSTON BREWERY, Philip Bajus, prop., 308 Wellington
Kingston Car Works Co., Wm. Irving, manager, Montreal
Kingston Charcoal & Iron Co., 40 Clarence

CITY OF KINGSTON. 57

KINGSTON COLLEGIATE INSTITUTE, Clergy
Kingston Cotton Manufacturing Co., Wm., Wilson, manager, foot Cataraqui
KINGSTON FOUNDRY, (Davidson, Doran & Co.,) cor Ontario & Union
KINGSTON GAS LIGHT CO., John Kerr, manager, 19 Queen
Kingston Hosiery Co., King w
KINGSTON HOSPITAL, Stuart
Kingston Lead Smelting Works, foot Orchard
Kingston & Montreal Forwarding Co., foot Earl
KINGSTON & PEMBROKE RAILWAY, Ontario
KINGSTON STREET RAILWAY OFFICE, A. McIlquham, 885 Princess
KINGSTON TIN WORKS, Jas. Reid, prop., cor Union & Division. (See adv.)
KINGSTON WATER WORKS, James Wilson, manager, Ontario w
Kirk Mrs. George, fancy goods, 75 Brock
Kirk James, helper, bds Bay
Kirk Samuel, laborer, Arch
KIRKPATRICK REV. FRANCIS W., M.A., rector St. James' Church, 158 Barrie
KIRKPATRICK GEORGE A., (Kirkpatrick & Rogers) 5 Emily
Kirkpatrick James, machinist, Loco. Works
Kirkpatrick John, gardener, Division
KIRKPATRICK J. S. (Kirkpatrick & Rogers) h cor Barrie and King
Kirkpatrick Michael, commercial traveller, Colborne
KIRKPATRICK & ROGERS, George A. Kirkpatrick, R. V. Rogers and J. S. Kirkpatrick) barristers and solicitors) 194 Ontario
Kirkpatrick Samuel, mariner, George
Knapp Fred, carpenter, 291 Princess
Knapp John, seed agent, bds Burnett House
Knapp Wm., boat builder, foot Ontario
KNIGHT A. P., M.A., rector Collegiate Institute, 208 William
Knight Wm. laborer, William
Knowles Henry, clerk, 234 Gordon
Knowles Mrs. Mary, 234 Gordon
Knox John, boiler maker, King e
Knox Wm., machinist, 276 Earl
Labat G., corporal "B" Battery, R.S.G.
Labossiere J. C., salesman, Wellington
Labie Gilbert E., trader, Earl
Lachance F. X., grocer, 259 Ontario, h 200 Bagot
Lachance Joseph, carpenter, Barrack
Lachance G., carpenter, Barrie
Lacroix Henry, cabinet maker, 499 Princess
Lafenier Joseph, grocer, Ontario
Lafenier Mrs. Lucy, 42 Gore
Lahey Wm., piano maker, 268 Gordon
Laing Stephen, carpenter, Nelson
Laird John, painter, 389 Division
Laird John, moulder, 389 Division
Laird Joseph, painter, 389 Division
Laidley George, saddler, 130 Queen
Lalonde Antonie, machinist, Bondhead
Lalonde Frank, blacksmith, cor Ontario & Place de Armes

Lalonde Frank, jr., blacksmith, cor Ontario & Place de Armes
Lalonde Louis, carpenter, 276 Sydenham
Lamb Jesse, fitter, Loco. Works
Lamb Richard, spinner, Johnson
Lamb Walter, mariner, 38 Division
Lambert Sam'l, carpenter, Park
LAMBERT THOMAS, (Lambert, & Walsh,) 338 Montreal
LAMBERT & WALSH, merchant tailors, 226 Princess
Lamoureaux Peter, broker, 355 King e
Landmann S., foreman Weber & Co., bds Burnett House
Landeryou John C., carpenter, Cherry cor York
Lane Benjamin, laborer, 35 Wellington
Lane Mrs. Catharine, grocer, 170 Bagot
Langdon Nathaniel, mason, Princess
Langdon Nathaniel, jr., mason, Victoria
Langley Henry, Earl
Langridge Stephen, laborer, Loco Works
Lanigan Andrew, city messenger, City Hall
Lansing Mrs Fanny, laundress, 148 Queen
Lake Ira, machinist, bds 103 Brock
Lake William, carpenter, Loco. Works
Lake Wm., moulder, 316 Queen
Lappage Wm., mason, Park
Lario Jos., cooper, 308 Wellington
Lark Edward, 125 William
Larking Henry, drover, bds St. Lawrence Hotel
LaRose Napoleon, machinist, William
Lasher Mrs. Henrietta, 868 Princess

Laturney Mrs Ellen, Princess
Laturney Geo., carter, 26 Johnson
LATURNEY JAMES, carriage maker and prop. Dominion Iron Ladder Co., 392 Princess, h Second
Laughern Francis, laborer, 61 Bay
Laughern Jas., mariner, 61 Bay
Lawrencell Jos., carpenter, Arch
Lawrencell Jos, corker, Barrie
LAVELL CHAS. H., M.D., 155 Brock
LAVELL MICHAEL, M.D., 267 Brock
Labery Patrick, laborer, 89 Earl
Lavie C., sergeant major "B" Battery, R.S.G.
Law Edw., rope maker, 85 Victoria
Lawless Jas., carter, 218 Gordon
Lawless Michael, mariner, 222 Earl
Lawless Peter, carter, 317 Johnson
Lawless P. J., bookkeeper, Gordon
Lawlor Jas., keeper K.P., Alfred
Lawlor Joseph, baker, Johnson
Lawencilla P., carpenter, Agnew's Lane
Lawson Mrs. Francis, Sydenham
Layton T. G., broom maker, Victoria
Leadbeater Wm., laborer, Wellington
Leaden Fred, machinist, Loco. Works
LEADER G. M., (Ohlke & Leader,) h head Johnson
Leahy B. J., grocer, 316 King o
LeDuc Oliver, spinner, Cotton Co.
Lee A. J., barber, 160 Princess
Lee   , hair dresser, bds St. Lawrence Hotel
Lee Geo., piano maker 2 Alma
Lee James, carpenter, Queen
Lee Jas., carpenter, 159 Johnson
Lee John, laborer, Sydenham
Lee Lyman, carpenter, 81 Queen

CITY OF KINGSTON. 59

Lee Joseph, stove mounter, Victoria Foundry
Lee Overton, laborer, 42 Elm
Lee Robert, carter, James
Lee Samuel, moulder, Victoria Foundry
Lee Samuel, blacksmith, Elm
Lea Sam'l M., clerk, Alfred
Legault Joseph, laborer, Loco. Works
LeHeup Edward, Young's Lane
LeHeup J. A., watchmaker, 68 Brock
Lemon Wm., teamster, Fire Hall
Lemmon John, moulder, Ontario
Lemmon Thomas, stoves, tinware, 355 King e
Lemmon Thomas, blacksmith, Second
LeMoode Peter, second hand dealer, 43 Princess
Lena Peter, 124 Queen
Lennon Felix, mechanic, Barrie
Lennon Felix, fireman, 3 upper George
Lennon John, moulder, Victoria Foundry
Lennon Patrick, laborer, 51 Main
Lennon Thos., blacksmith, 113 Colborne
Lennox Cooper, helper, 22 Bagot
Lennox Cooper, moulder, 22 Bagot
LeRicheux Alfred, bookkeeper, 286 Barrie
Leslie Jas. F., bookkeeper, George
Leslie Wm., lumber merchant, 57 George
Leslie Wm., engineer, 81 Gore
Lewers Robert, letter carrier, James
Lewis Fred, com. traveller 195 Earl
Lewis Mrs. Mary, 34 Union
LEWIS REV. BRO. NOVATIAN, teacher, Christian Brothers' School

LEWIS THOS G., (Wm. Lewis & Son,) h 195 Earl
LEWIS WM., (Wm. Lewis & Son,) h 195 Eearl
LEWIS WM. & SON. (William & Thomas G.,) sailmakers & ship chandlers, 271 Ontario
Lilly James, laborer, King e
Linaugh Thos., William
Linaugh Thos. jr., boiler maker, William
Liddell James, finisher, Earl
Lindsay John, shoemaker, 178 Princess
Lindsay Patrick, Second
Lindsay Thos., blacksmith, Queen
Lindsay Wm. J., boots and shoes, 170 Princess
Linegar Mrs. Ann, 284 Sydenham
Light Richard H., artist, Second
Linton Mrs. E., 83 Johnson
Linton Charles (Linton & Gilmore) h Brock
Linton & Gilmore (Charles Linton, Wallace Gilmore) carriage makers, 34 Princess
Linton John, laborer, 249 Earl
Lissons John W., carter, James
Little Mrs. Alice, Gore
Little Joseph, clerk, City Hotel
Little Robert, mariner, Barrie
Little Thomas, moulder, 208 Barrie
Little William, saloon keeper, cor Clarence and Wellington
Litton John, blacksmith, Loco. Works
LIVINGSTON C. & BRO., (Chas. & Wm. John,) merchant tailors, 69 Brock, h 189 Brock
LIVINGSTON CHARLES, SR., mayor, 189 Brock
Lloyd David, laborer, Loco. Works
Lloyd G., salesman, 353 Princess
Love Robt., butcher, cor Division & Adelaide

LONDON AND LANCASHIRE LIFE ASSURANCE CO., Thos. Mills, agent, 11 Clarence
Loftus James, mariner, 57 Ontario
LONDON RELIGIOUS TRACT SOCIETY, G. W. Andrews, depositor, 188 Wellington
Long Chas., foreman John M. Jackson, Queen
Long David, engineer, bds St. Lawrence Hotel
Long Mrs. Elizabeth, Beverly
Long Geo., storeman, Loco. Works
Longdon William F., bookkeeper, Wellington
Longuile Benj., mariner, bds St. Lawrence Hotel
Loscombe A. E. M., Deputy Crown Attorney, bds Burnett House
Love Robt., butcher, 426 Division
Lovick John, blacksmith, 146 Gordon
Lovick Salathre, turner, Loco. Works
Lovett J., finisher, Kingston Foundry
Lovett Jas., blacksmith, 72 Earl
Lovett Thos., moulder, 72 Ontario
Lovett Thomas, laborer, 16 Earl
Lowe Edward W., commercial traveller, 112 Earl
Lowe Wm., machinist, Cotton Co
Lowrey James, laborer, Queen
Lowrey William, laborer, cor James and Cherry
Loynes Mrs. Caroline, Barrie
LOYNES SHORE (Shore Loynes & Co.) h 186 Barrie
Ludlow Richd., carter, 107 King e
Lumb Richard, foreman spinning department, Hosiery Co
Lunn Thos., stone cutter, 269 Earl
Lyle John, laborer, Loco. Works
Lynch Mrs. M., 25 Johnson
Lynn Isaac, baker, Deacon

Lynden A., sergt.-instructor "B" Battery, R.S.G.
Lyons Charles, machinist, Loco. Works
Lyons Charles, saloon, Market Sq
Lyons Mrs. Elizabeth, Elm
LYSTER VERY REV. JAMES LL.D., Dean St. George's Cathedral, 58 King e
McAdam Thomas, turner, West
Macalister A., surveyor Customs, 181 King w
McAllister Jas., laborer, 16 Clergy
McArdell Jas., gunsmith, 378 King
McArdle Edward, laborer, 23 Upper Bagot
McArdle Joseph, stove mounter, 23 Upper Bagot
McArthur Adam, accountant, 254 Gordon
McARTHUR JAMES, manager Ontario Building and Savings Society, Clarence
McArthur John, pilot, 68 Ontario
McArthur John, mariner, 17 Colborne
McArthur William, potash maker, 85 Queen
McAuley George, mariner, Barrie
McAuley Mrs. S. P., King
McAULEY THOMAS, bookseller, stationer and bookbinder, 356 King, h 129 William (*see adv. opposite*)
McAvey Andrew, laborer, 219 Wellington
McBaine Angus, tailor, Johnson
McBlain David, foreman cloth room, James
McBlain George, laborer, James
McBride A., engineer, 190 Ordnance
McBride Jas., laborer, 92 Barrie
McBride James, 96 Barrack
McBride James, clerk post office, 98 Barrack

CITY BOOK STORE.

T. McAULEY

Invites special attention to his large stock of Educational Books used in the various Colleges, High Schools and Public Schools in Canada; Medical and Theological Books, besides a miscellaneous collection of Standard Books, to which is added every important work of interest as soon as published.

STUDENTS' NOTE BOOKS AND STATIONERY

ALWAYS ON HAND.

A large and well assorted stock of Note Books, Examination Books, MSS. Books, Exercise Books, Superfine Essay paper in all sizes, ruled to any pattern: Sermon Paper ruled to any pattern or cut to any size.

PRINTING AND BOOKBINDING.

All kinds of Printing, Books, Pamphlets, &c., done at short notice. Bookbinding in any style at low prices.

ORDER DEPARTMENT.

Any Book not in stock supplied at short notice. Books ordered from Great Britain and the Continent every mail. From the United States daily.

MAGAZINES, PERIODICALS, ETC.

Any Magazine, Newspaper or Periodical supplied to Order and mailed free of postage at lowest subscription price.

Liberal Discounts to Clergymen and Students. Special terms to libraries.

☞ Orders by mail promptly executed and sent postpaid.

T. McAULEY,

IMPORTER OF

BOOKS AND STATIONERY,

CITY BOOK STORE.

KINGSTON, - - - - ONTARIO.

McBride Joseph, carpenter, Chatham
McBride Robert, engineer, 190 Ordnance
McBride Samuel, carpenter, 192 Ordnance
McCabe Alex., gardener, 34 Barrie
McCabe John, tailor, s s Pine
McCabe Owen, laborer, Sydenham
McCabe T., finisher, Kingston Foundry
McCabe Thos., painter, 34 Barrie
McCaffery James, rope maker, 674 Princess
McCaige Neill, blacksmith, Queen
McCaine James, boiler maker, e s Nelson
McColl John, butcher, cor Durham & Park
McCammon Bros., (Jas. & Wm.,) livery keepers, City Hotel, Princess
McCammon Jas., M.D., Montreal
McCammon Jas., butcher, 268 Johnson
McCammon Jas., laborer, Princess
McCammon J., butcher, 72 Brock
McCammon John, butcher, 28 Upper Bagot
McCammon Robt., baker, 160 Bagot
McCammon Robt., baker, 54 William
McCammon S. A., letter carrier, 304 Johnson
McCammon Wm., butcher, 304 Johnson
McCardell Patrick, engineer, 37 Barrack
McCarter Mrs. Eliza, Brock
McCartney Alex, mason, Gordon
McCartney J., carter, 231 Gordon
McCartney Wm., carpenter, 349 Johnston
McCartney Wm., jr., machinist, 349 Johnson
McCarty Thos., teamster, Beverly
McCaugherty Hugh, laborer, Beverly
McColl Evan, 300 Gordon
McCaul Robt., engineer, Barrie
McCleary John, mariner, Barrie
McClennand John, teamster, King c
McConaghy Arch, mason, 21 York
McConaghy Hugh, blacksmith, 61 Queen
McConnell Richard, carpenter, 29 Colborne
Mc Connell J., hotel, 674 Princess
McConville Bernard, carter, 29 George
McCorkell Andrew, boat builder, Ontario
McCormick Armstrong, wines and liquors, 91 Princess, h Centre
McCormick Patrick, laborer, 46 Ordnance
McCormick Robert, clerk, 285 King w
McCormack Samuel, policeman, Montreal
McCormack Mrs. Sarah, Brock
McCormack Thos., fisherman, 51 Beverly
McCormick Thomas, scourer, Hosiery Com'y
McCRAE T. W., carriage maker, 479 Princess
McCUAIG REV. FINLAY, pastor Chalmers' Church, 127 Earl
McCullough George, carter, cor Brock and Alfred
McCullough James, laborer, York
McCullough James, jr., clerk, York
McCullough John, laborer, 20 Ellice
McCullough Samuel, moulder, cor Brock and Alfred
McCullough Wm., machinist, cor Brock and Alfred
McCullough William, carpenter, 33 Upper Bagot

CITY OF KINGSTON. 63

McCumisky Mrs. Alice, Wellington
McCummisky John, mariner, 154 Ontario
McCune Wm., machinist, Loco. Works
McCutcheon John, mariner, 221 Wellington
McCutcheon Wm., potash manuf'r, Wellington, h 85 Queen
McCutcheon Wm., baker, bds cor Princess & Barrie
McClyment A., salesman, 262 Queen
Mc Dermott John, carriage maker, cor Queen & King
McDermott Lawrence, baggage-master, Park
McDermott Patrick, cabinetmaker, 28 Brock
McDonald Arch J., 107 King e
McDonald Benjamin, pilot, Rideau
McDonald Mrs. Bridget, 408 Montreal
Macdonald Chas. W., clerk P.O., 33 Colborne
McDonald Chris, laborer, 86 Pine
McDonald Francis, mariner, 42 Charles
McDonald Geo., harness maker, 84 Princess h Wellington
McDonald Hector, painter, Johnson
Macdonald Hector, shoemaker, 125 Ordnance
McDonald Jas., shoemaker, 674 Princess
McDonald Jas., mariner, West
McDonald John A., mariner, 161 Montreal
McDonald John, reporter, Rideau
McDonald John, 240 Montreal
McDonald Miss Louise, Earl
McDonald Mrs. Mary, 303 Barrie
McDonald Robert, porter, Ontario
McDonald Wm., blacksmith, Car Works
McDonnell Mrs. Annie, 215 William
McDonnell Arch M., clerk, w s Collingwood
MACDONNELL G. M., Q.C. (Macdonnell & Mudie,) h Alfred
MACDONNELL & MUDIE (G. M. Macdonnell, Q.C., and John Mudie), barristers, 38 Clarence
McDougall Mrs. A., Union
McDougall Mrs. Flora, Union
McDowell Mrs. H., Gordon
McDowell Robt. J., agent, 473 Princess
McElhern Daniel, boilermaker, Union
McElhern Wm., carter, 48 Charles
McElhern Daniel, blacksmith, Loco. Works
McEwen Alex., carpenter, Earl
McEwen George, shoemaker, 282 Gordon
McEWEN & SON (Daniel and John F.) machine, engine and boiler manuf's, 54-6 Queen, h 32 Ordnance. (*See adv.*)
McFadden Alex., laborer, 433 Division
McFadden Dominic, hotel, 914 Princess
McFadden Edward, cabman, Montreal, nr Charles
McFadden Jas., carter, 58 John
McFadden Mrs. Margaret, 583 Division
McFarlane Mrs. Kate, Young's Lane
McFarlane Robt., shoemaker, 8 Colborne
McFaul John, machinist, Loco. Works.
McFaul R., dry goods, 180 Princess, h 20 Barrie
McGaghey James, wood worker, bds Division
McGann Mrs. Margaret, Princess

McGarrey James, melter, Loco. Works
McGaw J., salesman, (R. McFaul)
McGee Robt., driller, Loco. Works
McGill Arch., clerk, 21 Upper Bagot
McGill James, clerk 22 Upper Bagot
McGill S. C., real estate agent, 55 Clarence, h 13 King e
McGill Thomas, 38 Union
McGinn Robt., moulder, bds Island House
McGinn John, laborer, Stephen
McGinnis Francis, laborer, 38 James
McGinnis John, plater, James
McGinnis Owen, hotel keeper, 162 Ontario
McGladl Peter, mariner, 156 Rideau
McGlinn John, shoemaker, 137 Montreal
McGoldrick Michael, mariner, 92 Ontario
McGoldrick Michael, jr., boilermaker, 92 Ontario
McGowan Geo. A., tobaconist, 70 Princess
McGowan James, saloon keeper, Place de Armes
McGrath Mrs. Annie, 90 Arch
McGrath John, printer, *Whig*
McGrath Patrick, harness maker, bds 219 Princess
McGranahan R., laborer, Beverly
McGroevey James, machinist, Loco. Works
McGrigor James, mariner, Bagot
McGrogan Miss Alice, 190 Barrie
McGuire Anthony, butcher, 815 Princess
McGuire James, butcher, 815 Princess
McGuire John, engineer, bds St. Lawrence Hotel
McGuire Michael, marble cutter, Division
McGuire Thomas H., barrister, cor King and Brock, h Earl
McGurl Thos. H., teacher, First
McGurk Arthur, laborer, 30 Wade's Lane
McGurk Arthur, jr., laborer, 30 Wade's Lane
McIlquham Alexander, manager K.S.RR., cor Chatham and Elm
McIlquham Andrew, driver, 229 Victoria
McIlquoran Robert, blacksmith, Ontario
McIlroy James, painter, Bagot
McIlroy John, laborer, Montreal
McIlroy John, mason, King
McIlroy Joseph, salesman, 9 First
McIlroy Wm., laborer, 16 James
McIlroy Wright, agent, 9 First
McIntosh Daniel, V.S., 261 Bagot
McIntyre Alex., shoemaker, 110 Ordnance
McINTYRE JOHN, barrister, 304 King e, h Sydenham
McIntyre Miss Lucy, 304 Brock
McIntyre Neil, farmer, 231 Division
McIntyre Mrs. R. A., 70 Colborne
McIver Kenneth, clerk, 176 Sydenham
McIver J. B., bookkeeper, 4 Colborne
McIllwaine Samuel, machinist, Loco Works
McKane James, blacksmith, Loco. Works
McKague Neil, laborer, Loco. Works
McKay Donald, merchant tailor, 157 Princess
McKay Jas., tailor, 181 Colborne
McKay J., tinsmith, 181 Colborne
McKay John, brewer, King w
McKay John, sr., 111 Gore

McKay John K., jr., leather & hides, 162 Princess, h 218 Johnson
McKay Rev. Robt., Second
McKee Chas., laborer, Kingston Foundry
McKee John, laborer, 127 Division
McKee Thos., carpenter, 15 York
McKee William, mariner, Agnew's Lane
McKee William J., mariner, 256 Gordon
McKELVEY & BIRCH (John McKelvey and Samuel Birch) stoves, tinware, plumbers, gas fitters, etc., 71 Brock
McKELVEY JOHN (McKelvey & Birch) h Bagot
McKelvey R. J., book-keeper, Bagot
McKennie Alex., laborer, Car Works
McKenny William, carpenter, 431 Division
McKenzie John T. D., M.D., 367 Union
McKeown Mrs. grocer, 88 Clarence
McKillop Mrs. C., 28 Johnson
McKim John, laborer, George
McKim Peter, hide inspector, Clarence, res Cataraqui
McKinnon Donald, salesman, 62 Wellington
McLaren J., clerk G.T.R., Regent
McLaughlin J., confectioner, 256 Princess
McLaughlin Jas. A., laborer, 56 Montreal
McLAUGHLIN PATRICK, prop. Albion Hotel, cor Montreal & Queen

W. H. IRWIN & CO.,
DIRECTORY PUBLISHERS,
HAMILTON, ONT.

McLean Andrew, Ontario
McLean Neil, 310 Queen
McLennan Wm., teamster, King
McLeod Mrs. Ann, Bondhead
McLeod James, machinist, Johnson
McLeod Neil, Alfred
McLeod Mrs. Mary, 48 Colborne
McLeod Thos., machinist, Loco. Works
McLeod James, salesman, Earl
McLoud Robert, foreman, Loco. Works
McMahon A., rec. secretary and librarian, Mechanics' Institute
McMahon Adam J., clerk, Wellington
McMahon Alex., engineer, 34 Agnew's Lane
McMahon Andrew, Princess
McMAHON BROS. (John T. and Robert A.) hardware, 85-87 Princess, h 74 Wellington
McMahon Mrs. E. Earl
McMahon George, 260 King e
McMahon Geo., operator, Barrie
McMahon John, builder, 74 Wellington
McMAHON JOHN D., barrister, 36 Clarence, h Vaughn Terrace, 426 Princess. (*See card.*)
McMahon Mrs., Victoria
McMahon Mrs. M., 35 Wellington
McMahon Miss Nancy, 258 King e
McMAHON THOMAS, painter and paper hanger, cor Brock and Barrie
McMahon William G., clerk, cor Earl and Wellington
McMann James, salesman, Wellington
McManus Charles, keeper K.P., 50 Centre
McMANUS JAMES (G. M. Weber & Co.) h 74 Union
McManus John, 74 Union

McMaster James, laborer, 27 Upper Bagot
McMaster John, laborer, 27 Upper Bagot
McMenury Robert, laborer, 77 Queen
McMillan Arch., salesman, 308 Queen
McMillan Charles, 291 Brock
McMillan J., landing waiter Customs, Rideau
McMillan John, maltster, 398 King w
McMillan John, 803 Montreal
McMillan Malcolm, sailor, 119 Ordnance
McMillan Richard, pianomaker, Brock
McMillan Samuel, Wellington
McMorrison Frank, Loco. Works
McMullen John, boilermaker, 105 Ontario
McMullen John, moulder, Kingston Foundry
McMullen Joseph, blacksmith, 71 Gore
McMullen Richard, blacksmith, Barrie
McNally Michael, laborer, William
McNamee Wm., helper, William
McNAUGHTON BROS, (J. A., R. A.,) varieties etc., 175 Princess, h 40 Wellington
McNAUGHTON & CO., clothers, cor King & Princess
McNAUGHTON DUNCAN, 48 Wellington
McNAUGHTON JOHN, (McNaughton & Co.,) h 49 Clergy
McNaughton Wm., laborer, Bagot
McNeil A. W., plumber, 108 Clergy
McNeil Charles, laborer, Montreal
McNeil Chas., laborer, 77 Rideau
McNeil Charles, jr., laborer, 77 Rideau
McNeil Charles, keeper K.P., 230 Gordon
McNeil Hector, machinist, Loco. Works
McNeil John, moulder, 76 Johnson
McNeil Neil, plumber, 66 Brock
McNeil Neil, laborer, s s Charles
McNeil Wm., laborer, 77 Rideau
McPherson George, carpenter, Division
McPherson Miss H., 193 Brock
McPHERSON R., agent Department Immigration and Crown Lands, cor Ontario and William, h 124 Earl
McQuaid John, carpenter, John
McQuaid Mrs. Mary, laundress, 84 Queen
McQuade Wm., carpenter, Car Works
McQuade W., pianomaker, Rideau
McQuaig Neil, laborer, Agnew's Lane
McRae Joseph, carpenter, Kingston Hospital
McRae R. W. R., clerk, cor Wellington & Brock
McRAE WM., manager Pantry Grocery & Provision Co., h 184 Earl
McRAE W. R., (W. R. McRae & Co.,) h 184 Earl
McRAE W. R. & CO., grocers, cor Wellington & Brock
McRory Mrs. Mary, Barrie
McRiley Isabell, 4 Colborne
McRossie Wm., Canada Life Assurance Co., 48 Clarence, h Gore
McTaggart Miss M. S., millinery & dry goods, 110 Princess
McWater John, machinist, Loco. Works
McWhinney Hugh, laborer, 78 Ontario
Macarow P. H., clerk P.O., 40 Clergy

MACFADYEN REV. A. L., pastor Bethel Congregational Church, hd Brock
MACHAR JOHN MAULE, (Bawden & Machar) h 222 Johnson
Mack Jas., printer, *Whig*
Mackin Arthur, (Slaven & Mackin) h 189 Wellington
MACNEE & MINNES, wholesale dry goods, cor Princess & Bagot
MACNEE MRS., cor Union & Bagot
Macnee W. H., salesman, cor Union & Bagot
Madden Daniel, contractor, bds McGrath House
Madden Jas. W., tanner, Barrie
Madden Michael, engineer, 13 Charles
Madden Edward, laborer, Loco. Words
Magee Wm., caretaker Artillery Park
Maginn H., riding instructor, "B" Battery, R.S.G.
MAGUIRE HUGH, grocer, cor Princess & Montreal, h Gordon
Mahoney Michael, laborer, Wellington
MAHOOD WILLIAM JOHN, fancy goods, etc., 113 Princess, h 215 Queen
Maiden Mrs. C., 147 Colborne
MAIN RICHARD J., cabinet maker and upholsterer, 165 Princess
Mair Mrs. Ester, Arch
Makins Thomas, 22 Queen
Makins Wm., trader, 281 Barrie
Malefant Francis, driver, Rideau
Mallen Edward, porter, North
Mallen Lawrence, laborer, Park
Mallen Michael, trader, Bondhead
Malloy Jno., wood dealer, Clarence
MALONE GEO., accountant, 205 William

Malone Thos., cabinet maker, 208 King e
Maloney Jno., ice dealer, 79 Queen
Maloney John, blacksmith, 84 York
Maloney John D., tinsmith, Queen
Maloney John J., retired, Queen
Maloney M. J., bookkeeper, Queen
Maloney Pat'k, carter, 27 Bondhead
Manahan Dan'l, shoemaker, Johnson
Mandell David, carpenter, Arch
Mangham James, spinner, Cotton Co.
Manion Mrs. Mary, 174 Clergy
Manison John, moulder, Victoria Foundry
Maney James, mariner, 77 Queen
Marceau John, laborer, Rideau
Marchand Chas., laborer, Ontario
Marchand Edwin, engineer, Ontario
Marchildon H., cabinet maker, 211 Princess
Marlow John, laborer, King w
Marquette W., tailor, bds 103 Brock
Marriott George, 387 Brock
Marschand Charles, moulder, Kingston Foundry
Marrison Robert, stove mounter, Victoria Foundry
Marsh Alexander, laborer, Elm
Marsh John, driller, Loco. Works
Marsh, Jno., sr., gardener, 56 Elm
Marsh John H., grocer, 64 Elm
Marsh Wm., smith, Loco. Works
Marshall Delormay, builder, King
Marshall Edward, laborer, Park
Marshall Jas., shipper, cor Queen & Barrie
Marshall James W., salesman, cor Queen & Barrie
MARSHALL JOHN, (J. Muckleston & Co.,) Queen

Marshall Robt., blacksmith, Loco. Works
Marshall Sam'l, salesman, Queen
Marshall Sam'l, mason, York
MARSHALL WM., (J. Muckleston & Co.) h 68 Colborne
Marshall Wm., carter, 188 Division
Martin Alfred, 304 Queen
Martin Chas., mariner, 53 Charles
Martin David, clerk, 188 Sydenham
Martin David, carpenter, 188 Sydenham
Martin Jas., helper, (McEwen & Son)
Martin James, carpenter, 188 Colborne
Martin Mrs. Jane, Brock
Martin J. G. W., clerk Windsor Hotel
Martin John, carpenter, Brock
Martin John F., painter, 44 Upper Bagot
Martin John, river pilot, Charles
Martin Miss Harriet, teacher, 168 King e
Martin Mrs. R., 48 Colborne
Martin W. C., wholesale saddlery hardware, 214-16 Princess, h 198 Queen
Martin William, com. traveller, cor Bagot and Earl
Martin William, 188 Wellington
Martin William H., clerk, Clergy
Martinelle L., laborer, King e
Marvin Joseph, shipbuilder, 260 Montreal
Marvin Peter, moulder, 260 Montreal
MASON G. A., confectioner and fruiterer, 314 King e
Mason Henry, carpenter, 129 Bagot
Mason John, laborer, 264 Montreal
Mason Samuel, mariner, Princess
Massie James, V.S., Bagot

Massie John R., carpenter, 387 Barrie
Massie William, contractor, 81 Colborne
Matthews Jacob, engineer, 370 Brock
Matthews James, 242 Sydenham
Matthews Miss K., dressmaker, 77 Clarence
Maughen James, spinner, James
Maund Chas., wharfinger, Ontario
Mawhinney John, laborer, bds Albion' Hotel
Maxam A., stove mounter, Victoria Foundry
Maxam Alfred, painter, Balaclava
Maxam Geo., stove mounter, Victoria Foundry
Maxfield Thos., storeman, Johnson
Maxwell G. M., clerk, 58 Rideau
Maxwell Jas., carpenter, 255 Earl
Mayberry Miss Martha, 229 Wellington
Mayell John, merchant tailor, 78 Brock
Mayhew Mrs. Jessie, cor Elm & Alfred
Mayhew Lucas, auctioneer, Ontario
Mayne Miss Jessie, Sydenham
Mead Chas., checker G.T.R., bds Wellington
Meadows Edward, trader, 149 Brock
Meagher Mrs. Catherine, 184 Queen
Meagher G. G., salesman, 25 Wellington
Meagher Jas., trader, 117 George
Meagher Jeremiah, post office clerk, 25 Wellington
Meagher M., mariner, 79 Bondhead
Meagher Thomas, landing waiter Customs, 206 Montreal
MECHANICS' INSTITUTE, cor Princess and Montreal

MEEK ROBT., managing editor Whig, William
MEEK WILLIAM, sr., manager Whig office, 224 Sydenham
Meek William, jr., printer, 222 Sydenham
Meek William, carter, Elm
Meline Mrs. C., 300 Ordnance
Mellon J., sergeant "B" Battery, Artillery Park
Melville Mrs. Eliza, 204 Gore
Melville P. J., salesman, 204 Gore
Mevard Owen, laborer, 118 Ordnance
Menary Geo., carpenter, 158 Division
Mercer, Louis, cabinet maker, bds Albion Hotel
MERCHANTS' BANK OF CANADA, G. E. Hague, manager, cor King and William
Mercier Joseph, carpenter, Place de Armes
Merral Chas., engineer, Ordnance
Merrick Joseph, gardiner, Ellis
Merrick Mrs. Mary, 32 Wellington
Meritt Edw., moulder, 347 King e
Merrett, T. E., ledger keeper Merchants' Bank, h 158 Brock
Merter Peter, laborer, 146 Queen
METCALFE JAMES H., M.P.P., 280 Queen
Metcalfe John, butcher, res Williamsville
Metcalfe Richard, laborer, Loco. Works
METHODIST EPISCOPAL CHURCH, cor Brock & Montreal
Metiex Samuel, grain shoveller, Sydenham
Meveeton John, Gordon
Michael Mrs. M., laundress, Clergy
Middleton A. D., clerk, 55 Clergy
Middleton Lewis, 55 Clergy
Middleton Thomas, laborer, Clergy

MIDDLETON WILLIAM (John Henderson & Co.) h Gordon
Milk Joseph, tailor, 51 Chatham
Millan Mrs. Ann, hairwork, 70 Brock
Millan Bros. (Cornelius and Dennis) butchers, Montreal
Millan Dennis, moulder, Loco. Works
Millan Jeremiah, laborer, 91 Earl
Millan John, salesman, Queen
Millar A. M., salesman, 184 Princess
Millar H., stove mounter, Victoria Foundry
Miller Adam, carpenter, 200 Sydenham
Miller A. H., superintendent letter carriers, 82 William
Miller F. C., laundry, Princess, opposite City Hotel
Millar James, trader, 56 Rideau
Miller James M., hay presser, 56 Rideau
Miller Robert, carter, 96 William
Miller Robert, boiler maker, Boudhead
Miller S., carpenter, Car Works
Milligan George, machinist, 287 Division
Mills Bros., hatters and furriers, 154 Princess, h 150 Sydenham
Mills George, boiler maker, 386 Princess
MILLS GEORGE & CO., hats, caps and gents' furnishings, 170 Wellington
Mills George, smith, Loco. Works
Mills James, carpenter, Magdalen
Mills Mrs. Mary, 380 Brock
Mills John, sr., teacher, 424 Princess
Mills Robt., clerk, 424 Princess
Mills Samuel D., 428 Princess
Mills Thomas, clerk, Gordon
Mills Thomas, trader, 378 Brock

MILLS THOS., agent Fire Insurance Asssociation, London, Eng., and London & Lancashire Life Assurance Co., 91 Clarence
Milne John, laborer, 106 Ontario
Milne Mary, James
Milne Robert., laborer, Ontario
Milne Thos., engineer, 84 Division
Milne Thomas, mariner, Gordon
Milne Wm., fitter, Loco. Works
Milo Edward, carpenter, Johnson
Milo F. C. & Son, painters, 161 Queen
MINNES, JAMES, (Macnee & Minnes,) h 122 Bagot, op. Gore
Minnes John, laborer, Kingston Foundry
Minnes J. D., com. traveller, 495 Princess
Minnes W. T., salesman, 122 Bagot
Miscier Robt., bricklayer, Johnson
Mitchell Alex., laborer, Magdalen
Mitchell Mrs. Ann, Earl
Mitchell Arnold, salesman, bds 380 Barrie
Mitchell Isaac, 5 & 10 cent store, 78 Brock
Mitchell Jas., planer, Loco. Works
Mitchell James, mariner, Gore
Mitchell John, printer, 74 Earl
Mitchell J. C., builder, 380 Barrie
Mitchell Peter, carpenter, 28 Barrie
Mitchell William, baker, Barrie
Mockridge S., tailor, Barrie
Moffatt Mrs. E., 22 George
Moffatt Jas., machinist, 222 King
Moles Richard, laborer, Barrie
Monk Peter, driller, Loco. Works
Montgomery Robert, dyer, 225 Princess
Montgomery Mrs. William, second hand dealer, 295 Princess
Montgomery William, musician, 295 Princess
Montieth John, salesman, 70 Clarence
MONTIZAMBERT LT.-COL., C.A., Commandant "B" Battery and Assistant Inspector of Artillery, Tete du Pont Barracks
MONTREAL TRANSPORTATION COMPANY, J. Duncan Thompson, agent, foot Queen
Mooney Francis, machinist, Loco. Works
Mooney Robert, machinist, Loco. Works
Mooney Thos., foreman, Stuart
Mooers George, 500 Princess
Mooers Henry, grain merchant, foot Brock, h 90 Barrie
Moore A. R., clerk Bank Montreal
Moore Charles, (Moore & O'Connor,) h 151 Colborne
Moore Edward, sec.-treas. Kingston Car Works, 204 Albert
Moore Henry, mason, 222 Division
Moore Jas., bookseller & stationer, 172 Wellington
Moore Jas., clerk, 250 Barrie
Moore John, carter, 217 Gordon
Moore Mrs. Julia, Ontario
Moore Mrs. Margaret, boot fitter, 138 Colborne
Moore & O'Connor, (Chas. Moore and John O'Connor,) boots & shoes, 217 Princess
Moore Pat'k, laborer, Loco. Works
Moore R. M., manager Montreal Bank, h cor King and William
Moore Robt., carpenter, 104 Barrie
Moore Scott, laborer, Loco. Works
Moore Thomas, machinist, Loco. Works
Moore Thomas, grocer, Barrie
MOORE THOMAS, merchant tailor, 59 Brock, h 148 Earl
Moore T. W., salesman, Earl
Moore William John, machinist, 338 Queen

Morham Edward, tuner, Gordon
Morahan Bernard, saloon, cor Clarence and Ontario
Morahan Michael, laborer, cor Clarence and Ontario
Morahan Patrick, moulder, cor Clarence and Ontario
Moran Patrick, moulder, 84 Earl
Morcom Charles, operator, bds Wellington
Morgan Hugh, trader, 291 Princess
Morgan John, instructor, Bagot
Morgan William, moulder, Loco. Works
Morley Miss Mary Ann, Earl
Morris Emanuel, laborer, Barrie
Morris John, watchman, Kingston Foundry
Morris W. D., com. traveller, 122 Colborne
Morrison Frank, machinist, Princess
Morrison John, laborer, Stephen
Morrison John, moulder, 47 Main
Morrison Michael, flour and feed, 61 Brock, h 140 Johnson
Morrison Robert, laborer, Pine
Morrison Wm., carriage maker, 154 George
Morrisey John, laborer, 79 William
Morrisey John, moulder, Car Works
Mostyn Edwin, saloon, 78 Princess, h 111 Wellington
Mowat H. M., law student, 180 Johnson
MOWAT REV. JOHN B., M.A., professor Queen's College, 180 Johnson
Mowat Jno. J., laborer, 121 Queen
Mowat Robt., contractor, William
Moxley Jas., laborer, Loco. Works
Moxley Robt., blacksmith, 74 York
Moxley Wm., blacksmith, 86 York

Muckler Wm, moulder, Deacon
Muckleston Mrs. Ann, 226 King
MUCKLESTON J. & CO., (John S. Muckleston. Wm. Marshall, W. B. Dalton & John Marshall,) 71-73 Princess
MUCKLESTON JOHN S., (J. Muckleston & Co.,) h 55 West
MUDIE JOHN, (Macdonnell & Mudie,) h cor King & West
Mudie Wm. carpenter, 192 Gordon
Muldon Edward, laborer, Loco. Works
Mulholland Jas., engineer, Union
Mulholland John, finisher, Union
Mulholland Thomas, carpenter, 110 Barrie
Mullally Cornelius, laborer, 89 Wellington
Mullin Edward, salesman, 102 Barrack
Mullin James, grain weighman, Sydenham
Mullin John, laborer, 102 Barrack
Mullin Patrick, piano maker, 53 Bondhead
Mullet Mrs. Catharine, Charles
Mundie Wanen, blacksmith, Loco. Works
Mundell David E., clerk, 59 Arch
Mundell William, law student, 59 Arch
Munroe Charles, engineer, 58 Wellington
Murchison Colin D., tanner, 254 Montreal
Murdock Jas., carpenter, Maitland
Murdock Joseph, farmer, Perth Road
Murphy Mrs. Catharine, Agnew's Lane
Murphy D., laborer, 197 Colborne
Murphy J., landing waiter Customs
Murphy Jas., pensioner, 40 York
Murphy Jas., carpenter, 199 Montreal

Murphy James, machinist, Arch
Murphy Jas., carter, William
Murphy John, carpenter, 387 Alfred
Murphy John, painter, bds 840 Princess
Murphy Matthew, mariner, Montreal
Murphy Patrick, laborer, Loco. Works
Murphy Thomas, painter, 384 Division
Murphy Thos., river pilot, Charles
Murphy Thos., laborer, Montreal
Murphy Wm., laborer, 877 Princess
Murphy William, carpenter, 84 Johnson
Murray Francis, laborer, foot Wellington
Murray George, mariner, O'Kill
Murray Jas., mariner, 106 Clergy
Murray James, engineer, 336 Division
Murray James, post office clerk, 336 Division
Murray James, laborer, Victoria Foundry
Murray James, jr. (Eilbeck & Murray) h 336 Division
Murray Joseph, mariner, Rideau
MURRAY W. J. (Hardy & Murray) h Wellington, opp Model School
Murray Wm. J., carpenter, York
Muville Joseph, carpenter, cor Ontario and Clarence
Nancollies John, driller, Loco. Works
Nash T. W., chief engineer K. & P. Railroad
Naylor William, laborer, Earl
Neacus William, yardman, 28 Barrack
Nealy Mrs. M., laundress, Division
Neil Daniel, foreman dye house, Hosiery Co

Neill John, grocer, cor King & Earl
Neill Peter, teamster, Bondhead
Neilson H., surgeon-major, Tete du Pont Barracks
Neish Mary, Brock
Neish W., clerk Customs, 308 Johnson
Nelligan Bart, confectioner, 220 Princess
Nelson Miss Catharine, 258 King e
Nelson Miss Eliza, Earl
Nelson John, carpenter, bds St. Lawrence Hotel
Nelson John, carter, 152 Rideau
Nesbitt Duncan, carpenter, Main
Nesbitt James, policeman, cor Gordon & Johnson
Nesbitt Robert, policeman, cor Ordnance & Clarence
Neville George, bookkeeper, bds
Neville M. J., bookkeeper, K. & P. RR., bds Windsor Hotel
Nevin Wm., fitter, Bagot
NEW BURNETT HOUSE, J. W. Fralick, prop., Ontario
Newell Robt., mariner, Rideau
Newlands Isaac, law student, 506 Princess
Newlands Isaac, contractor, 184 Ordnance
Newlands George, builder, 506 Princess
Newlands Jno., mason, 165 Nelson
Newlands William, jr., architect, 83 Brock
Newlands Wm., mason, 153 Clergy
Newman Alex. D. T., baker, 322 King e
NEWMAN G. A., assist. secretary Canadian Engine and Locomotive Works, 212 King
Newman Joseph, salesman, 212 King e
NEWMAN R. J. J., baker, confectioner and fruiterer, 322 King e. (See advt)

Newman Robert, carpenter, 125 Montreal
Newman William, carpenter, 93 Wellington
Newman William, mariner, 277 King w
Newton John, carpenter, 60 Colborne
Newton Thomas, cabman, cor George & Centre
Newton Thomas, carter, cor George & Centre
Newton Wm., barber, bds 103 Brock
Newton William, salesman, 60 Colborne
Nickle William, 130 Earl
NICHOLSON REV. ALEX. B., B.A., professor Queen's College, cor Gordon and Union
Nicholson Amos, laborer, King w
Nicholson David, plasterer, Brock
Nicholson James, salesman, Brock
Nicholson Robert, carpenter, 332 Montreal
Nicholson Thomas, planing mills, 88 Union, h 346 Gordon
Nicholson William, telegraph operator, Montreal
Nicholson William, blacksmith, 3 Ordnance
Nicholson William J., carpenter, Union
Nicholson William, smith, Loco. Works
Nicoll John, 91 Bay
Nicolle John, clerk, Sydenham
NISBET FRANCIS, bookseller and stationer, cor Brock and Wellington
Nobes John, laborer, Wellington
Nobes Wm., carpenter, 52 Union
Noble Isaac, wood dealer, 344 Ontario, h 116 Rideau
Nokes Edward, teamster, Princess
Nokes Hy., broom maker, Victoria

Nolan James, sexton, 331 Brock
Nolan John, laborer, Barrie
Nolan John, laborer, 274 Sydenham
Nolan Mrs. Mary, 178 Clergy
Nolan Michael, mariner, 331 Brock
Nolan Patrick, telephone operator, 16 Place de Armes
Nolan Mrs., 16 Place de Armes
Nolies William, millwright, Loco. Works
NOON JOHN (Noon & Tyner) h 53 George
NOON & TYNER (John Noon and William W. Tyner) lumber merchants, 120 Ontario
Norris Samuel, broom maker, Sydenham
Norris William, clerk, 315 Brock
Norris W. H., salesman, 315 Brock
Northmore George, baker, 140 Victoria
Noyes Geo., stone cutter, Nelson
Nugent Edward, machinist. 241 Gordon
Nugent Edward, engineer, 241 Gordon
Nugent Mrs. Esther, 292 Montreal
Nugent James, agent, Ordnance
Nugent P., packer, Customs, 21 Johnson
Nugent Thos., trader, 21 Johnson
Nugent Wm., broker, 267 Princess
Nuttall Henry, com. traveller, Wellington
O'Brien Alex., tailor, 333 Princess
O'Brien Edward, laborer, 25 Division
O'Brien Henry, Windsor Hotel
O'Brien Jas., shoemaker, 80 Queen
O'Brien Jas., carpenter, Union
O'Brien Jno., laborer, 43 Colborne
O'Brien John, barkeeper, Windsor Hotel
O'Brien Jno., carter, 18 Bondhead

O'Brien John, shoemaker, Barrie
O'Brien John, laborer, n s Centre
O'Brien John, carter, Thomas
O'Brien John, planer, Loco. Works
O'Brien Lawrence, engineer, Union
O'BRIEN MARTIN, prop. Windsor Hotel, 205 Princess
O'Brien Michael, carriage maker, bds St. Lawrence Hotel
O'Brien Robert, laborer, Barrie
O'BRIEN THOMAS, secretary Windsor Hotel
O'Brien Thos., carpenter, Union
O'Brien Thomas, laborer, 34 Cherry
O'Connell Mrs. A., Agnew's Lane
O'Connell James, shoemaker, William
O'Connell John, shoemaker, 50 Magdalen
O'Connell Robert, shoemaker, Sydenham
O'Connor Daniel, mason, 216 Sydenham
O'Connor John, laborer, 80 Earl
O'Connor John (Moore & O'Connor) h 105 Union
O'Connor Miss N., 216 Sydenham
O'Connor Patrick, clerk, Barrie
O'Connor Thomas, mariner, West
O'Donnell Bryan, laborer, 246 Earl
O'Donnell John, Inland Revenue officer, 407 King
O'Donnell Patrick, grocer, 10 OKill
O'Donnell Wm., laborer, Johnson
O'Hara Henry, mariner, King c
O'Laughlin Mrs. Catharine, grocer, Market Square
O'Neil Arthur, teamster, cor Montreal & Bay
O'Neil Mrs. Bridget, 61 Bay
O'Neil James, laborer, Ontario
O'Neil James, laborer, 80 Earl
O'Neil James, laborer, Wellington
O'Neil John, laborer, 4 Patrick

O'Neil John, shoemaker, 274 Montreal
O'Neil Patrick, shoemaker, Rideau
O'Neil Philip, carpenter, Montreal
O'Neil Richard, machinist, Loco. Works
O'Neil William, laborer, Johnson
O'Reilly Geo., laborer, Loco. Works
O'Reilly Mrs. Mary Ann, Bagot
O'Reilly Mrs. Mary, grocer, Bagot
O'Reilly Patrick, shoemaker, Wade's Lane
O'Reilly Thomas, engineer, 82 Division
O'Reilly Wm., letter carrier, 170 Bagot
O'Reilly William, steward, Windsor Hotel
O'Shea John, trader, 87 Johnson
O'Toole Charles, laborer, 227 Wellington
O'Toole John, moulder, 41 King w
Oberndorffer Simon, cigars, 66-89-93 Princess, h 104 Queen
OCKLEY A. E., (Vincent Ockley & Sons,) h 115 Princess
OCKLEY JOHN, (Vincent Ockley & Sons,) 115 Princess
OCKLEY THOMAS. G., (Vincent Ockley & Sons,) h 115 Princess
OCKLEY VINCENT, (Vincent Ockley & Sons,) h 115 Princess
OCKLEY VINCENT & SONS, (Vincent, John V., Thos. G., A. E., grocers, china & glass etc., 115-7 Princess
Offord Mrs. Emily, 172 Clergy
Offord George, wholesale & retail boots & shoes, 117 Brock & 125 Princess, h 48 Clergy
OHLKE & LEADER, (Paul Ohlke & G. M. Leader,) picture manufacturers, Brock. (*See adv. under preface.*)
OHLKE PAUL, (Ohlke & Leader,) h hd Johnson

Oldfin John, gas fitter, 282 Wellington
Oldrieve G. S., (Oldrieve & Horn,) h cor Wellington & West
Oldrieve & Horn, (G. S. Oldrieve, Alex. Horn,) sailmakers, 263 Ontario
Oliver A. S., M.D., 351-353 King
Oliver Charles, Clergy
Oliver Charles, laborer, King nr Queen
Oliver Isaac, carpenter, Gore
Oliver Mrs. J. K., confectioner, Market Square, h 80 Gore
OLIVER LIEUT.-COL. JOHN RYDER, R.A., R.M. College
Oliver G. S., clerk Montreal Bank
Olsen Alex., laborer, Loco. Works
ONTARIO BUILDING AND SAVINGS SOCIETY, James McArthur, manager, Clarence
ORPHANS' HOME, 107 Union
Oram John, bookkeeper Union
Orr Mrs. Catharine, Johnson
Orr James, carpenter, Car Works
Orr Johnston, engineer, 37 Princess
Orr John, salesman, 213 Bagot
Orr J. L., boiler maker, Princess
Orser Edward, blacksmith, Loco. Works
Orser Horace, laborer, 137 Colborne
Orser Jas., laborer, Loco. Works
OSBORNE GEORGE, secretary-treasurer K. & P. RR., bds Burnett House
Ottawa Hotel, John Tierney, cor Ontario and Princess
Otto Joshua J., bookbinder, 34 Frentenac
Ouitice Stephen, moulder, Loco. Works
Outram Susan, 225 Wellington
Oulsnam T. H., salesman, Ordnance
Oulsomel Thos. H., clerk, Rideau
Overend Thomas, contractor, 287 Brock
Packer Joseph, machinist, Loco. Works
Packer Thomas, clerk, 28 Division
Page John, car inspector, Pembroke
Paladeau Henry, pilot, 104 Wellington
Paladeau L., letter carrier, 104 Wellington
Palmer George, carpenter, Gore
Palmer John, currier, Ford & Sons
Palmer Joseph, laborer, Alfred
Palmer Thomas, carpenter, Gore
Palmer Timothy, saloon, 202 Ontario
Pannell William, carpenter, Victoria Foundry
PANTRY GROCERY AND PROVISION CO., 174 Princess
Pappa Wm. J., printer, Colborne
Paradise Joseph, carpenter, King, nr Queen
Parideas Peter, carpenter, Ontario
Parke Thomas, barrister, 340 King
Parker Mrs. Fanny, 253 King e
Parker John, laborer, 253 King e
Parker Wm., fitter, Loco. Works
PARKHILL J. Y., grocer, 270 Princess
Parkin T. M., confectioner, cor Brock & Wellington
Parson John, laborer, Johnson
PATCH J. S., agent Canadian & American Express Co., cor King, Market Square
Patterson David, baker, bds cor Princess & Barrie
Patterson David J., carpenter, 601 Princess
Patterson Frank, mariner, cor Albert & Union
Patterson George, moulder, Union
Patterson John C., clerk, Gordon

Patterson John, salesman, bds 107 Wellington
Patterson Matthew, mariner, 275 King e
Patterson Wm., keeper K.P., Centre
Paul James, moulder, 26 Agnew's Lane
Payne Fred., laborer, King w
Paynter John, engineer, Earl
Peach Wm., mason, 284 Division
Pearce J. M., merchant, bds Windsor Hotel
Pedlar George, organ maker, 128 Union
Peller Frank, painter, Loco. Works
Pennell William S., carpenter, Princess
Penner Miss Elizabeth, 60 William
Pennington George, sail maker, Brock
PENSE E. J. B., prop. BRITISH WHIG, h 49 King e
Pense James P., post office clerk, 44 Colborne
Percy John, finisher, Kingston Foundry
Percy John, cabman, 106 Gore
Percy Mrs. Rachael, Barrie
Percy Thos., blacksmith, 106 Gore
Perdue John, laborer, Agnew's Lane
Perry Alfred, slater, Loco. Works
Perry Edward, pensioner, 111 Barrack
Perry Mrs. Ellen, 28 Division
Perry Jas., printer, 111 Barrack
Perry Miles, laborer, 105 Barrack
Perryman John, plasterer, 123 Queen
PETER REV. BRO., teacher, Christian Brothers' School
Peters Jas. C., fireman, Rideau
Peters Thos., (Johnson & Peters,) h 155 Wellington
Peters Wm., laborer, n s Charles
Petrie J. D., teller, Bank B.N.A.
Phelan Miss Catharine, 192 Clergy
Phelan Daniel, M.D., 901 Wellington
Phillips Miss M. L., first preceptress Collegiate Institute
Philips Thomas, hackman, 26 Place de Armes
Phippen Mrs. B. K., 204 Bagot
Phippen S. S., insurance agent, cor Princess and Montreal, h 85 Rideau
Pickering Thomas, laborer, 168 Bagot
Pickering William H., laborer, 421 Brock
Pidgeon Geo., clerk, 218 Gordon
Pidgeon G. H., messenger Customs, Gore
Pidgeon Geo. H., carpenter, Elm
Pidgeon Richard, 218 Division
Pierce Mrs. Margaret, Earl
Pillar William, Princess
PIPE WILLIAM, prop. Kingston Bottling Works, 261 Princess, h 285 Princess
Pogue Francis, fitter, Locomotive Works
Pogue George, mason, Ellice
Pogue Robert, shoemaker, 256 Earl
Pollic Mrs. A., 190 Ordnance
Pollic Hugh, clerk, 190 Ordnance
Pollic James, salesman, 190 Ordnance
Pollic Jno., tinsmith, 190 Ordnance
Pollett Francis, baker, 88 York
Pollett Thos., baker, Rideau
Polson N. C., (N. C. Polson & Co.,) h Sydenham
Polson N. C. & Co., druggist, 282-4 Princess
Pope Thos., shoemaker, 6 Hamilton's Lane
Porter A., driller, Loco. Works

CITY OF KINGSTON. 77

Porter Chas., storeman, 267 Ontario
Porter Mrs. Margaret, Chatham
Post John J., mechanic, Montreal
POST OFFICE, Jas., Shannon, postmaster, cor Clarence & Wellington
Potter Alex., mariner, Princess
Potter Henry, engineer, First
Potts John laborer, 57 Ontario
Pound Geo. D., baker, 11 Ellice
Pound John, laborer, 58 Colborne
Poutwicker Robt., laborer, bds 103 Brock
Powell J. W., photographer, cor King & Market Square
Powell W., architect, bds Burnett House
POWER & SON, architects, Wellington
POWER JOSEPH W., (Power & Son,) 72 Sydenham
Power Geo., W., clerk, cor Gore & King
Power Mrs. John, 157 Queen
Power Jonn, laborer, Albert
Power Mrs Mary, 57 Colborne
Power Patk., laborer, 181 Clergy
Power Patk., laborer, 290 Clergy
Power William, shipbuilder, King
Presnail Wm. & Bros. (William, Richard and Fred.) cigar manufacturers, 115 Brock
Preston West, stage owner, bds St. Lawrence Hotel
PRICE C. V., County Judge, 140 King e
Prickett John, blacksmith, 15 Gordon
Princliville Mrs. Sarah, Princess
Prettie Thomas, ropemaker, 451 Princess
Prettie Thos., driller, 451 Princess
Prevost Zotique, tailor, 55 Brock, h Earl
Pugh D. J., saddler, 212 Division
Pugh Frederick, salesman, 212 Division
Pugh J., corporal " B " Battery, Murney Tower
Pugh Wm., sexton, Wellington
Purdy James, organs & sewing machines, 246 Princess
Purdy Samuel, farmer, King
Purtell Jas., laborer, s s Charles
Purtell William., blacksmith, s s Charles
Putman Miss Louisa, King
Purvis John, laborer, 81 King w
Purvis Paul, moulder, 81 King w
PYKE JAS. W., sec. Can. Loco. & Engine Works, Earl
Pyman John, laborer, Young's Lane
Quartz John, sailor, bds Union House
Queen's Hotel, Andrew Dunbar, prop., 127 Brock
QUEEN'S UNIVERSITY & COLLEGE, cor Stuart & Arch
QUEEN SREET METHODIST CHURCH, cor Queen & Clergy
Quigley James, engineer, Charles
Quigley James, cabman, 218 Montreal
Quigley James, 815 Montreal
Quigley Joseph, Wellington
Quigley Miss Mary, Johnson
Quigley Patrick, machinist, Car Works
Quinn Mrs. Ellen, 47 John
Quinn Michael, pensioner, William
Quinn Michael, grocer, 306 King e
Quinn P. J., salesman, 268 Wellington
Quinlivan John, laborer, Wellington
RABAN CAPT. EDWARD, R.E., R.M. College
Rae William, piano maker, Earl
Raines Arthur, bookkeeper, Johnson

CITY OF KINGSTON.

Ramsay Alex., merchant tailor, 347 King e
Ramsay James, 232 Victoria
Ramsay Thos., bartender, Anglo American Hotel
Randell George, lighter, Barrack
Randall Henry, laborer, Union
Randall Jas., laborer, 18 Dufferin
Randell Jno., mariner, 18 Dufferin
Rankin Andrew, carter, 21 Rideau
Rankin William, Barrie
Ranton John L., clerk, Earl
Rass Wm., carpenter, Earl
Rathbun H. B. & Son., A Hoppins, agent, lumber dealers, foot Queen
Rathey James, blacksmith, Loco. Works
Rathey Robt., planer, Loco. Works
Rattenbury Jno., salesman, Union
Ratty Mrs. Elira, 117 Barrack
Ravenscroft Walter, laborer, William
Ray David, laborer, 336 Barrie
Raymond Charles, laborer, 25 Agnew's Lane
Raymond Nicholas, laborer, 25 Agnew's Lane
Raymond N., salesman, Queen
Raynard Mrs. Ellen, 218 Barrie
Rea Andrew, mariner, 190 Alfred
REDDEN JAMES, wholesale and retail groceries and provisions, 178 Princess, h Union, opp Park
Redmond Martin, laborer, 54 Magdalen
Reekie Robert, machinist, Loco. Works
Reed Frank, barkeeper, King e
Rees Bros., confectioners, 179-81 Princess
Rees Mrs. Caroline, Brock
Rees F. S., (Rees Bros.,) h 179 Princess
Rees George, baker, Brock
Rees Henry, teamster, Princess
Rees Mrs. Isabella, William
Rees Samuel, mason, Brock
Reeves John, hotel, Market Square
Reeves Mrs. Sarah, 209 William
Reeves W. & Co., gent's furnishings, 352 King e
Reeves Wilfred, (W. Reeves & Co..) h 352 King e
Regan Amos, finisher, Kingston Foundry
Regan Mrs. Elizabeth, 55 King w
Regan Jas., moulder, Kingston Foundry
Regan John keeper K.P., William
Regan Mrs. Mary, 41 Beverley
Regan Thomas, barkeeper, 111 Wellington
Reid Charles, timekeeper, Montreal
REID JAMES, prop. Kingston Tin Works, cor. Union & Division. (see advt.)
REID JAMES, furniture manfr. & undertaker, 254 Princess. (see advt.)
Reid James, grocer, Rideau
Reid James, hatter, Barrie
Reid John, machinist, Union
REID JOSEPH, cabinetmaker, 254 Princess
Reid Paul. carpenter, 35 Union
REID ROBERT, undertaker, 254-56 Princess
Reid Saml, foreman News, Queen
Reid Saml, foreman Loco. Works, 320 Queen
Reid William, carpenter, 290 Johnston
Reid Wm., moulder, Union
Reid W. H., butcher, cor. King & Brock, res Williamsville
Rendle Wm., fireman, Cotton Co.
Renton Jno., clerk P.O., 272 Earl
Renton T. T., bookkeeper, 272 Earl

CITY OF KINGSTON. 79

Renton W. J., com. traveller, 272 Earl
REYNER JOHN, dealer & tuner of pianos, 159 Princess, h 26 Barrie. (*See ad. inside front cover*)
Reynolds Mrs. Ann, 321 Victoria
Reynolds Geo., machinist, 301 Montreal
Reynolds Robert, mason, 321 Victoria
Reynolds Sampson, broom maker, 333 Victoria
Reynolds Thos., salesman, 37 York
Reynolds Wm., moulder, 351 Victoria
Ricaird Francis, currier, 571 Princess
Rice Miss Harriet, 69 Sydenham
Richards Steven, laborer, 142 Colborne
Richardson George (Jas. Richardson & Sons) 80 Gordon
Richardson James (Jas. Richardson & Sons) h 100 Stuart
Richardson James & Sons (James, George and Henry) commercial elevator, foot Princess
Richardson Mrs. Jane, 62 Earl
Richardson Mrs. Margaret, Johnson
Richardson Mrs., hair worker, 106 Princess
Richardson W. L., carver and gilder, 77 Brock, h 212 Princess
RICHELIEU AND ONTARIO NAVIGATION COMPANY, foot Johnson
RICHMOND & BOYDEN (James Richmond and Edward Boyden) dry goods, millinery and carpets, 118-120 Princess
RICHMOND JAMES (Richmond & Boyden) h 17 Union
Riddle Mrs. Margaret, Gordon
Ridley John, laborer, 74 Bondhead
Ridout Pen, clerk Federal Bank
Rigley James, laborer, 134 Union
Rigney William, groceries, 136 Princess, h 126 Johnson
Riley John, laborer, Bondhead
Riley Michael, laborer, Ontario
Roach Edward, laborer, Beverly
Roach E. H., druggist, Barrie
Roach John, laborer, 68 York
Roach John, tailor, 55 Colborne
Roach N., teamster, King w
Roach Wm., laborer, 39 King w
Robb Alex., machinist, Loco. Works
Robb Ephriam, butcher, cor. Patrick & Alma
Robb Mrs. Mary Anne, King e
Robb Wm., carter, 51 Pine
Robbs Jas., butcher, 284 Princess
Roberts A., quarter-master serg't "B" Battery, R.S.G.
Roberts E. T., time keeper, Loco. Works
Robertson Andrew, laborer, 344 Division
ROBERTSON BROS., china, glassware etc., 187 Princess
ROBERTSON B. W., (George Robertson & Son,) h 191 Brock
Robertson Mrs. E., Wellington
ROBERTSON DUNCAN, manager Bank B.N.A., 85 Wellington
ROBERTSON GEO. & SON., wholesale grocers, 183 Ontario
Robertson John, tailor, Stephen
Robertson John, Johnson
Robertson Samuel, tailor, 347 Division
Robertson Samuel, baker, 228 Division
ROBERTSON THOS. McKEAN Robertson Bros.) h Union
Robertson Thomas, Colborne
Robertson Wm., cor Gore & King
Robinson Alex·, tinsmith, King
Robinson Alex., boilermaker, Kingston Foundry

Robinson Alex., clerk, Barrie
Robinson Andrew, watchman, Loco. Works
Robinson Benj., laborer, O'Kill
Robinson Benj., druggist, 3 Clyde terrace, Sydenham
Robinson Benj., blacksmith, Loco. Works
Robinson Chris., merchant tailor, 191 Wellington, h 120 Brock
Robinson Mrs. Ellen, 298 Ontario
Robinson George, machinist, w s Collingwood
Robinson George, fireman, Park
Robinson George T., salesman, bds 47 Princess
Robinson G. W., carriagemaker, 283-5 Princess, h 247 Queen
Robinson James, finisher, Kingston Foundry
Robinson James S., painter, 279 Bagot
Robinson John, shoemaker, bds Albion Hotel
Robinson John H., agent, Balaclava
Robinson Robert, carpenter, bds St. Lawrence Hotel
Robinson Robert, carpenter, 27 King w
Robinson Robert, painter, King w
Robinson Robert, carpenter, Gordon
Robinson Thomas, clerk, w s Collingwood
Robinson Thomas, clerk, Ann
ROBINSON THOMAS D. (Wm. Robinson & Son) h 208 Queen
Robinson Thomas, landing waiter Customs, Ellice
Robinson Webb, 28 Charles
ROBINSON WILLIAM (William Robinson & Son) Division Court Clerk, h 279 Bagot
Robinson William, clerk, Dufferin
Robinson William, carpenter, King
Robinson Wm., shipper, (Macnee & Minnes.)
Robinson Wm. jr., painter, 8 Upper Bagot
ROBINSON WM. J., roompaper, 277 Bagot
Robinson Wm. J., boilermaker, Alfred
ROBINSON WM. & SON, (Wm. & Thos. D.) painters, 275 Bagot
Rochford A. jr., stovemounter, 79 Rideau
Rochford A. sr., engineer, 79 Rideau
Rockwell H. J., merchant tailor, 322 Princess, h 302 Queen
Rockwell W. A., Alice
Rodgers Geo., laborer, Loco. Works
Rodgers Wm. H., carpenter, 447 Albert
Rodenstine Mrs. E., William
Rogers Mrs. Ann D., King
Rogers James, blacksmith, Loco. Works
ROGERS REV. R. V., Church England, 189 Earl
ROGERS R. V., (Kirkpatrick & Rogers,) h 148 Barrie
Rogers Thos. H., messenger, 60 O'Kill
Rogers T. X., clerk, Federal Bank
Rollinson Walter, smith, Loco. Works
Ronan Thos., undertaker, 244 Bagot
Rooney Patrick, laborer, 278 Sydenham
ROSE EDWIN, boots & shoes, 138 Princess, h 88 Queen
Rose Miss Eliza, 216 Barrie
Rose Mrs. Mary, Union
Rose R. M., County Registrar, Court House, h 690 Princess
ROSS ALEX., dry goods, millinery, carpets, oil cloths etc., 128-30 Princess, h 236 Johnson

ROSS REV. DONALD, M.A., B.D., professor, Queen's College
Ross George, barkeeper, 111 Wellington
Ross James H., foreman news room *Whig*, 112 Barrie
Rossiter Charles, fitter, Loco. Works
Rothwell Hugh C., mariner, 120 Johnson
Rourk Peter, laborer, 43 Elm
ROUTLEY JOHN, tobacconist, 173 Princess
ROUTLEY W. K., tobacconist, 173 Princess
Rowan Robert, engineer, Barrie
Rowcroft Samuel, foreman spinner, Charles
ROWLAND FLEMING, collector of Inland Revenue, Market Square, h 160 Earl
Rowlands Mrs. Jane, 85 George
Roy Richard, tailor, Barrie
Ruberry Patrick, laborer, 13 Agnew's Lane
RUDD T. G., hardware, 202 Princess. (*See adv.*)
Runians N. E., grocer, 242 Princess
Rushford Alex., engineer, 63 Queen
Rushford Jas., mariner, Bondhead
Rushford Joseph, grocer, Gordon
Rutherford C., moulder, Alfred
Rutherford John, laborer, Loco. Works
Rutherford Mrs. Margaret, Clergy
Rutherford Robert, carriagemaker, 270 Division
Rutherford Thos., moulder, Alfred
Rutherford Thomas, bookkeeper, Second
Rutherford Thos., laborer, Second
Ruttan Henry M., Brock
Ryan Andrew, harness maker, bds 219 Princess
Ryan Capt. B., 79 Clarence
Ryan Geo., machinist, Car Works
Ryan James laborer, Earl
Ryan John, mariner, 24 Ellice
Ryan John, jr., mariner, 24 Ellice
Ryan Mat., smith, Loco. Works
Ryan Patrick, laborer, Beverly
Ryan Wm., laborer, 24 Ellice
Ryan Wm., mariner, Wade's Lane
Ryan W. F., laborer, Loco. Works
ST. ANDREW'S CHURCH, Presbyterian, cor Princess & Clergy
ST. FRANCES, Mother Superioress, Convent of the Congregation de Notre Dame
ST. GEORGE'S CATHEDRAL, Episcopal, cor King & Johnson
St. John Mrs. J., 270 Sydenham
ST. LAWRENCE HOTEL, Hen'y Grimshaw, prop., cor King & Queen
ST. MARY'S CATHEDRAL, Roman Catholic, cor Johnson, & Clergy
ST. THECLA, M. M., superioress St. Mary of the Lake Convent
Sabre Bros., hay pressers, foot Brock
Salt John, carpenter, Magalen
Salter Joseph, second-hand dealer, 332-4 Princess
Sands James, butcher, hd Division
Sands J. S. (J. S. Sands & Son) h 175 Wellington
Sands J. S. & Son (J. S. and W. C.) merchant tailor, 175 Wellington
Sands W. C. (J. S. Sands & Son) h 169 Clergy
Sands Thomas, mariner, King w
Sanderson George, tailor, King e
Sargent F. R., clerk, Vine
Sarsfield George, boots and shoes, 207 Princess, h Sydenham
Saunders Edward, hotel, 144 tario

SAUNDERS HERBERT JAS., M.D., M.R.C.S., 244 King e
Saunders J., butcher, 346 Princess
Saunders J., laborer, 420 Division
Saunders John, laborer, Gore
Saunders John, butcher, 87 Elm
Saunders Joseph, driver, Division
Saunders Mrs. J. C., 246 King e
Saunders Wm., tinsmith, 318 Brock
Savage Henry B., painter, 166 Bagot
Savage James, stovemounter, Victoria Foundry
Savage John, 79 York
Savage Mrs., dressmaker, 215 Princess
Savage Thos. & Sons, (Thomas, Henry B., Thos. jr.,) painters, 78 William
Sawyer Ontario, salesman, h 12 Earl
Sawyer W. A., salesman, cor. Earl & Wellington
Sawyer Wm., artist, 72 Earl
Scanlan John, printer, *Whig*
Scanlan Patrick, pensioner, n s Centre
Scanlan Wm., printer, *News*
Scanlan Mrs. Mary, 100 Wellington
SCANTLION FRANCIS, manager A. Caldwell & Son, bds Windsor Hotel
Schroder John, pork butcher, 80 Brock
Scobell Fred, mail clerk, 401 King
Scobell Fred, laborer, 167 Montreal
Scott Mrs. Ann, 301 Alfred
Scott Colin, drawing master, Collegiate Institute
Scott David, packer, 80 Johnson
Scott Mrs. Eliza, cor Ontario & Queen
Scott Jas., machinist, Loco. Works
Scott Mrs. Janet, King e
Scott John, mason, 440 Division
Scott John, painter, bds Albion Hotel
SCOTT N. K., grocer & wine merchant, cor Princess & Bagot, h 142 Johnson
Scouse John, painter, 267 Johnson
Scrutton Edw., laborer, Johnson
Seal John, carpenter, 76 Bondhead
Seaton Richard, laborer, 128 Queen
Selby Chas., blacksmith, William
Self Samuel, pound keeper, 219 Earl
Sergeant Robt., clerk, Hamilton's Lane
Servis Jno, currier, (Ford & Sons.)
Settington Fred, moulder, Loco. Works
Sexton F., agent, bds St. Lawrence Hotel
Sexton Patrick, mariner, Union
Shanahan Mrs Ellen, 91 Rideau
Shanahan James, blacksmith, Union w
Shanahan John, Ocean saloon, cor. King & Clarence
Shanahan John, laborer, 39 Division
Shanahan Patrick, hotel, 148 Ontario
Shanahan Wm., saloon keeper, 76 Princess
Shargrove Peter, laborer, Barrie
SHANNON JAMES, postmaster, 47 George
SHANNON LEWIS W., prop. *Daily News*, 89 George
SHANNON ROBT. W., barrister, 67 Princess, h 89 George. (*See card.*)
SHANNON WM., assistant postmaster, 381 Queen
Sharkey John, laborer, Joseph
Sharp Andrew, laborer, Ontario
Sharp Fred., tuner, Brock

D. McEWEN & SON,
Machine, Engine and Boiler Works.

ENGINES AND BOILERS
—MANUFACTURED FOR—

STEAM YACHTS, TUGS, OR MILLS,
and Fully Guaranteed.

MINING REPAIRS CONSTANTLY ON HAND.

REPAIRING OF ENGINES AND BOILERS A SPECIALTY.

WORKS, 54 & 56 QUEEN STREET,
KINGSTON. ONTARIO.

THE BIG CAKE BAKERY.

R. J. J. NEWMAN,
Fancy Cake and Bread Baker, Confectioner, &c.,

AND DEALER IN

Fruits of all Kinds in their Season,
OYSTERS, &c., &c.

Wedding, Windsor, and all Kinds of Large Cakes Made to Order at Lowest Rates.

IN OUR REFRESHMENT DEPARTMENT WE TAKE THE LEAD.

DINNERS AND LUNCHES SERVED AT ALL HOURS HOT OR COLD.

Ice Cream, Soda Water, and other Drinks Kept in Season.

☞ Boats and Hotels promptly supplied. All orders strictly attended to.

322 King Street, Kingston.

SIGN OF THE BIG CAKE.

Sharp Harry, salesman, 400 Brock
Sharp Joseph, second-hand dealer, 119 Brock
Shaver Stanley, machinist, Loco. Works
Shaw A., chief clerk Customs, 190 Gordon
Shaw Andrew, bookkeeper, Johnson
SHAW FELIX, dry goods, carpets etc., cor Princess & Wellington, h 113 Bagot
Shaw Jas., salesman, 33 Johnson
Shaw Jas., chandler, 33 Johnson
Shaw J. M., salesman, Barrie
Shaw John, coroner, 185 William
Shaw Joseph, laborer, 45 Colborne
SHAW ROBERT, barrister & solicitor, 169 Princess
Shaw Samuel, carter, 291 Earl
Shaw Samuel, Clergy
Shaw W. J., salesman, 33 Johnson
Shea Mrs. M., Bagot
Shea Wm., machinist, 28 Arch
SHEDDON CO., (LIMITED,) George Young, agent, cor. Ontario & William
Sheldon & Davis, photographers, 336 King e
Sherlock J. M., merchant tailor, 223 Princess, h 254 Queen
Sherman W. E., clerk, bds Gore
Sherridan Bernard, grocer, 245 Wellington
Sherrock James, sailor, bds St. Lawrence hotel
Sherwood James, cabman, 85 King w
Sherwood John, bookkeeper, 85 King w
Sherwood Wm., tinsmith, 85 King w
Shibley George, agent, 60 Arch
Shibley Schuyler, Bagot

Shiels John, tinsmith, 258 Rideau
Shields John, tinsmith, 89 Queen
SHORE LOYNES & CO., grocers, 266 Princess
SHORT CAPT. & BT.-MAJOR C. J., "B" Battery Tete du pont Barracks
Shufflebothan Walter S., grocer, 466 Montreal
Siler John, machinist, Johnson
Siler Wm., slotter, Johnson
Silkworth Melvin, cutter, 213 Princess
Sinclair Miss Charlotte, 212 Sydenham
Sinclair John, blacksmith, Loco. Works
Sinclair Robt., laborer, Frontenac
Sinclair Robert, driver, Sheddon Co.
SINGER MANF'G CO., F. W. Irwin, manager, 238 Princess
SIMMONDS MRS. A., dress & mantlemaker, 228 Princess
SIMMONDS ALFRED, second-hand book dealer & stationer, 228 Princess. (See advt.)
Simmons Alfred, grocer, 23 King w
Simmons Mrs. Ann, widow, 382 Brock
Simmonds Geo., machinist, Loco. Works
Simmons William, mariner, 141 Montreal
Simpson Arch, hotel, cor Ontario & Queen
Simpson Bernard, carpenter, 6 Rideau
Simpson C., corporal "B" Battery, R.S.G.
SIMPSON ISAAC, J.P., private banker & real estate, insurance, notary public, etc., 55 Clarence
Simpson James, cabman, Centre
Simpson Jno., shoemaker, Ontario
Sinnard, Louis, tailor, King e

Sinnott John, laborer, 32 Johnson
Sinnott Miles, cabman, King e
Sinnott Thos., cabman, 32 Johnson
Sissons John, laborer, Loco. Works
Sissons Wm., laborer, Cotton Co.
Skelton Anthony, shoemaker, 460 Montreal
Skelton John, painter, 460 Montreal
Skinner Henry, wh. druggist, 171 Princess, h 154 John
Skinner James, fitter, Loco. Works
Skinner James, locksmith, Union
Skinner Wm., salesman, 126 Earl
Slater Frank, plasterer, 143 Colborne
Slater Thomas, boilermaker, Montreal
Slater Thomas, laborer, 73 York
Slaven James, (Slaven & Mackin), h 189 Wellington
Slaven John, harnessmaker, bds 219 Princess
Slaven & Mackin, (James Slaven, Arthur Mackin,) merchant tailors, 189 Wellington
Slevin Michael, tailor, Bagot
Sleeman Henry, mason, Alfred
Sleith Saml., mason, 304 Johnson
Sleman William, mason, Princess
Slimmons John, stove mounter, Victoria Foundry
Sloan Alex,, laborer, 293 Montreal
Sloan Robert, engineer, 255 King e
Smallridge George M., carpenter, 169 Victoria
Small Philip H., policeman, Alfred
Smart John, laborer, Johnson
Smeaton Alex., engineer, 86 Queen
Smeaton Charles, tanner, George, nr Montreal
Smeaton J. R., grocer, 59 King w
Smith Mrs. A. F., millinery, 86 Division
Smith Alexander, Johnson
Smith Miss Ann, 413 King e
Smith Arch. J., clerk, Johnson
Smith Arthur M., Union
SMITH BROS.. (Charles & John,) watchmakers & jewellers, 345 King e, h 733 Princess
Smith Chas. F., student at law, Rose Lawn
Smith Mrs. Caroline, Princess
Smith Edward, 22 Chatham
Smith Edw., fitter, 22 Chatham
Smith Mrs. Elizabeth, 32 Upper Bagot
Smith F. T., bookkeeper, 86 Ontario
Smith George, watchmaker 733 Princess
Smith Henry, cab driver, 22 Place de Armes
Smith Henry, mariner, 257 Johnson
Smith Henry, fitter, Loco. Works
SMITH H. STALLERAFFE, bookbinder, 43 Brock, h 65 Gore
Smith James, blacksmith, First
Smith Miss Jane, 304 Brock
SMITH JOHN, book & job printer, 349 King e
Smith John, hide dealer, 56 Brock, h 79 Wellington
Smith John, trader, 46 York
Smith John, blacksmith, Loco. Works
Smith Joseph, tailor, 40 O'Kill
Smith Joseph A., tailor, King e
Smith Mrs. L., 149 Colborne
Smith Mrs. Mary, 457 Union
Smith Patrick, engineer, Park
Smith Patrick, grocer, Ontario
Smith Robert, teamster, 56 Albert
Smith Robert, laborer, 132 Bay
Smith Robert W., machinist, Loco. Works
Smith Samuel, spinner, Cotton Company

Smith Samuel, moulder, Loco. Works
Smith Thomas, carpenter, bds Albion Hotel
Smith Thos., blacksmith, King w
Smith William, blacksmith, Car Works
Smith William, laborer, cor Ann and Bagot
Smith Wm. H., carpenter, Brock
Smylie John, moulder, Locomotive Works
Smythe A. H., knitter, Hosiery Co
SMYTHE E. H., LL.D., barrister and solicitor, 192 Ontario, h 3 Westbourne Terrace,
Smythe James G., mariner, 55 William
Smyth William S., clerk general delivery, P.O., 132 Johnson
Snodden Alexander, policeman, cor Johnson and Gordon
Snowden William, builder, 232 Gordon
SNOOK T. L., barrister and solicitor, 332 King
Snyder Mrs. Alice, Deacon
Sommerville Francis, engineer, Second
Somerville Frank, carpenter, 214 Sydenham
Somerville Wm., salesman, 169 Colborne
Sowards James, hotel, 212 Montreal
Sourley Charles, laborer, 20 Bondhead
Spade Amos, inside porter, New Burnett house
Spang Charles, farmer, 390 Princess
SPANGENBERG F. W., watchmaker, jeweler, &c., 347 King e, h 86 Wellington
Spankie William, Brock
Sparks R. E., dentist, 230 Princess

Spence Charles, gardiner, Victoria
SPENCE & CRUMLEY, (D. M. Spence, Edward Crumley,) dry goods & millinery, 132-4 Princess. (See advt. front cover.)
SPENCE D. M., (Spence & Crumley,) h 132 Princess
Spence John, laborer, 25 Agnew's Lane
Spence John, currier, River
Spence R. A., carpenter, Car Works
Spence Wm., grocer, 224 Princess
Spencer A., 182 Queen
Spencer Abram, grinder, Cotton Co.
Spencer Mrs. M., 278 Sydenham
Spencer Levi B., contractor, 104 Bagot
Spencer Lewis, boilermaker, Queen
Spencer Lucas, boilermaker, 52 Colborne
Spereman James, inland revenue officer, Brock
Sperry Frank, clerk, St. Lawrence Hotel
Spriggs H. J., salesman, 238 Gordon
Spottswood George, saloon, 186 Wellington
Sprowell John, mariner, 64 Ontario
Stacey James, clerk, Division
Stacey John, pensioner, 209 Alfred
Stacey Wm., tinsmith, 209 Alfred
Stafford R., messenger Bank British North America
Stagg Albert, planer, Loco. Works
Staley Charles, mariner, Maitland
Staley Charles, nut tapper, Loco. Works
Staley Mrs. Harriet, Johnson
Staley Hy., laborer, Loco. Works
Staley Martin, carpenter, Simcoe
Staley Captain M., hotel keeper, cor Princess and Barrie

Stamford Thomas, laborer, 123 Montreal
Stansberry John, driver, Shedden Company
Statley George, musician, King, nr Queen
STEACY EDWARD T. (Walsh & Steacy) h Bagot
Steacy James, bookkeeper, 267 Division
Steacy Joseph, salesman, Bagot
Stearne P., fur dealer, foot Brock
Stephens Wm., mariner, 25 Pine
Stethem W. J., com. traveler, West
Stevenson A. D., mariner, 359 Brock
STEVENSON & CO., piano manufacturers, cor Princess & Ontario
STEVENSON H. J., manager Stevenson & Co.. h 58 William
Stevenson Mrs. Lucy, 237 Wellington
Stephenson Thomas, bookkeeper, Wellington
Stewart G., staff pay serg. " B " Battery R. S. G.
Stewart James, finisher, Kingston Foundry
Stewart James, agent, King w
Stewart John M., 68 Clergy
Stewart Richard, machinist, King
Stewart William, station agent, K. & P. RR., Barrack
Stewart William, jr., porter, K. & P. RR., Barrack
Stillman D. H., barber, 161 Princess
Stobart E. H., laborer, Montreal
Stobart H., stove mounter, Montreal
Stokes Wm., laborer, 30 Barrack
Stone John H., laborer, Park
STRACHAN ARCH., hardware, 193 Princess, h 98 Bagot
Strachan John, laborer, Gordon
Strachan John G., post office clerk, 248 Division
STRACHAM M. & SON, lumber, sash, doors, &c., 55 Gore
Strainge W., grocer, 147 Montreal
Strange Fred., clerk Federal Bank
Strange Frank, clerk, 132 King w
Strange H., sergt. " B " Battery, R.S.G.
Strange J. C., clerk P.O., Wellington
Strange J. M., clerk, King
Strange John, King w
STRANGE O. S., M.D., cor King & Union
STRANGE & STRANGE, (Maxwell Wm. & John,) insurance agents, 57 Clarence, h 132 King
Stansbury Jno., carter, s s Charles
Stratford Henry, taxidermist, 354 Princess
Stratford Mrs. Margaret, grocer, cor Princess & Clergy
Strong Anthony, machinist, Montreal
STROUD BROS., (J. B. Hawley, manager,) tea merchants, 109 Princess
Stroughton Mrs. E., King w
Struthers Clinton, driver, bds St. Lawrence Hotel
Stuart Alex., hotel keeper, 805 Montreal
Stuart John, watchman, Magdalen
Sturgess Edwin, carpenter, 424 Division
Suddard Edward, porter G. T. R., Elm
Sughrue John, pilot, 114 Queen
Sullivan Mrs. Catherine, 72 Barrack
Sullivan Dennis, detective, Rideau
Sullivan Jeremiah, laborer, 51 Bay
Sullivan John, laborer, 94 Gore
Sullivan John, painter, 75 Ontario

Sullivan Michael, M.D., 860 King e
Sullivan Michael, carpenter, 169 Montreal
Sullivan Mrs., 178 Barrie
Sullivan Mrs. Mary, Ontario
Sullivan T., saloonkeeper, 208 Wellington
Sullivan Thomas, saloonkeeper, 154 Rideau
Sullivan Wm. H., barrister, cor King & Market Sq., h William
Sullivan W. O., engineer, William
Sutherland Alex., boots & shoes, 103 Princess
Sutherland M. J., (Fenwick Hendry & Co.,) h 134 Earl
Sutherland R., shoemaker, 30 Elm
Sutherland Samuel, clerk, 190 Clergy
Swaine John, baker, 94 York
Swaine Mrs. Mary, 314 Johnson
Swan George T., grocer, 29 Ellis
Swan Samuel, planer, Loco. Works
Swanston Adam, baker, cor Princess & Barrie
Sweeney John, laborer, 83 Johnson
SWIFT JAMES, coal dealer, foot Johnson, h 134 King w
Swift James F., clerk, King w
Swift John, engineer, 68 Ontario
Swift Joseph, clerk, 224 King o
Switzer Peter, laborer, 63 Queen
SYDENHAM ST. METHODIST CHURCH, Sydenham, between William & Johnson
Tait Joseph, mason, 87 Charles
Tait Joseph G., mason, York
Talbot Anthony, broom maker, 30 Chatham
Talbot Henry, 251 Victoria
TANDY H., supt. Can. Loco. & Eng. Works, h Wellington
TASCHEREAU LIEUT. & BT.- MAJOR, J. E. M., "B" Battery, Tete du Pont Barracks

Tarrant Jas., laborer, 47 Colborne
Tarrant John, carpenter, Deacon
Tassell Chas., builder, Clergy
Taylor Mrs. B., Ontario
Taylor Edward, finisher, Kingston Foundry
Taylor Geo., laborer, 427 Division
Taylor Henry, tinsmith, Stuart
Taylor J. H., asst. superintendent K. & P. RR., 93 Queen
Taylor Jonathan, carter, 8 Ellice
Taylor John, finisher, Kingston Foundry
Taylor Joseph, boat inspector, 68 George
Taylor Mrs. P., 430 Brock
Taylor Samuel, steam fitter, McEwen & Son
Taylor Wm., painter, Car Works
Telgmann Miss D., musical teacher, 103 Queen
Tetlock John, carpenter, 127 Montreal
Theobald J. A., barber, 167 Wellington
Thibodo Augustus, 22 Ontario
Thierault Chris. J., engineer, Earl
Thom James, salesman, Gordon
Thomas Wm., shoemaker, Princess
Thompson Alex., bookkeeper, Queen
Thompson Alex., carpenter, 71 Ontario
Thompson Charles, policeman, Earl
Thompson David, mechanic, Earl
Thompson Frank, mariner, 177 Sydenham
Thompson Frank, fitter, Loco. Works
Thompson George, wh. liquors, 331-3 King o, h 210 Queen
Thompson Jacob, sailor, bds 47 Princess
Thompson James, clerk, Queen

CITY OF KINGSTON. 89

THOMPSON J. DUNCAN, agent Montreal Transportation Co., h 22 Colborne
Thompson Miss Mary, King
Thompson Robt., clerk, G. T. R, Johnson
Thompson Thos., clerk, Frontenac
Thompson Wm., mariner, 23 Bondhead
Thompson Wm. W., carpenter, 86 Upper Bagot
THOMSON ROBERT, freight agent, G.T.R., h Johnson
Thorn Benjamin, carpenter, 186 Division
Thornton Edward, 528 Ontario
Thornton John, grocer, 503 Princess
Thornton Mrs. Mary, 2 First
Thornton Samuel, hotelkeeper, cor Ontario & Brock
Thornton Wm., carpenter, Car Works
Thornton, Wm. J., machinist, s s Pine
Thurman John, pensioner, 55 John
Thurston Henry, engineer, 166 Barrack
Tierney Bros. (Owen and John) teas, wines, &c., 261 Ontario
Tierney John, Ottawa Hotel, cor Princess and Ontario
Tierney John (Tierney Bros.) h 179 Queen
Tierney Owen (Tierney Bros.) h Ontario
Tierney Patrick, clerk, bds Burnet House
TILLINGHAST T. C., merchant tailor, 79 Brock, h 81 Wellington. (See advt.)
TILLINGHAST T. J., bookkeeper, 81 Wellington
Tindall Thomas, laborer, James
Tinnes William, laborer, Princess
Tisdale Samuel, laborer, Arch
Titus George, mariner, Union
Tobins Richard, laborer, Gore
Tobin Thomas, moulder, 405 King
Todd Robert, shoemaker, Ontario
Tomkins Mrs. A., Young's Lane
Tomlinson Henry H., carpenter, Simcoe
Tooher Thos., hotel keeper, 312 Montreal
Towers Wm., laborer, William
Town Mrs. 314 King e
Townsend Thomas, laborer, 34 Upper Bagot
TOYE R. H., baker and confectioner, 302 King e, h 102 Queen
Tracy Francis, blacksmith, 38 Rideau
Treneer John, laborer, Earl
Trainer Enoch, laborer, Barrie
Trainer Mrs. Jane, 215 Earl
Travis Joseph, carpenter, 78 Queen
Traynor James, carpenter, Car Works
Trendell John, trumpet major, "B" Battery, R.S.G.
Trowell John, mariner, Wellington
Tucker John, 196 Sydenham
Tucker Thomas, laborer, 16 Bondhead
Turbet J., grocer, cor Barrie & Earl
Turcott Alfred, carpenter, Gore
Turcott Nicholas, laborer, Earl
Turnbull Alex., painter, bds 47 Princess
Turnbull Thomas sr., engineer, Kingston Foundry
Turner Daniel, bookkeeper, bds St. Lawrence Hotel
Turner D. C., bartender, 143 Princess
Turner G. W., shipper, 103 Wellington
Turner Mrs. Isabella, Wellington

CITY OF KINGSTON.

Turning Thos., laborer, bds 103 Brock
Turpin H., laborer, 146 Colborne
Turpin Mrs. Jane, tailoress, 146 Colborne
Tuttle John, mariner, n s Centre
Tutton Fred., machinist, Sydenham
Tweddell John, merchant tailor, 125 Princess, h 200 Queen
Tweed Thomas, 47 Arch
Twigg John gardener, 19 Gordon
Twiss Francis, carter, 117 Barrack
TWITCHELL M. H., United States consul, 82 Clarence, h 26 Wellington
Twohey Mrs. Ann, 264 Earl
TWOHEY REV. P. A. (Roman Catholic) 225 Johnson
Tye Isaac, laborer, Victoria Foundry
Tyeo John, laborer, Alfred
TYNER WILLIAM H. (Noon & Tyner) h 84 Union
Tyo Stephen, mariner, cor Montreal and Stephen
UNITED STATES CONSULATE OFFICE, M. H. Twitchell, consul, 82 Clarence
Upper Joseph, contractor, King
Urquhart Arch, com. traveller, 112 Montreal
Urquhart Wm., stone cutter, 112 Montreal
Vair George T., salesman, 330 Johnson
Vanarnam Chas. A., confectioner, 850 King
Vanarnam Gideon, trader, 25 Earl
Vandewater John, agent, 46 Durham
Vandewater John, carpenter, Car Works
Vandewater, R. W., general insurance agent, office Stevenson & Co's piano factory, h 49 George
Vandussen Wm., laborer, Ordnance
Vanluven Thos., county treasurer, Princess
Vanwinkle Jacob, carpenter, Montreal
Vanorder John, laborer, Loco. Works
Varault Mrs. Margaret, Earl
Varney Richard, hotel, King w
Varney Wm., moulder, Loco. Works
VAN TASSEL W. A., manager Haines & Locket, h 134 Princess
Veal Elijah, painter, 154 York
Veal Elijah, painter, 173 Nelson
Veevers Henry, grinder, Cotton Co
Vick David, laborer, Stephen
VICTORIA FOUNDRY, Chown & Cunningham proprs., cor King & Queen
Villiers Major Henry, D.A.G., King w
Vince Samuel, finisher, Kingston Foundry
Vince Wm., engineer, 19 Ontario
Virtue Mrs. Mathew, laundress, 269 Division
Vital Mathew, mason, Division
Voigt F. C., clerk, P. O., 226 Johnson
Voigt Henry C., accountant, 226 Johnson
Volume James, shoemaker, 59 Elm
WADE HENRY, druggist, cor King & Brock, h 89 Gore
Wade Thomas, carpenter, 89 Gore
Waddell D. A., harnessmaker, 287 Wellington
Waddell Robert, 316 Johnson
WADDINGTON BROS., (Wm., Geo. & Henry,) butchers, 318 King e, res Bath road. *(See advt.)*
Wagar T. S., turner, 94 Division

CITY OF KINGSTON. 91

WAGGONER BROS., (Joseph & John,) proprs. Waggoner House, 298 Ontario
WAGGONER HOUSE (Waggoner Bros.) 298 Ontario
WAGGONER JOSEPH, clerk Waggoner House
Waite Willoughy, laborer, Sydenham
Waite Wm., carter, Sydenham
Waldron George R., broommaker, Second
Waldron John, laborer, 189 Colborne
WALDRON RICHARD, dry goods, cor Wellington & Brock, h 190 Bagot
Walen Patrick, tanner, n s John, nr Montreal
Wales Robert, 135 King w
WALKEM RICHARD, (Walkem & Walkem,) h 60 Barrie
WALKEM & WALKEM, (Richard T. Walkem, Q.C., & Joseph B. Walkem,) barristers, 93 Clarence. (*See card.*)
Walker Mrs. Catharine, 12 Clergy
WALKER MAJOR GEORGE ROBERT, R.E., R. M. C.
Walker J. S., salesman, 214 Queen
Walker Mrs. Sarah, 232 Sydenham
Wallace Mrs. Andrew, boarding, 103 Brock
Walling E., sergeant "B" Battery, Fort Henry
Walsh A., corporal "B" Battery, Fort Henry
Walsh Edw. A., printer, *Whig*
WALSH EDWIN, salesman, 338 Montreal
Walsh George, loom fixer, Montreal
Walsh Jas., moulder, Loco. Works
Walsh Jas., cabman, Johnson
Walsh Jas., loom fixer, Montreal
Walsh Jas. H., Montreal, nr James
Walsh John, laborer, William
Walsh John, jr., carter, William
Walsh John J., 76 Gore
Walsh Max., polisher, 194 Sydenham
Walsh Mrs. Mary, laundress, foot Queen
Walsh Michael, butcher, 310 King e, h 624 Princess
Walsh Mrs. M. H., millinery, 354 King, h 76 Gore
WALSH PATRICK J., (Walsh & Steacy,) h 57 Arch
Walsh Patrick, coal dealer, cor Ontario and Barrack, h Ontario
Walsh P. H. W., salesman, 57 Arch
Walsh Robert, clerk, William
WALSH & STEACY (Patrick J. Walsh and Edward T. Steacy) dry goods, etc., 106 Princess
Walsh Thomas, foreman weaver, Montreal
Walsh Wm., mechanic, Montreal
Wandell Mrs. Martha, 138 Victoria
Wannocott Robert, laborer, n s Charles
WARD JOHN, grocer, 337 Princess, h Johnson
Ward John, salesman, bds Beaupre's Hotel
Ward John, laborer, 31 Bondhead
Ward Maurice, carpenter, Johnson
Ward Prestly, blacksmith Wade's Lane
Ward Thomas, butcher, Princess
Ward Wm., engineer, Barrie
Warden Mrs. Catherine, 135 Colborne
Warrick Chas. J., carpenter, 84 Arch
Warrick Mrs. Mary, 86 Arch
Washington Thos., marble cutter, Johnson

Waters Geo., clerk Bagot
Waters John, baker, 83 Rideau
Waters Wm., driver Shedden Co., 19 O'Kill
Watham Philip, laborer, 293 King
Watkins George, 252 Victoria
Watkins John, stone cutter, 136 Colborne
Watson Benjamin, 250 Gordon
Watson Geo., laborer, 413 Johnson
WATSON JOHN, M.A., LL.D., professor Queen's College
Watson Mrs. M., Brock
Watson Thomas, sailor, bds 188 Colborne
Watson William, shoemaker, 136 Colborne
Watson William J., confectioner, 282 Princess
Watt James, shoemaker, 403 King
Watt James, carter, Earl
Watt Mrs. Martha, n s Charles
Watts John, laborer, Loco. Works
Webb George, laborer, Kingston Hospital
Webb William, laborer, Young's Lane
WEBER G. M., (G. M. Weber & Co.,) h 186 Wellington
WEBER G. M. & CO., (G. M. Weber & Jas. McManus,) piano manufacturers, 42 Princess (See adv.)
Webster, Bates & Co., (W. J. Webster & J. J. Bates,) manufacturers brooms, blacking etc., 265 Ontario
Webster E. W., bds Windsor Hotel
Webster W. J., (Webster, Bates & Co.) Montreal
Weir James, steward K. P., 27 Pembroke
WEIGHTS & MEASURES OFFICE, C. B. Crysler, inspector, 45 Clarence

Welch Charles, marblecutter, 185 Division
Welch E. R. & Son, (E. R. & Fred.,) proprs. Canada Marble Works, cor Princess & Clergy
Welch E. R., (E. R. Welch & Son,) h 179 Division
Welch Fred., (E. R. Welch & Son,) h 4 Vaughan Terrace
Welch John, accountant, 67 Earl
Welch Patrick, carpenter, 37 Princess
Wells Henry, harnessmaker and livery keeper, 53 Princess
Westlake John P., tailor, 385 Johnson
Whalen Patrick, beamer, William
Whalen Mrs. Margaret, William
Wharin William, 188 Ordnance
Wheeler Joseph, pianomaker, 90 Bondhead
Whitcher C. H., broker, 271 Princess
Whitcomb Mrs. M., Brock
White Benj., carpenter, 98 Barrack
White Miss Eliza, William
White H. B., clerk, bds Burnett House
White J. T., district agent Canada Life Assurance Co., 48 Clrrence, h cor Earl & Gordon
White Mrs., cor Ontario & Clarence
White Robt., dyer, 79-89 Princess
White Mrs. S., 108 Barrack
WHITE S. P., tobacconist, 123 Princess
Whitehead A., carpenter, Car Works
Whitehead D. R., com. traveller, 79 Colborne
Whitehead J., laborer, n s Centre
Whitehead Jas., real estate agent, cor King & Brock
WHITING JOHN L., B.A. (Britton & Whiting) h 152 Bagot

CITY OF KINGSTON.   93

Wilkins John jr., laborer, 16 George
Wilkinson George E., (Geo. M. Wilsonson & Son,) 165 Queen
Wilkinson George M., (Geo. M. Wilkinson & Son,) h 165 Queen
Wilkinson Geo. M. & Son, (H. J. & G. E.,) grocers, 201-3 Princess & 178-80 Wellington
Wilkinson H. J. (Geo. M. Wilkinson & Son,) h 73 William
Wilkinson Mrs. Mary, Park, cor Victoria
Williams Edward, wood merchant, 23 Earl
Williams H., laborer, Loco. Works
Williams John, laborer, 24 Wade's lane
Williams Manley, hotel, Ontario, cor Queen
Williams Mrs. M., Earl
Williams Thos., moulder, Loco. Works
Williamson Adam, carpenter, 115 Gore
Williamson F., mariner, Barrack
WILLIAMSON REV. JAMES, M.A., LL.D., Vice Principal Queen's College, 136 Earl
Williamson James, moulder, 38 Collingwood
Willis James, blacksmith, Loco. Works
Wills —, barber, 221 Princess
Willoughby James, laborer, Brock
Wilmot Edward, blacksmith, 200 William
Wilmot Henry, carpenter, 200 William
Wilmot Nathaniel, blacksmith, 39 Montreal, h 141 Ordnance
Wilson Bros. (H. W. and R. J.) druggist, cor Princess and Montreal, h Union, opp Drill Shed
Wilson Bros. (Thos. C. and Wm.) livery keepers, 120 Clarence
Wilson Charles, laborer, Loco. Works
Wilson David, printer, 196 Bagot
Wilson Edward. 211 Colborne
Wilson Edward B., Second
Wilson George, laborer, Colborne
Wilson G. F., stone cutter, 81 Colborne
WILSON REV. HENRY, D.D., Church of England, s s Gore
WILSON REV. J., Methodist Episcopal, Division
WILSON JAS., manager Water Works, 28 Barrie
Wilson John, gardener, 9 Upper James
Wilson J. F., laborer, 302 King w
Wilson Joseph, mason, 52 Bay
Wilson Robert, blacksmith, Loco. Works
Wilson Mrs. Sarah E., 138 King e
Wilson Thomas, stove mounter, Victoria Foundry
WILSON W. J., druggist, (successor to Heath & Gunn,) 185 Princess
Wilson Wm., manager Kingston Cotton Company, Montreal
Wilton Henry, harness maker, 167 Princess
WINDSOR HOTEL, Martin O'Brien, prop., 205-9 Princess
WINGFIELD & CO., registry office for unemployed, real estate insurance & collectors, 9 Montreal
WINGFIELD JAMES,(Wingfield & Co.,) 9 Montreal
Wisdom Jno, laborer, Loco. Works
Wisdom Jno.,carpenter, 489 Alfred
Wishart John, engineer, Arch
Wonham P. C. R., bookkeeper, Bank Montreal
Wood Mrs. Ann, 793 Montreal
Wood Bros., (H. A. W. & T. W.) watchmakers, 236 Princess

Wood Charles, driver, Chatham
Wood George, laborer, Beverly
Wood Chester, carpenter, 793 Montreal
Wood Mrs. Mary, Chatham
Wood Samuel, laborer, Park
Wood Thomas, tailor, Gore
Wood Wm., gardener, 390 Princess
Woodford James, blacksmith, Loco. Works
Woodhard James, hd Princess
Woodrow Wm., laborer, Gore
Woods Charles, printer, 134 Chatham
Woods George, laborer, King w
Woods L. M., 7-cent store, 101 Princess
Woods Mrs. Mary, 203 Wellington
Woods Samuel, laborer, Car Works
Woollard Miss Charlotte, 629 Princess
Woollard Peter, mariner, Ontario
Woollard Wm., salesman, 619 Princess
Woollard Wm. J., clerk, 619 Princess
Wooton John, pensioner, 303 Montreal
Wormworth Wm., piano maker, Clergy
Worsley Lt.-Col. P. W., 35 Centre
Worth J., farrier sergeant "B" Battery, R.S.G.
WRIGHT CLARK (Clark Wright & Son) h 21 Colborne
WRIGHT CLARK & SON, (Clark and C. W.,) hatters and furriers, 132 Wellington
WRIGHT C. W., (Clark Wright & Son,) h 21 Colborne
Wright George, carpenter, 110 Barrack

Wright John, carter, 303 King w
Wright John, gardener, 270 Johnson
Wright John, 26 Place de Armes
Wright Mrs. R. H., card printing, 107 Brock
Wright Robert H., carpenter, 107 Brock
Wright William, butcher, 258 Princess
WURTELE LIEUT. ALFRED GEORGE GODFREY, C.M., R.M. College
Wrigley John, rollercoupler, Cotton Co.
Wylie George, carpenter, 28 Place de Armes
Yates Mrs. Elizabeth, 64 William
Yates James, carpenter, 258 Earl
Yates Joseph, printer, 64 William
Yeadow Henry, laborer, Union
Youlden Henry, engineer, Rideau
Young George, shoemaker, 198 Colborne
Young George, shoemaker, Second
YOUNG GEORGE, AGENT The Sheddon Co. (Limited), 216 Gordon
Young Henry, moulder, Loco. Works
Young Mrs. Jane, Rideau
Young John, M.D., 232 Princess
Young Richard, mason, 269 Gordon
Young Stephen, currier, 43 Dufferin
Young William, laborer, Pine
Young William., 291 King
Yule James, bookkeeper, 105 Gore
Zeigler George, brewer, 38 Upper Bagot
Zimmerman Nicholas, foreman, Loco. Works

ESTABLISHED 1858.

HENRY BRAME,
Leading Undertaker,

No 251, corner Princess & Sydenham Streets, Kingston, Ont. All branches of undertaking attended to. Has constantly on hand all kinds of

COFFINS & CASKETS,

Both wooden and metallic. A complete stock of SHROUDS of every description, and all things appertaining to his line. Keeps always for use the best quality of embalming fluids. His Hearses are first-class. Funerals conducted in the city and county on most reasonable terms.

W. H. IRWIN & CO.,

Directory Publishers & Publishers' Agents,

HAMILTON, ONTARIO.

City of Hamilton, published every February	$2.50
City of Kingston, published every two years	2.00
City of Brantford and County of Brant	2.00
County of York	2.00
County of Perth	2.00
County of Waterloo	2.00
County of Simcoe	2.00
County of Halton	1.50
County of Wentworth	2.00

Directories of Montreal, $3; Toronto, 3; Quebec, $2.50; City of Guelph and County Wellington, $3; London (Ont.) $3. Sent on receipt of Price.

SUBSCRIBERS' CLASSIFIED BUSINESS DIRECTORY.

ALE, BEER AND WINE BOTTLERS.
Harback H. A., 69 Princess
Pipe W., 285 Princess

ARCHITECTS.
Power & Son, Wellington

AUCTIONEER.
Hutcheson James E., 86 Brock

BANKS.
Bank British North America, City Hall
Federal, cor Wellington & Clarence
Merchants, King e
Montreal, King e

BANKERS.
Carruthers Bros., 44 Clarence
Fraser Donald, 342 King e
Simpson Isaac, 55 Clarence

BARRISTERS AND SOLICITORS.
Agnew James, City Hall
Britton & Whiting, 69 Clarence
Kirkpatrick & Rogers, 194 Ontario
McIntyre John, 304 King e
Macdonald & Mudie, 38 Clarence
MacMahon John D., 36 Clarence
Shaw Robert, 169 Princess
Smythe E. H., 192 Ontario
Snook T. L., 332 King e
Walkem & Walkem, 93 Clarence

BOOK BINDERS.
McAuley Thomas, 356 King e
Smith H. Stalleraffe, 43 Brock

BOOKSELLERS AND STATIONERS.
British & Foreign Bible Society Depository, G. S. Hobart, 155 Princess
Henderson John & Co., 88 Princess
London Tract Society, G. W. Andrews, 190 Wellington
McAuley Thomas, 356 King e
Nisbet Francis, Brock cor Wellington
Simmonds Alfred, 228 Princess

BOOTS AND SHOES.
Armstrong D. F., 141 Princess
Haines & Lockett, 184 Princess
Rose Edwin, 138 Princess

BREWERS.
Bajus P., 308 Wellington
Kelly, McKay & Daunt, King w

BUILDING AND LOAN COMPANIES.
Frontenac Loan & Investment, 49 Clarence
Ontario Building & Savings, Clarence

CITY OF KINGSTON.

BUTCHERS.

Waddington Bros., 318 King e

CARRIAGE MANUFACTURERS.

Brown J. W. & Co., 308 Barrie
Laturney James, 392 Princess
McCrea. T. W., 479 Princess

CARTAGE AGENTS.

Shedden Co., (limited) George Young, agent, cor Ontario & William

CARVERS AND GILDERS.

Ohlke & Leader, Brock

CHEMISTS AND DRUGGISTS.

Hobart G. S., 135 Princess
Wade Henry, cor King & Brock
Wilson W. J., 185 Princess

CHINA, GLASSWARE ETC.

Ockley Vincent & Sons, 115-7 Princess
Robertson Bros., 187 Princess

CLOTHIERS AND GENTS' FURNISHERS.

Anis W. G., 86 Princess
Dunbar & Co., 100 Princess
Lambert & Walsh, 226 Princess
McNaughton & Co., cor King & Princess

CONFECTIONERS, ETC.

Gardiner J. O. & Co., cor Earl & Division, manufacturers
Mason G. A., 314 King e
Newman R. J. J., 322 King e
Toye R. H., 302 King e

DENTIST.

Clements Leonard, 140 Wellington

DRY GOODS.

Bowes & Bisonette, 204 Princess
Cousineau F. X. & Co,, 80 Princess
Hardy & Murray, 176 Princess
Macnee & Minnes, wholesale, cor Princess & Bagot
Richmond & Boyden, 118-20 Princess
Ross Alex., 128 Princess
Shaw Felix, cor Princess & Wellington
Spencer & Crumley, 132-4 Princess
Waldron Richard, cor Wellington & Brock
Walsh & Steacy, 106 Princess

ENGINE AND BOILER MANUFACTURERS.

McEwen & Son, 54 Queen

EXPRESS COMPANIES.

American Express Co., cor King & Brock
Canadian Express Co., cor King & Brock

FORWARDING COMPANY.

Montreal Transportation Co., J. Duncan Thompson, agent, foot Queen

FOUNDERS AND MACHINISTS.

Chown & Cunningham, Victoria Foundry, cor King & Queen
Eavidson, Doran & Co., 37 Ontario

FURNITURE MANUFACTURERS AND DEALERS.

Brame Henry, 251 Princess
Drennan W. M., 75 Princess
Jackson John M., 113 Brock
Main R. J., 165 Princess
Reid James, 254 Princess

JOHN A. McMAHON,
Solicitor, Notary &c.,
36 Clarence St.,
KINGSTON.

Money to Loan at Lowest Rates.

R. W. SHANNON, M.A.,
Barrister, Solicitor &c.

OFFICE:
'DAILY NEWS' BUILDING,
KINGSTON, - - ONTARIO.

WALKEM & WALKEM,
(Richard T. Walkem, Q.C., Jos. B. Walkem.)

SOLICITORS &c.

93 Clarence Street,
KINGSTON, - - ONTARIO.

L. CLEMENTS, L.L.S.,
DENTIST.

OFFICE AND RESIDENCE:
Opposite Post Office, Wellington St.

Established in Kingston in 1857.

GROCERS.

Browne James & Co., wholesale, Ontario
Farrell Thomas, Market Square
Gunn A. & Co., wholesale, 125-7 Ontario
McRae & Co., cor Wellington & Brock
Maguire Hugh, cor Princess & Montreal
Oakley Vincent & Sons, 115-17 Princess
Pantry Grocery & Provision Co., 174 Princess
Parkhill J. Y., 270 Princess
Redden James, 178 Princess
Robertson Geo. & Son, wholesale Ontario
Scott N. K., cor Princess & Bagot
Shore Loynes & Co., 266 Princess
Stroud Bros., 109 Princess

HARDWARE.

Chown A., 252 Bagot
Corbett John, cor Princess & Wellington
Hamer John, 55 Princess
Horsey R. M., 189 Princess
McMahon Bros., 85-7 Princess
Muckleston A. & Co., 71-3 Princess
Rudd T. G., 202 Princess
Strachan Arch., cor Princess & Montreal

HATS AND CAPS.

C. O. D. Store, 206 Princess
Galloway James, 84 Princess
Mills Geo. & Co., 170 Wellington
Wright Clark & Son, 132 Wellington

CITY OF KINGSTON.

HOTELS.

Albion P. McLaughlin, cor Montreal
British American, H. McFaul, cor King & Clarence
Waggoner House, Waggoner Bros., 298 Ontario
New Burnett House, W. Fralick, Ontario
St. Lawrence, Henry Grimshaw, cor King & Queen
Windsor, Martin O'Brien, 205-9 Princess

INSURANCE COMPANIES AND AGENTS.

Accident Ins. Co., J. P. Gildersleeve, 42 Clarence
Boiler Inspection & Ins. Co., J. P. Gildersleeve, 42 Clarence
Caledonia Fire, J. P. Gildersleeve, 42 Clarence
Commercial Union Assurance, fire & life, Strange & Strange, 57 Clarence
North British Mercantile Ins. Co., M. Flanagan, City Hall
Ontario Mutual Life Association, James Wingfield, 9 Montreal
Royal Canadian, fire & marine, J. P. Gildersleeve, 42 Clarence
Royal Fire & Life Ins., Strange & Strange, 57 Clarence
Standard Life Assurance, J. P. Gildersleeve, 42 Clarence
Tontine Mutual Benefit Association, James Wingfield, 9 Montreal

IRON LADDERS.

Laturney, 392 Princess

LOCOMOTIVE WORKS.

Canadian Locomotive & Engine Co., Ontario

LUMBER DEALERS.

Caldwell A. & Son, cor Ontario & Place de Armes
Noon & Tyner, Ontario
Strachan M. & Son, 55 Gore, and Barriefield

MERCHANT TAILORS.

Dunbar & Co., 100 Princess
Lambert & Walsh, 226 Princess
Livingston C. & Bro., 69 Brock
McNaughton & Co., cor King and Princess
Moore Thomas, 59 Brock
Tillinghast T. C., 79 Brock

MUSIC DEALERS.

Carey Wm. & Son, 159 Princess
Henderson John & Co., 88 Princess
McAuley Thomas, 356 King e

PHOTOGRAPHER.

Henderson Henry, 90 Princess

NEWSPAPERS.

British Whig, 336 King e
Chronicle & News, 67 Princess
Daily News, 67 Princess
Queen's College Journal, College Building
Weekly British Whig, 336 King e

PAINTERS AND PAPERHANGERS.

McMahon Thomas, cor Brock and Bagot
Robinson Wm. & Son, 275 Bagot

PHYSICIANS AND SURGEONS.

Fee Samuel H., 405 Princess
Fenwick K. N., 141 King e
Garrett Richard Wm., B.A., 201 Wellington

Irwin Chamberlen, cor King and William
Lavell C. H., 155 Brock
Lavell M. 267 Brock
Saunders H. J. 244 King e
Strange O. S., cor King & Union

PIANOS AND ORGANS.

Carey W. & Son, 159 Princess
George Joseph, 110-14 Gore
Stevenson & Co., cor Princess and Ontario
Weber G. M. & Co., 42 Princess

PLANING MILLS, SASH AND DOORS.

Strachan M. & Son, Barriefield

PRINTERS, BOOK AND JOB.

Baillie Bros., Wellington
British Whig, 336-40 King e
Daily News, 67 Princess
Smith John, 349 King e

ROOMPAPER AND PAPERHANGERS.

Robinson Wm. J., 277 Bagot
McMahon Thomas, cor Brock and Bagot

SECOND HAND BOOKS.

Simmonds Alfred, 228 Princess

SEWING MACHINES.

Cunningham John, 348 King e
Singer, F. W. Irwin, 238 Princess

STEAMSHIP LINES (OCEAN).

Dominion, J. P. Gildersleeve, 42 Clarence
Inman, J. P. Gildersleeve, 42 Clarence
National, J. P. Gildersleeve. 42 Clarence

STOVES, TINWARE, ETC.

Chown & Cunningham 248 Bagot
McKelvey & Birch, 71 Brock
Reid Jas., cor Union and Division

TINSMITH (MANUFACTURING.)

Reid Jas., cor Union and Division

UPHOLSTERING (MAUFACTURING.)

Jackson John M., 113 Brock

UNITED STATES CONSUL.

Twitchell M. H., 32 Clarence

TOBACCO, CIGARS, ETC.,

Routley W. H., 173 Princess
White Samuel P., 128 Princess

UNDDRTAKERS.

Brame Henry, cor Princess and Syrenham
Reid James, 254 Princess

VABIETIES.

McNaughton Bros., 175 Princess
Mahood Wm. J., 113 Princess
Woods L. M. 101 Princess

VINEGAR MANUFACTURERS.

Haaz Bros., 130-2 Ontario

WATCHMAKERS AND JEWELERS.

Johnston Albert E., 192 Wellington
Smith Bros., 345 King e
Spangeberg F. W, 347 King e

COUNTY
—OF—
FRONTENAC.

This County is bounded on the north by Renfrew, on the south by the River St. Lawrence, on the east by Lanark and Leeds, on the west by Hastings, and on the south-west by Lennox. It consists of the Townships of Barrie, Bedford, Clarendon & Miller, Hinchinbrooke, Howe Island, Kennebec, Kingston, Loughboro, Olden, Oso, Palmerston and North and South Canonto, Pittsburg, Portland, Storrington, Wolfe Island, and the incorporated Villages of Portsmouth and Garden Island.

The County of Frontenac was named after the founder of the first settlement in Upper Canada, Count de Frontenac, who built a fort on the banks of the Cataraqui in July, 1673.

In 1674 De la Salle obtained from Louis XIV., King of France, the fort and four leagues of land along the border of Lake Frontenac (Ontario), the two islands in front, and the interjacent islands. On the 27th of August, 1758, Colonel Bradstreet took possession, and from that date commenced the British rule. In 1874 the U. E. Loyalists commenced to settle in this County. The first settler was Captain Grass, who took up land in Kingston Township. After the war of 1812 Sir John Johnson selected the shores of the Bay of Quinte and vicinity for discharged soldiers and others, who settled here in large numbers. The County includes every variety of land, and is rich in minerals. The back townships are now open for settlement, and, with the extension of the Kingston and Pembroke Railway, the County will in the course of a few years have a much larger population than at present. Number of acres about 600,000; population about 16,000.

COUNTY COUNCIL, 1883.

D. J. WALKER, Esq., Inverary P.O., Warden.

BARRIE.—Tapping, T., reeve, Hardinge.
BEDFORD.—Tett, B., reeve, Bedford Mills.
CLARENDON & MILLER.—Dawson, G. W., reeve, Plevna.
HINCHINBROOK.—McKeever, J., reeve, Godfrey.
HOWE ISLAND.—Quinn, J. H., reeve, Howe Island.
KINGSTON.—VanLuven, A. P., reeve, Murvale. T. Buck, deputy reeve, Cataraqui.
KENNEBEC,—Williams, J., reeve.
LOUGHBORO.—Woodruff, J., reeve, Rutledge, J., deputy-reeve, Loughboro.
OSO.—Bourk, W., reeve, Oso Station.
OLDEN.—Flynn, Robert, reeve, Mountain Grove.
PALMERSTON & NORTH AND SOUTH CANONTO.—McKenzie, J., Mississippi.
PORTLAND.—Denison, George, reeve, Hartington. Murton, J., deputy reeve, Murvale.
PITTSBURGH.—Patterson, R. S., reeve, Kingston. Whitney, T., deputy reeve, Pittsferry.
STORRINGTON.—Walker, D. J., reeve, Inverary. Shannon, R., deputy reeve, Sunbury.
WOLFE ISLAND.—Hogan, T., reeve; Grant, D., deputy reeve, Wolfe Island.
GARDEN ISLAND.—Calvin, D.D, Reeve.
PORTSMOUTH.—Adams, J., reeve.

COUNTY OFFICERS.

D. J. Walker, Warden; C. V. Price, Judge; William Ferguson, Sheriff; B. M. Britton, Clerk of Peace and County Attorney; John Fraser, County Court Clerk and Deputy Clerk of Crown and Pleas ; R. M. Rose, Registrar; Thos. F. Vanluven, Treasurer; F. Elkington, County Clerk; John Agnew, M.A., M.D., Inspector of Public Schools; C. H. Corbett, Esq., Governor of Jail; A. S. Oliver, M.D., Surgeon of County Jail; Auditors: E. N. Gurney and A. Brown, Treasurer's Accounts; Thos. Hogan, F. Elkington, Administration of Justice Accounts; John Ashley, Court House Keeper.

TOWNSHIP CLERKS.

BARRIE.—W. Deighton .... Cloyne.
BEDFORD.—R. Cook .... Fermoy.
CLARENDON.—E. Playfair .... Plevna.
HINCHINBROOK.—J. Hamilton .... Parham.
HOWE ISLAND.—M. Melville .... Howe Island.
KENNEBEC.—W. Patterson .... Arden.
KINGSTON.—John Simpson .... Cataraqui.
LOUGHBORO.—J. Wilson .... Sydenham.
OLDEN.—M. W. Price .... Arden.
OSO.—H. Rigney .... Maberly.

PALMERSTON.—J. Elkington, M.D.................................... Ompah.
PITTSBURG.—Chas. Belwa .... Barriefield.
PORTLAND.—J. Donnelly .... Harrowsmith.
STORRINGTON.—A. Richie... Inverary.
WOLFE ISLAND.—F. A. Hatfield .... Wolfe Island.

DIVISION COURT CLERKS.

No. 1, Wm. Robinson, Kingston; 2, P. McKim, Cataraqui; 3, Charles Ruttan, Loughboro; 4, Alex. Grant, Verona; 5, D. J. Walker, Inverary.

AGRICULTURAL SOCIETY.

COUNTY OF FRONTENAC AGRICULTURAL SOCIETY.—R. J. Dunlop, President, Kingston; J. H. Metcalfe, 1st Vice-President, Kingston; D. J. Walker, 2nd Vice-President, Kingston; Isaac Simpson, Treasurer, Kingston; Francis Elkington, Secretary, Kingston.

47th BATTALION.

Geo. A. Kirkpatrick, Lieut.-Colonel; George Hunter, Henry R. Smith, Majors; W. M. Baillie, Adjutant; John R. Smith, Surgeon; James McCammon, Asst.-Surgeon.

No. 1, STORRINGTON.—Robert Huton, Captain; Alex. Sharp, Lieutenant.
No. 2, INVERARY.—Joseph Healey, Captain; David James, Lieutenant.
No. 3, ELGINBURG.—Charles N. Spooner, Captain; Charles Irvin, Lieutenant.
No. 4, PORTSMOUTH.—Thomas Kelly, Captain; Edwin Atrons, Lieutenant.
No. 5, BARRIEFIELD.—James Byrne, Captain.
No. 6, WOLFE ISLAND.—I. H. Bradford, Captain; M. A. Kemp, Lieutenant
No. 7.—Elijah Joyney, Captain; N. P. Joyney, Lieutenant.

→J. P. TETT & BRO.←

Merchants,

Millers,

Lumbermen,

BEDFORD MILLS, ONTARIO.

N. CAVERLY,

GENERAL MERCHANT

AND ISSUER OF

MARRIAGE LICENSES,

INVERARY.

Applications Strictly Confidential

TOWNSHIP OF BARRIE.

Acres assessed, 13,422. Population, 458.

See also the following Villages in the Township: Hardinge, Harlowe.

☞ The letter *t* in italics signifies tenant; all the rest are owners.

	Post Office		Post Office		Post Office
Armstrong John,	Cloyne	Grey Robert,	"	Roy James,	Cloyne
Armstrong Thos.,	"	Hawley, Peter,	Cloyne	Salmon Wm.,	"
Benny John,	"	Herbert George,	"	Scott Robert,	"
Benny Wm.,	Harlow	Kennelly Edw.,	"	Snaw Robert,	Plevna
Benyard Robert,	Cloyne	Kennelly John,	"	Snider Bilins,	Cloyne
Bishop Albert,	Harlow	Killenbeck Wm.,	Plevna	Snider Joshua,	"
Bishop Edgar,	"	Lake Daley,	Cloyne	Spencer Amos,	Harlow
Bishop Geo.,	Cloyne	Lake Henry,	"	Storey Peter,	Cloyne
Bishop Richard,	Harlow	Loux Abraham,	Harlow	Tapping James,	Harlow
Bosley Frs. sen.,	Cloyne	McCausland Wm.,	Cloyne	Tapping Thos sr.	Harding
Bosley Frs.,	"	McGregor Chas.,	"	Tapping Thos.,	"
Bott Ernest,	"	McLaren Finlay,	"	Teal Nelson,	" *t*
Bott George,	Harlow	McLaren Wm.,	"	Thompson Andrew,	"
Brown David,	"	McMillan Donald,	"	Thompson Couglas,	"
Brown Irwin,	"	Maynard John,	"	Thompson Joel,	"
Burgess Phil,	Cloyne.	Maynard Wm.,	"	Thompson John,	"
Campbell Arth,	Harlow	Meeks Andrew,	"	Thompson Samuel,	"
Clifford John,	Cloyne	Meeks Dennison,	"	Vanalstine Bernard,	"
Cole Frank,	"	Miller Adolphus,	"	Vanalstine James,	"
Cole Fred,	"	Miller Francis,	"	Vanalstine Roy,	"
Cole Lafayette,	"	Mitchell John,	"	Warren James,	"
Cole Orlando,	"	Morgan Daniel,	Harlow	Wartman Secord,	"
Connor Geo.,	Harlow	Morgan Edward,	"	Webb Joseph,	"
Cornell John,	Cloyne	Neal Thomas,	"	Weese David,	Cloyne
Cuddy Sam,	Harlow	Pettiford Hugh,	Cloyne	Wheeler George.	Harlow *t*
Cummings W.,	Cloyne	Perry John,	"	Whiteman Thos.,	"
Curtiss N.,	Harlow	Perry Thomas,	"	Wicksware Alph.	Cloyne
Deighton Wm.,	Cloyne	Pipe John,	Harlow	Williams N.,	Tamworth
Dalyea Alex,	Harlow	Pipe William,	"	Winters Abraham,	Cloyne
Delyea Isaac,	Cloyne	Richardson A.,	Cloyne	Winters Albert,	"
Dempsey Thos.,	"	Richardson George,	"	Winters John sen,	"
Dempsey Wm.,	"	Richardson Thomas,	"	Winters John,	"
Earl John,	Harlow	Rosenbloth Aug.	Harding	Winters Thos.,	"
Eustace David,	"	Rosenbloth Chas.	"	Wise William,	Harlow.

TOWNSHIP OF BEDFORD.

This Township contains some very good land, and in some parts of the Township large quantities of iron ore are found.

Number of acres assessed, 49,523. Population 1,404.

See also the following villages in the Township: Bedford Mills, Tichborne.

☞ The letter *t* in italics signifies tenant; all the rest are owners.

	Post Office		Post Office		Post Office	
Algnire Dan,	Westport	Brennan Peter,	Fermoy	Daley Peter,	Glendower	
Anderson Jas,	Fermoy	Brewster Dan,	"	*t*	Donnegan M,	Kingston
Anderson W,	Gleudower	Brewster Wm,	Bed Mills	*t*	Donohue Jas,	Glendower
Asselstine Thos,	Westport	Bridgen Sam,	Parham	*t*	Donohue Jer,	Westport
Asselstine W sr,	Glendow'r	Brswn Alpheus,	Glendow'r		Donohue John,	"
Asoelstiue W jr,	"	Burkett Wm,	Fermoy	*t*	Donohue Ptk,	Glendower *t*
Atcheson John,	Westport	Bualey John,	"		Doran Wm,	Quebec
Atcheson Robt,	"	Burns John,	Bedf. Mills		Egan Ptk,	Fermoy
Atcheson Wm,	"	Burns Hugh,	"		Ewing John,	Westport
Bain Israel,	Fermoy	Burns Thos,	"		Fitzgerald Edw,	Fermoy
Barker Noah,	"	Callaghan Jas,	Westport		Fitzgerald Thos,	"
Barr Carson,	"	Callaghan John,	"		Fitzgerald W,	Glendower
Barr Edward,	"	Callaghan Michael,	"		Fluke David,	Bedf. Mills
Barr Geo,	"	Cameron John,	"		Forrester Wm,	Fermoy
Barr James,	"	Campbell John,	Fermoy		Fox Geo,	"
Barr Wm,	"	Carr Edw,	Bedford Mills		Frame Thos,	Parham
Barr Wm jr,	"	Canley Patk,	Westport		Frawley Mica,	Glendower
Barrett Jas,	"	Coate Alex,	Fermoy		Frawley Timothy,	"
Barrett Wm,	"	Coate Joseph,	"		Garden Jas,	Belford Mills
Bateman Henry,	Westport	Connell J,	Bedford Mills		Garvin Francis,	Fermoy
Bedore Edw,	Fermoy	Connell Sam,	"		Garvin Thos,	"
Bedore Jos jr,	"	Conners Jas,	Glendower		Gauhan Mich,	Wastport
Bedore Jos sr,	Parham	Conners John,	"		Gillerby Jas,	"
Bedose Louis jr,	"	Conners Michael,	"		Golden Edw,	Fermoy
Bedore Louis sr,	Fermoy	Cooke Robt,	"		Good Fra.	Parham
Bedore Maguire,	"	Coulter Ben,	Glendower		Good George,	Glendower
Bennett John,	"	Coulter Daniel,	"		Good Robt,	"
Boland Frs,	"	Coulter James sr,	"		Gray W H,	"
Botting Ben,	"	Coulter James	"		Green Thos,	" *t*
Botting John	"	Cornwall Edw,	Parham		Hamilton Jacob,	Fermoy
Botting Richard,	"	Conway Dan,	Fermoy	*t*	Hamilton Jas,	Bedf. Mills
Bradley Wm,	"	Crow Martin,	Glendower		Hamilton Geo.	Fermoy
Bradshaw Geo,	Parham	Crozier Thos,	"		Hamilton Geo,	Parham *t*
Bradshaw Wm,	"	Crozier Wm,	"		Hamilton Wm.,	"
Brash, Geo,	Westport	Curle Robt,	Parham		Hannon John,	Fermoy.
Brash Henry,	"	Cutting John,	Fermoy		Hanson Henry	"
Brash John,	"	Daley John sr,	Glendower		Harrington D,,	

TOWNSHIP OF BEDFORD.

Name	Post Office	Name	Post Office	Name	Post Office
Harrington Tim,	"	McCew Frs,	Westport	Sheltz Peter,	Parham
Hastings John,	Parham	McCew Ptk,	"	Shillington H,	Fermoy
Hastings Thos,	Glendow'r	McDonald Mich,	Parham	Shillington Jas,	"
Hastings Wm,	Parham	McFarland Geo,	Opinion	Shillington, Joh	"
Hempton J G,	"	McGinnis Geo,	Parham	Shillington, Jos,	"
Hickey Patk,	"	McGowan Thos,	Fermoy	Snook, Oliver,	"
Hickey Thos,	Fermoy	McGregor Jno,	Parham	Songest John,	Parham
Hopkins Aaron,	Glend'r	McKeaver Jas,	Glend'r	Sparks Rich,	Fermoy
Howes Francis	"	McNeil Jas,	Fermoy	Stafford Dan,	Parham
Howes Geo,	Parham	McNichols John,	Glend'r	Starr Elijah,	Bedf'd Mills
Howes Rich,	"	McNichols Ptk,	"	Steele John	"
Hunter Alfred	"	McNichols Walt,	"	Stinson Carson,	Fermoy
Hunter James,	Opinion	Madden Jno,	Westport	Stinson Robt,	"
Hunter John,	Parham	Mararity Denis,	"	Stonas Jab,	Bedf'd Mills
Jennings John,	Glend'r	Mararity John	"	Stonas Robt,	"
Jones Epan,	D'Arcy	Mullviehilly J,	"	Stonas Wm,	"
Jones John,	"	Miss Wm,	Glendower	Studdifun W,	Parham
Jones Jos,	"	Mitchell Louis,	Bed. Mills	Swabrick Wm,	"
Jones Jus,	"	Murphy Jas,	Fermoy	Sweetman Thos,	Fermoy
Jones Step,	Westport	Murphy Patk,	"	Taggart J, jr,	Westport
Jones Wm,	"	Murphy Pete,	"	Taggart J,	"
Judge Patk,	"	Murray Jas,	"	Tehan Morris,	"
Judge Wm,	"	Murray John,	"	Thompson Ab,	Fermoy
Keith Sylv r,	Westport	Neley Barney,	Glend'r	Thompson Art,	"
Relly Francis,	Parham	Nicholson Edw,	Opinion	Thompson Ezra,	Parham
Kelly James,	"	Nicholson Jas,	Fermoy	Thompson Geo,	Fermoy
Kelly Michael,	Glendower	Nicholson John	"	Thompson Henry	"
Kelly Terr,	"	Nicholson Peter	"	Thompson Jas,	"
Kennedy David,	Westport	Noonan Jas,	"	Thompson J W,	Westport
Kennedy John,	"	Noonan John	"	Thompson Jos,	Fermoy
Kennedy John,	Parham	Noseworthy J,	Glend'r	Thompson Sam,	"
Kennedy Sam,	"	Nowland Jno,	Fermoy	Thompson Thos,	"
Ketch Wm,	Fermoy	O'Brian J M,	Bedf'd Mills	Thompson Wm,	"
Kiley John,	Glendower	O'Connor Mich,	Fermoy	Tierrney John,	"
Diley Patk,	"	O Connor Morris,	"	Toban John,	Westport
Kirpatrick J,	Bedf'd Mills	Page Alfred	"	Toban Thos,	"
Kirpatrick R,	Fermoy	Patterson, Robt,	"	Truelove, Jas,	Fermoy
Kish John,	"	Patterson W,	Westport	Tuppins Jno,	Westpor
Lake N C,	Parham	Peters Elias,	Eermoy	Tuppins Thos,	"
Lamarsh Ben,	Bedf. Mills	Piereon Almond,	Parham	Turner Francis,	"
Lee Wm,	Fermoy	Pool Samuel,	Bedf'd Mills	Walker D J,	Parmey
Lemon And,	Glendower	Porter Wm,	Fermoy	Walker W J	"
Lemon Jno,	Bedf'rd Mills	Quinn Henry,	"	Welsh Owen,	Fermoy
Lewis Hugh,	Fermoy	Ranvall Peter,	Parham	When And W,	"
Lunn John,	Parham	Reid Robt,	"	Wilson Henry,	Bedf Mills
Lushaw Luke,	Bedf. Mills	Rielly Hugh,	Fermoy	Wilson Jas,	Fermoy
Lynn R W,	Fermoy	Rielly, Jas,	"	Wilson Wm,	"
McCalester John,	Fermoy	Riley Steph,	Parham	Woods, Wm,	"
McCalester Simeon,	"	Rogers C J,	Fermoy	You Leon,	Bedford Mills
McCarty Daniel,	Westport	Robinson T,	"	NON RESIDENTT,	
McCarty Daal jr,	"	Scanlan Terrance	"	Adams & Co,	Fermoy
McCarty John	"	Scanlan Terrance	"	Bawden Jos,	"
McCarty Michael	"	Sears D,	Bedford Mills	Blair John,	Bedford Mills
McCann Ptk,	Fermoy	Sears Hez,	"	Blair Robt,	Westport
McCeaver Henry,	Glend r	Sears Horace	"	Blair Wm,	"
McCeaver Wm,	"	Sears Lyman	"	Connell Sam,	Fermoy
McCew Edw,	Westport	Sears Wm,	"	Controy Patk,	Parham

TOWNSHIP OF CLARENDON AND MILLER.

	Post Office		Post Office		Post Office
Curry John,	Parham	Kelly John,	Glendower	Shields & Donnelly,	"
Deane Wm,	Kingston	Kennedy Wm,	Westport	Sukler Nil,	Westport
Drummond & Co,	Fermoy	Ludlow D,	"	Simpson Is,	Kingston
Duncan Wm,	Westport	Ludlow Jas,	"	Trian Ca,	Bedford Mills
Ewing Thos,	"	Lynch Jas,	"	Walker J,	Fermoy
Finn Edw,	Parham	McCollum Neil,	"	Webster, Wm,	"
Fredenburg W H,	Westp't	McCornish Geo,	"	Whalen Jno,	Westport
Hamilton Wm,	Fermoy *t*	McCowon John,	Kingston	Whitmarsh Edw,	"
Hunt Weston,	Quebec	Machar John,	Fermoy	Whitmarsh Noah,	"
Hutchins Alp,	Bedf Mills	Murphy John,	Westport	Wiggins S C,	Parham
Hunter Wm,	Parham	Pixley Henry,	Kingston		

TOWNSHIP OF CLARENDON AND MILLER.

Acres Assessed ———. Population, 650.

See also the following Villages in the Township; Ardock, Plevna.

☞ The letter *t* in italics signifies tenant; all the rest are owners.

Albert John, Plevna	Freeler Edw, Ardoch	Lemker Carl, Plevna
Armstrong John "	Freeler Joseph, "	Lemka Justin, "
Armstrong Robt., "	Gamble Robt, Plevna	Lamka Robert, "
Babcock Wm., "	Gardis Wm, Ardoch	Lemka Wm, "
Baker John, "	Gilmour Wm, "	Lepel F H, "
Barton John, "	Godkins Jos, "	Lloyd Joseph, "
Barton S. C., "	Gowan Jas sr, "	Londry And, "
Barton Wm., "	Gowan James, Plevna	Lyons Abel, Ardoch
Bawler John, "	Gowan John, "	McDonald Arch, Plevna
Bennett John, "	Grant Wm, "	McDougall Chas, Ardoch
Boyce Wm, "	Hanes Edw, "	McGregor John, Plevna
Bremner James "	Hartman Wm, Ardoch	McKinnon John, Ardoch
Briscoe John "	Haskell John, "	McLaren David, "
Britton B. M, Kingston	Haskell R L, "	McLaren Peter, "
Brown Amos, Plevna,	Hawes Stephen, Plevna	McLellan Alex, "
Brown Lewis, "	Hicks Reuben, Ardoch	McPherson Don, Plevna
Bucher Alex, "	Hicks Timothy, "	McQueen M, "
Card Egerton, "	Hill Marvin, Plevna	Mallory Almer, Ardoch
Card James, "	Holden Marvin, "	Mallory David, Plevna
Card Joseph, "	Holmes George, "	Mallory Rich, "
Campbell Jas, Ardoch	Jacob E R, Ardoch	Mallroy W, "
Cheetom Aaron, Plevna	Jennerette Amos, "	Martin Chas, Ardoch
Clegget Thos, "	Johnson Arth, "	Martin Garret, "
Cousins Robt, "	Johnson Jas, Plevna	Martin Wm C, "
Cousins Thos, "	Kellar Fred, Ardoch	Meeks Damen, Plevna
Dovy Harwill, Ardoch	Kellar James, Plevna	Meeks Joel, "
Davy Manson, Plevna	Kellar Peter, "	Meeks Josephus "
Dawson Abram, "	Kellar Philip, Ardoch	Meeks Pythias "
Debroys Wm, "	Killinbeck W, Plevna	Miller Alex, Ardoch
Denny Fras, Ardoch	Kring Leonard, "	Mitchell Sam, Plevna
Dick R F, Plevna	Kring Watson, "	Mosier David, "
Douglas John, "	Lawrence H H, "	Muldoon Jas, "
Ferris Joseph "	Leeman Levi, "	Muldoon Robt sr, "

TOWNSHIP OF HINCHINBROOKE.

	Post Office.		Post Office.		Post Office.
Muldoon Robt,	Plevna.	Smith Wm,	Ardoch.	Thompson Jer.,	Plevna.
Ohlman Leo sr,	"	Spike James,	"	Thompson Wm,	Ardoch.
Ohlman Leo	"	Stalker Alex,	"	Vankoughnet Geo,	"
Ohlman Joseph	"	Stalker Isaiah,	"	Vankoughnet John,	"
Ohlman Michael	"	Stalker James,	"	Ward James sr,	"
Powley Jas,	"	Stalker John,	"	Ward James,	"
Preidom Anthony,	Ardoch	Stalker Andrew,	"	Ward Luke,	Plevna
Quackenbush G A,	Plevna	Stewart Samuel,	"	Watkins Robt,	Ardoch
Quackenbush N,	" t	Storing Isaac,	Plevna	Watson Joseph,	"
Quackenbush Phil,	"	Storing John,	"	Weber George,	"
Quackenbush R S,	"	Struthers Jos,	"	Weber Michael,	"
Shaw William	"	Struthers R M,	"	Wensley Edw,	"
Shinner John,	"	Swager Hubert	"	White Isaac,	"
Shinner Joseph,	Ardoch	Tait Thos,	Plevna	White Robt,	"
Simpson Isaac,	"	Terry Jacob,	"	White William,	"
Smith Chas,	"	Thompson Amos,	"	Wood Ira,	"

TOWNSHIP OF HINCHINBROOKE.

This Township is comparatively new, and some of the land is very rich and fertile. Among the first settlers was Mr. John McKnight, who took part in the rebellion against the enemy in 1837.

Number of acres assessed, 59,183. Population, 1,101.

Post Offices: Cole Lake, Godfrey, Parham.

☞ The letter *t* in italics signifies tenant; all the rest are owners.

	Post Office.		Post Office.		Post Office.	
Alexander S,	Tichborn	Campbell Jno.,	Cole Lake	Craig Robert,	Godfrey	t
Allen Thos,	Parham	Campbell Jas,	Godfrey	Creamer Jos,	Parham	t
Alton Samuel,	"	Campbell Oscar,	"	Croft John,	"	
Babcock Chas,	Godfrey	Card Damon,	Parham	Cronk Manasseh,	"	
Babcock Israel,	"	Card John,	Enterprise	Cronk Solomon,	"	
Babcock Jacob,	Parham t	Card Titus,	Parham	Cronk Sylvester,	"	
Babcock John,	"	Carroll Jas sr,	Enterprise	Cronk Wm,	Enterprise	
Beattie Dawson,	Parham t	Carroll James,	"	Cronk Wilson,	Parham	
Beattie John,	Godfrey	Carroll John,	"	Dawson Jas,	Godfrey	
Bertrim Alex,	Parham t	Carroll John,	Godfrey	Deer John,	"	
Bertrim Wm,	"	Carroll Peter,	Enterprise	Delouksie P,	Enterprise t	
Black Wm,	Godfrey	Carroll Wm,	Godfrey t	Dermott Josh,	Parham	
Breen Thos,	Enterprise	Casmey Richard,	"	Dillon James,	Enterprise	
Breen Wm,	"	Claxton Jno,	Cole lake	Donohue Ptk,	"	
Bridgen Sam,	Godfrey	Claxton Wm,	Parham	Donohue Ptk,	Godfrey	
Brown J,	Tichborne	Clow Oliver,	"	Doyle Ptk,	Enterprise	
Brown Lotus,	Godfrey	Clow Wm,	"	Drader Jacob,	Godfrey	
Buckley Thos,	"	Colter Jos,	"	Draffin James,	Parham t	
Buckley Wm,	"	Conaway Michael,	"	Draffin Samuel J,	" t	
Bush Alex,	"	Connolly Timothy,	"	Duggan Cor,	Enterprise	
Bush John,	"	Cooper Roland,	"	Estes Wm,	Parham	
Bush Nicholas,	"	Cox George sr,	"	Fairfield R A,	Godfrey	
Butrell George,	"	Cox George,	" t	Finn Anthony,	Enterprise	
Campbell Jas,	Cole lake	Cox James,	"	Finn Edward,	"	

TOWNSHIP OF HINCHINBROOKE.

Name	Post Office	Name	Post Office	Name	Post Office
Finn John,	Enterprise	Judge Wm,	Godfrey	Ruttan James,	Parham
Finn Patrick,	"	Keats Ths,	Cole Lake	Ruttan John,	"
Finn Peter,	"	Kelly Owen,	Godfrey	Scales, Benj.	"
Fisher James,	"	Kenehan Wm,	"	Shellington J,	Godfrey
Fitzgerald Wm,	Godfrey	Kennedy Jas,	Cole Lake	Shellington John	"
Forbes George,	Parham t	Kennedy John	"	Shibley H F,	"
Frawley Patk,	Cole lake	Kennedy Jos,	Godfrey	Shibley Schuyler,	"
Freeman B C,	Godfrey	Kennedy Thos,	Cole Lake	Shirtliff S M,	Parham
Freeman Wesley,	"	Killins George	"	Sholtz Parker,	Godfrey
Genge Thomas,	"	Killins Geo W,	"	Sills Chas,	Parham
Giles G W,	"	Killins Robt,	"	Simkins Enoch,	Godfrey
Giles John,	"	Kingston Paul,	Godfrey	Simkins Geo,	Parham
Gilchrist David,	"	Knox Robt,	"	Simkins Isaac,	Godfrey
Gilchrist John,	"	Lake Walter,	"	Smith David,	Parham
Godfrey Chester,	"	Lanty Ptk,	Enterprise	Smith Henry,	"
Godfrey Coleman,	"	Lee Philip,	Parham	Smith Henry,	Godfrey
Godfrey James,	"	Lee Wm,	"	Smith H K,	Parham
Goodberry Chs,	" t	Leslie David,	Godfrey	Smith Hugh,	"
Goodfellow David,	"	Leslie John,	"	Smith Reuben,	"
Goydfellow D,	Parham	Leveck Sam,	Enterprise	Snider Alex,	Godfrey
Goodfellow John,	"	McCattry Jas,	"	Snider Buson,	"
Goodfellow S,	Godfrey	McCaffry Philip,	" t	Snider Car,	"
Gregory Thos,	"	McGowan Jas,	Parham	Snider Davis,	"
Grey Hugh,	Parham	McGowan Joseph,	"	Snider David,	"
Haddock Alf,	Godfrey	McGuire John,	" t	Snider Jesse,	"
Haley James,	Enterprise t	McKeever Hy,	Godfrey	Snider Sager,	" t
Hamilton John,	Parham	McKeever Jas.	"	Snider Thos,	"
Hamilton Wm,	Godfrey	McKnight John sr,	"	Summers Thos,	Enterp
Harper Samuel,	"	McKnight John,	Cole lake	Steel W,	Parham t
Hartman Shem,	Parham t	McKnight Warren,	"	Storms Henry,	"
Hastings Jno,	Godfrey	McLean D C,	Parham	Swarbrick Geo,	"
Hempton Thos,	Tichborn	McMahon Alex,	Cole lake	Swarbrick Henry, sr	"
Hempton Thos,	Parham	McMahon John,	"	Sarbrick Henry, jr,	"
Herring Jason sr,	"	McUmber Eli,	Parham	Swarbrick Jas,	"
Hickey James,	Godfrey	McUmber Wm,	"	Switzer Chris,	Godfrey
Hickey Stephen,	"	Martin Elisha,	Godfrey	Switzer, Orran,	Parham
Hill James sr,	"	Mathews Adam,	"	Switzer Wm,	"
Hill James,	"	Moore Harry,	"	Tallant E,	Godfrey
Hill John,	"	Moran Michl,	Enterprise	Tallant John,	" t
Hooper D,	"	Neadow Peter,	Parham	Tallant Thos,	"
House Andrew,	Parham	Neadow Robt,	"	Thompson Edw.	"
House George,	"	Nefcey T,	Godfrey	Timmins John,	Enterp
Howard Chs,	Godfrey	Parton Rich,	Enterprise	Timmins Peter,	"
Huguson And,	Enterp t	Peters Benson,	Cole Lake	Trayner Hugh	"
Huguson John,	" t	Peters Eben,	Parham	Tummons Denis,	Godfrey
Innis James,	Parham	Peters Miles,	Cole lake	Turner Patk,	Parham
Irvin Wm,	Godfrey	Peters R H,	Enterprise	Vaness James,	"
Jackson Oran,	Parham	Peters Stephen,	Cole Lake	Vanluven J,	"
Jeffey Edw,	Godfrey	Pridgen Thos,	"	Vanvolkenburgh H,	" t
Jeffey George,	"	Reppard Geo,	Parham t	Vanvolkenburgh R,	" t
Jeffey James,	"	Reynolds, Chas,	Godfrey	Vine Edw,	Godfrey
Jeffey Joseph,	"	Reynolds Henry,	"	Wager Asley,	Parham t
Jeffey Wm,	"	Rodgers F E,	"	Wager Chas,	" t
Jenkins Chs,	Tichborn	Rolley Jos,	Enterprise	Wager Clinton,	"
Judge Edw,	Godfrey	Rolly Larrey,	"	Wager David,	"
Judge Michael,	"	Ruttan Chas,	Parham	Wager Henry,	"

	Post Office.		Post Office.		Post Office.
Wager Hiram,	Parham	Wager Redford,	Parham	Watson Joseph,	Parham
Wager James,	" *t*	Wager Sandford,	"	Watson Thos,	" *t*
Wager Jerome,	"	Wager Thos,	"	Webster W J,	"
Wager John,	" *t*	Wager Wolford,	"	Weldon Douglas,	Godfrey
Wager Oscar,	"	Walker Jas,	Godfrey	Whalen Jas,	Enterprise
Wager Philip,	"	Warner Chs,	Parham		
Wager Philip C,	"	Warner Sidney,	"		

TOWNSHIP OF HOWE ISLAND.

This Township consists of an Island in the St. Lawrence River, nearly opposite Pittsburgh, and contains about 8,000 acres. Population 314.
See also the following Villages on the Island: D'Arcy, Howe Island.

☞ The letter *t* in italics signifies tenant; all the rest are owners.

	Post Office.			Post Office.			Post Office.	
Amol Wm,	D'Arcy		Goodfriend John,	D'Arcy		Norris Thos,	Howe Is'd	
Amstead Amos,	"		Goodfriend Peter,	"		O'Brien James,	"	
Baillie Geo,	" *t*		Greer Wm,	"		Pickett Michael,	D'Arcy	
Baillie Jno,	Howe Isl'd *t*		Gunn A,	Kingston		Prior John,	"	
Breof John,	"		Hoskins Wm,	D'Arcy		Prior Thomas,	" *t*	
Bobia Louit,	"		Johnston Wm,	"		Prior Timothy,	" *t*	
Bobia Peter,	"		Kane Matt, sr,	Howe Is.		Quinn Joseph,	"	
Cadeau Joseph,	"		Kane Matt,	D'Archy		Radford I H,	Kingston	
Cassidy Donald,	"		Kane Patrick,	"		Rochford Jos,	Howe Is'd *t*	
Cassidy John,	"		Kane Thomas	"		Rochford Leo,	D'Arcy	
Cassidy Peter,	"		Kelly John,	Howe Is'd *t*		Simpson Arch,	Howe Is'd	
Clancy Thos,	"		Kelly Wm,	"		Simpson John,	"	
Clark James,	"		Keyes Robt,	D'Arcy		Simpson Robt,	"	
Clixby Smith,	"		Lachance Adolphus,"			Sughrue John,	D'Arcy	
Compow Michael,	G. I.		Lachance Joel,	"		Sughrue Mortimer,	"	
Cox John,	Howe Island		Lavis Chas,	Howe Is'd, *t*		Sughrue Wm & John,"		
Cronkhite S,	"		Lavis John,	" *t*		Sughrue W J,	"	
Driscoll James,	D'Archy		Lavis Simon,	" *t*		Thompson Richd,	"	
Driscoll John	"		McDonald Angus,	D'Arcy		Turcott James,	" *t*	
Donohue Dan,	Kingston		Mahony Jas,	Howe Is'd *t*		Walker Payson,	" *t*	
Foley John,	Howe Island		Mahony Patk,	" *t*		Welsh Chs,	Howe Is'd *t*	
Garrow Israel,	D'Arcy		Marshall Alex,	D'Arcy		Welsh Joseph,	"	
Gillespie Robert	"		Melville Mich,	Howe Is'd *t*		White Joseph,	D'Arcy	
Gollagly John	"		Norris Jas sr,	D'Arcy *t*		Wilson John,	Howe Is'd	
Gonneau Joseph	"		Norris Jas jr,	Howe Is'd				
Goodfriend John, sr "			Norris Patrick,	"				

TOWNSHIP OF KENNEBEC.

Acres Assessed 3,477. Population, 971.

See also the only Post Office in the Township: Arden; all the rest are marked.

☞ The letter *t* in italics signifies tenant; all the rest are owners.

Andrew Thos,
Arney James,
Arney John,
Babcock David,
Babcock John,
Babcock Norman,
Baker C C,
Baker John,
Baker Wm,
Barker Henry,
Barker Joseph,
Barker Samuel,
Black James,
Boomhowr Albert,
Boomhowr Andrew,
Boomhowr Gilbert,
Boomhowr Jas, sr & jr
Boomhowr Nelson,
Broomhowr Paul,
Broomhowr Walter,
Bolt George,
Camp Solomon,
Card Hiram,
Card Miro,
Card William,
Clancey Andrew,
Clancey Alex,
Clapper Henry,
Clark Alva,   *t*
Clark Anson,
Clark Daniel,
Clark George,
Clark John,
Clark Nelson,
Clark Sylvester,
Clarke William,
Clark S E, South Bay
Chown —, Kingston
Cunningham —, Kingston
Daniels Alex,
David Daniel,
Davy Wm,
Daley Edwin A,
Deline Edward,
Ellis John,

Fraser Duman,
Gardiner Walter,
Gaylord Levi,
Gendran John,
Gendran Jos,
Godfrey Adam,
Godfrey Jno,
Gonyean C M,
Grange Alf,
Grange Jno,
Gray James,
Green Al E,
Green Chas,
Green Robt,
Green Wm,
Haines Geo sr,
Haines Geo jr,
Hartwick Millett
Hartwick Samuel
Hawley Chas.
Hawley Luther,
Hawley William,
Hays Edgar,
Hays Geo,
Helm Geo,
Hinchley N H,
Hogan David,
Hooper Henry,
Huffman Isaiah,   *t*
Hughes Peter,
Johnsou Frank,
Johnson Jno,
Kellar Benj,
Kellar Geo sr,
Kellar Geo jr,
Kellar James,
Kellar Jos,
Kellar Leon,
Kellar Moses,
Kellar Wm,
Kirk James,
Knight David,
Knight Samuel,
Knight Wm,
Loyst Chris,

Loyst Calvin,
Loyst John,
Loyst Joseph,
Loyst Peter,
Loyst Simeon,
Loyst Wm,
Lucas John,
Lyman Wm,
McAuslin Jno,
McGuirld Ptk,
McHenry John,
McRory John,
Miller Addison,
Miller Alph,
Miller Geo,
Miller Joseph,
Miller Wm,
Monds Glen,
Monds David,
Moore Jacob,
Mosier Daniel,
Mosier Peter,
Newton Elisha,
Newton George,
Newton Richard,
Osborn David,
Osborn Hiram
Parks George,
Parks Ira,
Parks James,
Parks James M,
t Parks Wesley,
Parks Wm,
Paul Wm J,
Patterson Wm,
Pearson John,
Pearson John N,
Peterson Jas,
Peterson John,
Peterson Nelson,
Peterson Wm,
Presley James
Pringle Wm,
Rathbun F & Son,
Rathbun H B,

Rogers John,
Schoolcraft Wm,
Scott Daniel sr,
Scott Daniel,
Scott David,
Scott James,
Scott Wm, *t*
Scriver David,
See Charles,
Shorts Felix,
Thompson Andrew,
Thompson Gilbert,
Thompson James, *t*
Thompson Isaiah,
Thompson Peter,
Thornton H E,
Tryon Nelson,
Vandewaters John

Vanness Henry,
Vanness Hiram,
Vanvolkingburg M,
Vanvolkingburg S,
Walker R E,
Wart J R,
Williams J M,
Williams L D, Camden
Williams M A, Croyden
Wood David,
Wood Ebenezer,
Wood Elias *t*
Wood George,
Wood Isaiah,
Wood John,
Wood John M,
Wood Miles, *t*
Wood Kedben,

Wood Wm,
Woodcock Christopher,
Woodcock David J,
Woodcock David W,
Woodcock David, jr,
Woodcock Edward,
Woodcock George, sr,
Woodcock George, jr,
Woodcock Gilbert,
Woodcock Henry,
Woodcock John O,
Woodcock Manson,
Woodcock Miles, *t*
Woodcock Nelson,
Wookcock Sidney,
Woodcock Thos,
York Benjamin,
Yeomans Thos,

TOWNSHIP OF KINGSTON.

This township was first settled in the year 1784 by Captain Grass. Acres assessed 50,126. Population 2,418.

See also the following Villages in the Township: Cataraqui, Collins Bay, Elginburg, Glenburnie, Glenvale, Portsmouth, Sharpton, Westbrook.

☞ The letter *t* in italics signifies tenants, fs, farmers' sons and o. occupiers; all the rest are owners.

	Post Office		Post Office		Post Office
Abbott George,	Kingston	Asselstine Jus, Westbr'k *t*		Benjamin E, Westbrook	
Abbott Jas,	"	Asselstine K, Wilton		Bennett Wm, Glenburnie *t*	
Abbott Robt,	Elginburg	Aylsworth Albert, Odessa		Bennington Geo, Glenvale	
Abrams Jonathan, Catar',		Babcock Corn, Sharpton		Berry David, Millhaven,	
Adsit Geo, Westbrook, fs,		Babcock D, Wilton		Berry Jas H, Cataraqui,	
Adsit Wm, Westbrook,		Babcock Darius, Sharpton		Berry John, Cataraqui,	
Ahern Wm, Kingston,		Babcock Peter, " *fs*		Black Andrew, Cataraqui	
Aikin Clark, Collinsby,		Babcock Sam, " *fs*		Black John, Cataraqui	
Aitkin Robt, " *t*		Baker Chas, Collinsby *fs*		Black Patrick, Kingston	
Alberton John, Elginburg		Baker Jas, "		Blacklock Wm, jr, Glenb.	
Alport Henry, Westbrook		Baker John, Cataraqui *t*		Blacklock Wm, sr, "	
Armstrong C, Elginburgh		Baker J F, Portsmouth *t*		Bolton John, Kingston *t*	
Arnoll Ed, Cataraqui		Baker Sam, "		Borance James, Elginburg	
Anold Hy, " *t*		Bell Alex, Westbrook		Borance John, Glenvale *t*	
Ash John B, Elginburgh *t*		Bell Ashford, Sharpton		Borance Robt, Elginburg *t*	
Ashley Alvan, Collinsby		Bell Charles, "		Borance Thos, " *t*	
Ashley C, "		Bell F W, "		Boyd Arch, Glenburnie *fs*	
Ashley G W, "		Bell James H, " *fs*		Boyd James, " *fs*	
Ashley John, " *t*		Bell John, "		Boyd John, " *fs*	
Ashley John W, " *t*		Bell P M, Westbrook		Boyd Solomon, "	
Asselstine Abram, Wilton		Bell Wm, Sharpton		Boyd Robt, Kingston	
Asselstine John, Collinsby		Belt Wm, Cataraqui, *t*		Bracker Walter, "	

Name	Post Office	Name	Post Office	Name	Post Office
Braden John sr,	"	Collins Wm,	Elginburg,	Dennis Thos, Collinsby,	
Braden John jr,	"	Compton Chas, jr, Kings,		Donnelly David, Portsm.	
Braden Wm,	"	Compton Chas, sr,	"	Doolin Mich, Kingston.	
Bradshaw W C, Cataraqui		Compton Ed.	"	Doolin Patrick,	"
Bramaigan John, Kingston		Conely John, Wilton		Doolin Thos, Kingston	
Breathen Thos, Sharpton		Cook Ed,	Cataraqui,	Doolin Wm,	
Breck Ira, Kingston o		Cook Henry.	"	Dorsey Ed, Westbrook	
Brewer B, California		Cook James,	"	Dougherty Geo, Elginburg	
Brewer Geo, Elginburg		Cook Joseph,	"	Dougherty Jas,	"
Brewer Philip,	"	Cook Wm,	"	Dougherty John, Cataraqui	
Bridge And, Westbrook,		Cook Wm.	Westbrook,	Draper Geo, Barriefield	
Bridge Corn, Cataraqui,		Coombs John, Westbrook		Draper John, Glenburnie	
Briggs Thos, Kingston,		Cooper Richard, Kingston		Draper Rich,	"
Brown Geo,	"	Cordukes Jno, Westbrook		Draper Thos, Barriefield	
Brown Henry, Cataraqui,		Cordukes R T, Cataraqui		Driscoll Den, Glenburnie	
Brown John,	"	Corrigan Dennis, Kingston		Driscoll Jeremiah,	"
Brown Sam, Kingston,		Counter Chas, Elginburg		Driscoll John	
Brown Thos, Westbrook t		Counter Geo,	"	Duffin Jas, Westbrook	
Bryant Edward, Kingston		Cousins Thos, Collinsby t		Duffy Jas, Kingston t	
Bryant Frances,	"	Craig A J, Glenburnie ƒs		Dunlop John,	"
Bryant John,	"	Craig James	"	Edwards Thos, Elginburg	
Bryant Rueben,	"	Craig Robt,	"	Egan Michael, Kingston	
Bryant William,	"	Craig Wm,	"	Ellerbeck Jos, Glenvale t	
Buck Edwin, Elginburg		Croft George, Kingston		Elliott Edwin, Kingston ƒs	
Buck Thos, Cataraqui,		Crosier Thos,	"	Ellion John C,	" ƒs
Buck Thos G, " fs		Cummins D, Wilton		Elliott ,	"
Buck Wm, Wilton, t		Cummins Jer, Wilton		Elliott Smith,	" ƒs
Burke Mich, Kingston,		Cunningham H, Glenburni		Elliott Hugh, Kingston ƒs	
Burke Thos, Kingston.		Curson Jas, Cataraqui		Elliott John,	"
Burnett Angus, Cataraqui		Dalton Hy,	"	Elliott Wm,	" ƒs
Buruett Wm,		Daly John, Glenburnie		Ely Samuel, Cataraqui o	
Burnside E, Elginburg t		Darragh G, Mt Chesney t		Ely Wm jr,	" ƒs
Bushell I, Glenburnie t		Darragh Robt,	"	Ely Wm sr,	"
Bushell Jas, Kingston		Daudy John, Kingston		English Anthny, Kingston	
Caines Jas, Elginburg t		Daudy Wm,	"	Everett John, Collinsby	
Caldwell And, Cataraqui		Davey James Murvale		Fair J M, Glenburnie ƒs	
Caldwell Wm, Elginburg t		David J W, Cataraqui ƒs		Fair, M J, Kingston	
Camic Wm, Glenburnie		David Wm, Kingston		Fair R H, Glenburnie ƒs	
Caruthers John, Glenvale		David Z, Cataraqui		Fair W J,	"
Caruthers John A, "		Davidson Joseph, Glenvale		Fairbank Oliver, Cataraqui	
Cashman J, Elginburg ƒs		Davis Isaac, Murvale		Fairbank O H,	"
Cashman Michael, "		Davis John, Kingston o		Fee Wm, Kingston	
Cashman W, Glenburnie		Davis Wm, Murvale		Fenwick Geo, Kingston,	
Clagg Joseph, Cataraqui		Dawson Barnabas, Collin,		Ferguson Dan, Glenburnie	
Clark John, Glenvale		Dawson Jas, Elginburg		Ferguson Daxid, Murvale	
Clark S D, Odessa		Dawson John,	"	Ferguson Geo,	"
Clark Wm, Collinsby		Dawson Rueben, Collins,		Ferguson Hugh,	"
Cliff Joshua, Kingston		Dawson Tim, Elginburgh		Ferguson J W,	"
Clavey Robt, Odessa		Day Calvin, Portsmouth,		Ferguson Prof, Kingston	
Clyde Thos, Cataraqui,		Day Henry, sr, Elginburg		Ferguson R G, Murvale,	
Clyde Wm, "		Day Henry, jr, "		Ferguson Wm, Glenburn.	
Cochrane Chas, Glenbur,		Day, P W, Collinsby,		Ferris Chas, Portsmouth,	
Cochrane James, "		Day Sidney, Portsmouth,		Ferris Ed,	"
Coglin Isaac, Elginburgh		Day Wm, Collinsby,		Ferris Jonathan,	"

TOWNSHIP OF KINGSTON.

Post Office	Post Office	Post Office
Ferris John H, Kingston	Gibson John W, Kingston	Hamer John, Kingston
Ferris John, "	Gibson Robt, Glenvale	Hamilton David, Cataraq'
Ferris Joseph, Kingston,	Giery Wm, Glenburnie	Hammond W, Glenvale t
Ferris J P H, "	Glassford Alex, Glenvale	Harker D C, Sharpton fs
Ferris Neil, Cataraqui,	Glassford Jas, Glenburnie	Harker John, "
Findlay Jas, Cataraqui,	Glassford John, Glenvale	Hawkie Robt, Mt Chesney
Fisher Wm, Kingston,	Gordon Chris, "	Hawkie Thos, "
Fizzell John, Collinsby,	Gordon Jas, Cataraqui	Harkness Sam, Kingston
Flanigan Jas M, Kingston	Gordon Jas, Glenvale	Harpell Geo, Cataraqui
Flanigan John, jr, "	Gordon Thos, Mt Chesney	Harpell Henry, "
Flanagan John, sr, "	Gordon Wm, Odessa	Harpell Geo, "
Fogg, Albert, Cataraqui,	Gorrie Jos jr, Cataraqui	Harpell Jacob B, "
Fogg Donald, "	Gorrie Jos sr, "	Harpell Jacob G, "
Ford Wm, Kingston,	Gossage Geo, Cataraqui t	Harpell John. "
Forsyth Robert, "	Gould Wm, Kingston	Harpell John J, "
Forsyth Thos, Collinsby	Gowdy Jas, " t	Hartrick J, Portsmouth t
Fowler Daniel, Glenburn'	Graham Al, Portsmouth fs	Harvey Henry, Cataraqui
Fowler Jas., Mt. Chesney	Graham Chris, " fs	Harvey James, "
Fowler, Joseph, "	Graham David, Elginburg	Hawley B, Collingby t
Fowler John, Murvale,	Graham Ed jr, Portsm'th fs	Hay Chas, Glenburnie
Fowler Mich, Mt. Ches',	Graham Ed sr, "	Hay John, "
Fowler Mich, jr, "	Graham Hy, '	Healey Joseph, Glenvale
Fowler Ptk, Mt Chesney	Graham John, Portsmouth	Healey Thos H, "
Fowler Thos, " fs	Graham John, Elginburgh	Heath Peter, Westbrook t
Fraser Donald, Kingston	Graham Luke. Glenburn'	Heaton John, Cataraqui
Fraser Sch, Collinsby t	Graham Matthew, "	Heaton Shadrack, "
Frazer Tim, Glenvale	Graham Thos, "	Hennessy John, "
Gallagher D, Kingston fs	Grass Chas, Portsmouth	Hennessey Martin, "
Gallagher John sr, "	Grass Dan, Westbrook,	Henry Henry S, "
Gallagher John jr, "	Grass F P, Portsmouth	Hickey Jas jr, Kingston fs
Gallagher Wm, "	Grass Horace, Collinsby	Hickey Jas sr, "
Gale John, "	Grass John, Portsmouth	Hickey John, " fs
Gardiner Francis, "	Grass John, Collinsby	Highland G W, Westbrk fs
Gardiner Jac'b, Westbrook	Grass Mich, Westbrook	Highland J E, Cataraqui t
Gardiner Jas, Kingston	Grass Peter, "	Highland Robt jr, " fs
Gardiner John, Westbrook	Grass R J, Portsmouth	Highland Robt sr, "
Gardiner Jos, " fs	Grass Wm, "	Highland Wm, "
Gardiner W jr, " fs	Green John, jr, Kingston	Hines Jas, Cataraqui
Gardiner W sr, "	Green John, sr, "	Hippauf Chas, Westbrook
Gardiner W E, Kingston fs	Green Wm, Kingston fs	Hogan George, Cataraqui
Garrett Wm, Collinsby t	Grimason Thos, Cataraq'	Hogan Henry, " fs
Gaskin capt J W, Kingston	Guess Barnabas, Elginb'	Hogan Jas, K Mills fs
Gates Geo, Westbrook	Guess E F, "	Hogan John, Cataraqui "
Gates Jas F, " fs	Guess F B, Murvale	Hogan John, sr, K Mills
Gates Wm, "	Guess Fergus, "	Hogan Ptk, Cataraqui
George Chas, Kingston	Guess Francis, Elginburg	Hogan Thos, K Mills
George Rich, "	Guess James, "	Hooper John, Cataraqui
George Robt, "	Guess M P, "	Hooper William, Catara'
George Wm, "	Gunning Sidney "	Horn John, Simcoe Is,
Gibson Albt, Glenvale fs	Gurney A M, Cataraqui t	Horning Arnold, Elginbu'
Gibson James, Kingston	Hafner Ecrad, "	Horning Geo, "
Gibson Jas H, Cataraqui	Hafner Philip " fs	Horning Jacob, Murvale
Gibson John, Glenvale t	Hafner Wm, Kingston	Horning John, "
Gibson John C, " fs	Hafner Mich, Portsmouth	Horning Rich, Glenvale

TOWNSHIP OF KINGSTON.

	Post Office		Post Office		Post Office
Horning Sheldon,	Murva'	Knapp Peter,	"	McDonald J A, Collinsby	t
Horning Wm,	Elginburg	Knight Arch, Cataraqui		McDonald Robt, jr, Cata.	
Howie Ar jr, Westbrook	t	Knight Jonathan,	"	McDonald Robt, sr,	"
Howie Arch sr,	" t	Knight Jonathan,	" t	McEwen Wm, Westbrook	
Howie Alex, Westbrook	t	Knight Lewis, Westbrook		McFarlaud Geo, Elgin.	
Howie Jas,	" t	Knight Robt, Cataraqui	t	McGowan Geo, Sharpton	
Howie John	" t	Lake Amos K, Elginburg		McGrouse John, Kingston	
Howie James, Glenvale	t	Lake Cyrus, Glenvale	t	McGurl S, Cataraqui	
Houstan Wm J, Wilton	t	Lake Wm, Elginburg		McGuire Ptk, Kingston	
Hunter Alfred, Glenburnie		Laland Leon, Collinsby	t	McIntosh Alex, Glenburn	
Hunter Fred,	"	Lampkin Elgin, Cataraqui		McIntyre Neil, Kingston	
Hunter Fred,	" fs	Langwith Joseph, Glenvale		McIver And, Cataraqui	
Hunter Geo,	"	Lasee John, Collinsby		McIver Hen, S, Cata,	fs
Hunter John, Wilton		Lasee Joseph, Collinsby		McKecknie Robt, Sharpt'	
Irvine Chas, Elginburgh		Lashford Philip,	" t	McKendry J, Mt Chesney	
Irvine Hy,	" fs	Lawson Geo, Elginburg		McKim Geo, Catarqua	t
Irvine John,	"	Lawson Hy, Sharpton	t	McKim Miles, Westbrook	
Irvine Wm, Murvale		Lawson Jos, Elginburg	t	McKim Peter, Cataraqui	
Irvine Wm, Elginburg	fs	Lea Geo, Odessa		McLaughlin R, Barriefield	
Jackson Jethro, Cataraqui		Leatherlaud J, Elginburg	t	McMichael Al, Cataraqui	
Jackson John, Kingston		Lee Israel, Murvale		McMichael O,	"
Jackson John, Collinsby		Lee James,	"	McMillen J jr, Kingston	
Jackson Wm, Cataraqui		Lemmon Hir, Westbrook		McMillen John sr,	"
Jackson Wm, Elginburg		Lemmon Thos,	"	McQuay And, Cataraqui	
Jamieson Wm, Mill Point		Leonard Ant, Glenvale	fs	McRowe F J,	"
Johnstoh Geo, Kingston		Leonard J A,	"	McRowe Jacob,	"
Johnston Hugh, Cataraqui		Leonard John	"	McRowe James	"
Johnston John,	"	Leonard Syl, Mt Chesney		McRowe Wm,	" fs
Johnston Orl, Kingston fs		Leoney Jas, Cataraqui		McVity Thos, Collinsby	
Johnston Wm, Elginburg		Leslie Wm, Kingston		McVity Wm,	" fs
Jones John, Kingston		Lilles And, Glenburnie	t	McWaters, J, Portsmouth	
Jones Owen, Kingston	t	Lilly Wm, Wilton,		Mabee Benj, Odessa	
Joyner Don, Cataraqui fs		Lindsay Jas, Elginburg	fs	Madigan Michl, Kingston	
Joyner Elijah,	"	Lindsay Robt,	"	Main Wm, Sharpton	
Joyner Jas, Cataraqui	fs	Liston Thos, Glenburnie		Manion Ptk, Wilton	fs
Joyner O, Cataraqua	fs	Lyon Alex, Collinsby	t	Manion Peter, Wilton	
Joyner Stewart,	" fs	Lyster Anthony, Cataraqni		Marks Wm, Portsmouth	
Juniac Francis, Elginburg		Lyster rev Dean, Kingston		Marshall Frs, Westbrook	
Kairnes Den, Cataraqui fs		McAdoo A W,	"	Marshall Jno, Mt Chesney	
Kairnes P jr, Cataraqui fs		McAdoo H,	" fs	Marshall Rt,	"
Kairnes Ptk sr,	"	McArthur Chas, Sharpton		Marshall Rt jr,	"
Keenan Dan, Kingston		McCallum Arch, Kingston		Marshall Wm, Westbrook	
Keenan Felix jr,	"	McCallum Jas,	"	Martin Dawson, Wilton	
Keenan Felix sr,	"	McCallum John,	"	Martin E R,	"
Keenan Thos,	"	McCallum N, Glenburnie		Martin John, Glenvale	
Keenan Thos jr,	" fs	McCameron J, Cataraqui		Martin Miles, Odessa	
Kemp Geo,	"	McCannell Jas, Kingston		Martin Sam, Wilton	
Kendall Wm, Cataraqui		McCartney Wm,	"	Martin Thos, Glenvale	
Keon Wm, Sharpton		McClement Wm, Murvale		Martin Wm, Wilton	
Keyes John, Kingston		McCormack Frs, Collinsby		Motthews R S, Kingston	
Kiell Well, Elginburg	t	McCormack P J, Kingston		Maxwell Robt, Sharpton	
Killoran James, Kingston		McCormack W, Collinsby		Meacham Geo P, Elginb'	
Kirkpatrick Jas,	"	McDonald And,	" fs	Merrer John, Belleville	
Knapp Jas, Elginburg		McDonald D W, C'linsby fs		Metcalfe John, Kingston,	

TOWNSHIP OF KINSTON.

Name	Post Office	Name	Post Office	Name	Post Office
Metcalfe Wm,	Kingston	Peters John E,	Wilton *fs*	Robinson Hy,	Glenvale
Miller A A,	Sharpton	Petifore Rich,	Cataraqui *t*	Robinson Thos,	Kingston
Millsop David,	Sharpton	Petifore Wm,	" *t*	Robinson Wm,	Kingston
Millsop Wm,	"	Pillor Wm jr,	Glenvale	Rose Benj,	Westbrook
Mobie John,	Cape Vincent	Pillor Wm sr,	Kingston	Rose P,	
Moham Arth,	Elginburg	Pope John L,	Elginburg	Rowe Wyman,	Cataraqui *t*
Mohan Michael,	Murvale	Porter Geo,	"	Ryan Martin,	Wilton
Mohan Peter,	" *fs*	Porter John,	Cataraqui	Ryan Michael,	"
Moon Jas,	Glenvale	Porter John,	Elginburg	Sandercock J,	Westbrook
Mooney Thos,	Collinsby *t*	Potter John,	K Mills	Sands Henry,	Kingston
Moore Ed,	Mt Chesney	Powary Albert,	Cataraqui	Scott Joseph,	Westbrook
Moore John,	Mt Chesney	Powley I D,	Cataraqui	Scrivens John,	Cataraqui
Moore Thos,	Kingston *t*	Powley Jacob,	Elginburg	Scrivens Joseph,	"
Moore Robt,	Glenvale	Powley Jacob,	Cataraqui	Scrivens Jos sr,	"
Morley John,	Westbrook	Powley Jas,	"	Sears Geo,	Kingston
Morton Joseph,	Kingston	Powley Jas B,	Westbrook	Sears Robt jr,	"
Mundle John,	Westbrook	Powley J W,	Cataraqui	Shannon D,	Glenburnie *fs*
Mundle John,	"	Powley Thos,	Elginburgh	Shannon H,	Westbrook *fs*
Murphy Alex,	Elginburg	Purdy Chas,	Cataraqui	Shannon J P,	Westbrook
Murphy Francis,	Elginbu'	Purdy David	"	Shannon Robt,	Glenburnie
Murton F,	Portsmouth *fs*	Purdy Herbert	"	Shannon Wm,	Westbrook
Murton Jas,	Murvale	Purdy John,	Kingston	Shannon W,	Glenburnie *fs*
Murton John,	Portsmouth	Purdy Philip,	Cataraqui	Sharp Alex,	Mt Chesney
Myers Thos,	Glenvale	Purdy S,	Elginburg	Sharp Thos,	Sharpton
Nelson Thos,	Kingston	Purdy Val,	Cataraqui	Sharp T J,	Sharpton
Nelson Wm,	Cataraqui	Quelch John,	Westbrook	Shaw Jas,	Kingston *o*
Nelson Wm,	Lyn	Quick Edward,	Elginborg	Sheehan Denis,	Westbrook
Newlands Geo,	Kingston	Quigley Jos,	Mt Chesney	Sheehan Mich,	"
Newlands Wm,	Kingston	Rankin Hugh,	Collinshy	Sherbino Frs jr,	Glenvale
Nicol Geo,	Cataraqui *fs*	Rappee Chas,	Kingston	Sherbino Frs sr,	"
Nicol Wm,	" *fs*	Raycroft Math,	Glenvale	Sherbino Joseph,	"
Nicholas Sidney,	Murvale	Raycroft Wm,	"	Sherbino Robt,	"
Nisbett Jas,	Kingston	Raymond Hud,	Sharpton	Shewall A B,	Cataraqui *t*
Noble Chas,	Elginburgh	Reddan C,	Portsmouth *fs*	Shibley S,	Wilton *t*
Northoven John		Reddan Geo,	" *fs*	Shoreclift Wm,	Glenburn'
Nugent Peter,	Collinsby	Reddan Jas,	" *fe*	Shortell John,	Pittsburgh
Orneal Sam,	Cataraqui	Reddan John,	"	Silver Chas,	Cataraqui
Orr John, jr,	Collinsby *t*	Reddan Miles,	Wilton	Silver Sidney,	Westbrook
Orr John, sr,	"	Reddy Ed,	Cataraqui *t*	Simmons Geo,	Collinsb' *t*
Orser Emanuel, jr,	Elgin'	Redpath Geo,	Kingston	Simpson, Ernest,	Cata' *fs*
Orser Emanuel, sr	"	Reese E.	Cataraqui	Simpson Harry,	"
Orser Isaac,	Cataraqui	Reeves Robt,	Kingston	Simpson Isaac,	Kingston
Orser Kenneth,	Elginbur'	Reid Henry,	Kingston	Simpson John,	Cataraqui
Orser Peter,	Glenvale	Reid John,	Glenburnie	Smith Aaron,	Glenvale
Orser Thos,	"	Reid Matthew,	Cataraqui	Smith Allen,	Westbrook
Ovens James,	Elginburgh	Reid Robt,	Glenburnie	Smith Arch,	Kingston
Patterson Capt F,	Kingst'	Reid W H,	Kingston	Smith Champion,	Westb'
Patterson Geo,	Mt Chesn'	Remmington Lewis,	"	Smith Chas,	Elginburg
Patterson John,	Mt Ches'	Richardson Wm,	Glenva'	Smith David,	" *fs*
Paterson W,	Mt Chesney	Richardson E D,	Kingston	Smith Geo,	Murvale *t*
Perkins G H,	Elginburg	Riley Alfred,	Cataraqui	Smith Geo W,	Westbrook
Peters Geo,	Westbrook	Risbridger Geo,	Kingst' *fs*	Smith Hy,	Collinsby
Peters Hugh,	Wilton *t*	Risbridger Thos,	Kingston	Smith Hor,	Cataraqui *fs*
Peters John	"	Robbs James,	"	Smith Isaac,	Westbrook

TOWNSHIP OF KINGSTON. 117

Name	Post Office	Name	Post Office	Name	Post Office
Smith Isaac, Westbrook	fs	Swift Mich, Glenburnie		Walpole John, Westbrook	
Smith James,	"	Thomas Wm, Westbrook		Walter Jas jr, Elginburg	t
Smith James,	" fs	Thompson D. Mt Chesney		Walter Jas sr	"
Smith James, Cataraqui	t	Thompson J, Elginburg	t	Walter Wm,	" t
Smith John, Elginburg		Thompson J, Mt Chesney		Ward Jon, Portsmouth	
Smith Joseph, Cataraqui		Thompson J, Kingston	t	Ward John, Cataraqui	
Smith L,	" t	Thompson T, Mt Chesney		Ward Jos, Elginburg	t
Smith Nath, Westbrook		Topliff Geo, Glenvale	fs	Ward P E, Portsmouth	fs
Smith Nelson,	"	Topliff Thos,	"	Ward Thos, Kingston	t
Smith P, Glenvale	t	Topliff Well,	" fs	Ward Wm, Cataraqui	t
Smith Peter, Westbrook		Trennaman Jno, Kingston		Ward W E, Portsmouth	fs
Smith Rich, Collinsby		Trundell Chas, Cataraqui		Wartman B A, Collinsby	
Smith Robt, Westbrook	fs	Trundell C A,	"	Wartmen C, Glenvale	
Smith Sam, Collinsby	o	Trundell Frs, Collinsby		Wartman C D,	"
Smith Thos, Cataraqui	t	Vair Geo, Glenburnie		Wartman E, Portsmouth	fs
Smith capt W, Cataraqui		Vair John,	"	Wartman Hy,	"
Smith Wm,	" t	Vair Robt,	"	Wartman H E,	"
Smith Wm, Portsmouth	t	Vanardon Abr, Kingston		Wartman Hir, Elginburg	
Smith Wm, Glenvale		Vanardon Isaiah,	"	Wartman J, Portsmouth	
Smith W J, Cataraqui	fs	Vanardon Jas,	"	Wartman John A.	" fs
Snook Hy, Westbrook		Vanardon John,	"	Wartman Sidney,	"
Sparhem Wm. Cataraqui		Vanardon Math,	"	Watson Geo, Kingston	
Spooner C N, Glenburnie		Vanardon Thos,	"	Watts Henry, Glenvale	
Spooner Reuben,	"	Vanluven A P, Murvale		Watts Samuel, Kingston	
Spooner Wm,	"	Vanluven John,	"	Watts Sam N,	" fs
Sproule J A, Westbrook		Vanluven Mich,	"	Wellburn M, Portsmouth	
Sproule James	"	Vanluven T F, Kingston	o	Wellburu Wm,	" fs
Sproule Joseph, jr,	"	Vanluven Zara, Murvale		White Geo E, Portsmouth	
Sproule Joseph sr,	"	Vean Wm C, Glenburnie		Wilders Art, Kingston	
Sproule Thos,	"	Vroman Ed, Murvale		Wilders Geo,	" fs
Sproule Wm,	" fs	Vroman John, Murvale		Wilders Henry,	" fs
Stanley Wm, Cataraqui		Waddington G, Kingston		Wilders Joseph,	" fs
Stevens Abram, Westbro'		Waddington H,	"	Williamson John, Glenb.	
Stevens Thos, Westbrook		Waddington W,	"	Williamson Wm,	"
Stewart Jos,	"	Waggoner D, Glenburnie		Wilson Geo, Portsmouth	
Stewart Sam, Westbrook		Waggoner H,	"	Wilson Henry, Glenvale	t
Stewart Wm, Elginburgh		Walkem Joseph, Kingston		Woodruff Chas, Elginbur'	
Stigney Thos, Glenvale	t	Walkem Rich,	"	Woodruff John, Elginbur'	
Still David, Westbrook		Walker Geo. Wilton		Wright Dan. Westbrook	
Stoddard Arth, Elginburg		Walker Hiram,	"	Wright Geo, Westbrook	
Storms John C, Wilton		Walker John, Glenburnie		Wright John,	"
Strabenzie Col, Kingston	o	Walker J P, Wilton		Young Jas, Glenvale	
Summerville T, Sharpton		Walker N H,	"	Young, John,	"
Summerville W,	"	Wallace Hugh, Westbrook		Young R R,	"

TOWNSHIP OF LOUGHBORO.

This Township contains 52,000 acres, the greater portion of which is covered with lakes, the principal one being Loughborough Lake. It also contains several very productive mines which are being developed. Nnmber of acres assessed, 49,231; population 1,904.

See also the following Villages in the Township: Desert Lake, Loughboro, now called Sydenham, Perth Road, Oates, Railton. Spaffordton.

	Post Office.		Post Office.		Post Office
Abrams Benj,	Desert L	Blake G O S,	Spaffordton	Christopher Hen,	Lough'
Abrams J J,	"	Blake Jas O,	" *fs*	Clark And,	"
Albertson Jno,	"	Blake John,	Loughboro	Clark Chas,	"
Alderbeck Rich,	"	Blakesly Alb,	" *t*	Clark Henry,	Wilmur
Alton John,	Loughboro	Booth J K,	"	Clark John,	Loughboro
Amey Adam,	"	Botting Wm,	"	Clement Geo,	"
Amey Adam, jr,	Wilmur	Bailey Henry,	"	Clough Owen,	Perth Road
Amey Albert,	Desert Lake	Boyce David,	Wilmur *t*	Clowe M,	Loughboro
Amey John,	Spaffordton	Boyce Jacob,	Loughboro	Coleman Michael,	"
Amey Miles,	"	Boyce Martin,	Spaffordton	Collins James,	"
Amey Nelson jr,	Wilmur	Boyle Peter,	Railton	Collins Arthur,	" *t*
Amey Peter,	Perthroad	Brady Chas,	Perthroad	Collins Wm,	Loughboro
Ansell G W,	Loughboro *t*	Brawley Jas,	Loughboro	Conoly Tim,	Wilmur
Arthur Geo,	Perthroad *t*	Brawley Jose,	" *t*	Conway Pat,	Railton
Ashley Abram,	Loughboro	Brawley Thos,	"	Corkill Wm J,	Perthroad
Aykroyd Benj,	Wilmur	Brawley Wilson,	"	Cosgriff Dan,	Wilmur
Aykroyd Geo,	"	Brown David,	" *t*	Cosgriff Jas,	Spaffordton
Aykroyd Sam,	Railton *fs*	Buck Albert,	Loughboro	Cosgriff Joseph,	" *fs*
Aykroyd Wm,	Wilmur	Buck B,	Perth Road *t*	Cosgrove James,	Oates
Babcock Cy,	Perthroad *t*	Buck Benoon,	Spaffordton	Counter Hy,	Spaffordton
Babcock David,	"	Buck Geo,	Railton	Cox, Hy,	Loughboro
Babcock J N,	"	Buck Harvey	"	Cox H J,	"
Babcock K K,	", *fs*	Buck Nelson,	Wilmur	Cranston Chas,	Railton
Backus Syl,	Loughboro *t*	Buck S P	Spaffordon	Cranston Levi,	Railton
Baker John S,	Wilton	Buck Tim,	"	Creighton Hugh,	Loughb'
Barnett Art,	Loughboro	Buse Wm,	Loughboro *t*	Creighton John,	"
Barrett Chas,	" *t*	Buttermore Wm,	P Road	Darling Avory,	Perth Rd'
Benn Elgen,	Spaffordton *t*	Caldwell T D,	Loughboro	Darling Ira, jr,	"
Benn Nelson,	" *t*	Caldwell Thos,	"	Darling Ira, sr,	"
Bennett W sr,	Dessert L. *t*	Campbell Arthur,	P Road	Davey Adam,	Loughboro
Blackford H A,	Wilton	Campbell Wm,	"	Davey S,	"
Blake Colburn,	Loughbo'	Carcallion Thos,	Lough'	David Dan,	"
Blake Dan,	"	Carey Francis,	Spaffordt'	David Wm,	"
Blake Geo S,	"	Chown Lewis,	Loughboro	Davis J W,	"

Post Office	Post Office	Post Office
Deeks Jas, Perth Road	Grooms Mich, Loughboro	Johnston W, Perth Road
Deer George, Wilmur	Guess Anson, "	Joyce Rich, Spaffordton.
Deer Henry, Loughboro	Guess B S, "	Joyner Rich, Loughboro
Dennie L, Loughboro	Guess F, " *fs*	Kavanagh Fred, Perth R'.
Detlor B, " *t*	Guess Fergus, Wilmur	Kavanagh Geo, Perth Ro'
Detlor Geo, " *t*	Guess Geo W, Loughboro	Keely Francis, Railton
Detlor W S, "	Guess J B, "	Keller Harvey, Oates *fs*
Devana Pat, Spaffordton	Guess J N, Loughboro	Kelly John, Loughboro
Deyo Dan, Dessert L	Guess Leignton, "	Kelly Thos, Loughboro
Deyo James, " *fs*	Guess Sidney, "	Kemp George, " *t*
Deyo Schylor, "	Guess Wm E, "	Kemp M, " *fs*
Deyo Sidney, "	Guess Wm S, "	Kemp Wm, "
Dixon John R, Loughboro	Guess Wilmot, "	Kennedy Alf, " *fs*
Donald John, Wilmur	Guthrie John, Perth Road	Kennedy Robt jr, "
Donald P, Loughboro *t*	Guthrie Waltrr, jr, "	Kennedy Robt sr, "
Donovan John, Railton	Guthrie Walter, "	Kennedy Wm sr, Wilmur
Donovan T jr, "	Guthrie Wm, "	Koen Alex, Oates
Donovan T sr, Spaffordton	Hadley Hiram, Perth R	Koen James, "
Duff Chas, Perth Road	Hagerman Abram, Lough	Koen John, "
Duff Wm, "	Hagerman Ed, Loughboro	Koen Michael, "
Dulmage Geo, Loughboro	Haley Thos, Loughboro	Keon Robt, "
Ennis Geo, Perth Road	Harker Ed, Perth Road *t*	Koen Wm, " *fs*
Ennis James, "	Harker Geo, "	Koen Wm M, " *fs*
Ferguson Robt, Wilmur *t*	Harris Joseph. "	Kibby John, Spafford'n *fs*
Ferguson W, Perth Road	Hart Arthur, Spaffordton	Kibby Rich, "
Foize Michael, "	Hart Chas, Oates	Lacey Jos, Perth Road *fs*
Foxton Fred, "	Hart Wm, Spaffordton	Lacey Mich, "
Foxton J jr, "	Hartman Syl, Perth Road	Lacey W P, Loughboro *t*
Foxton J sr, "	Hendershot —, Loughbo'	Lahey Jas, "
Fraser Kenneth, Loughb	Henderson John, Perth R	Lake D W, "
Freeborn John, "	Henry David, Wilmur	Lawrence Ed, " *t*
Freeman Alpheus, Lough'	Hobbs Syl, Perth Road	Lawrence Jno, "
Freeman J M, "	Hobbs Wm, Loughboro	Lawrence T, "
Freeman John R, Wilmur	Hogan Mich, Perth Road	Lawrence Tim sr, "
Freeman J W, Loughbora	Hogon Patrick, Wilmur	Lawrence Wm, "
Freeman P W, "	Holden John, Perth Road	Lawson Fred, "
Freeman Sam, "	Holland T P, Loughboro *t*	Lawson Jos, Spaffordton
Freeman Stephen, "	Homer Hy, "	Leatherland J, Loughboro
Freeman Wm W, "	Horning J W, "	Lee Luke, " *t*
Gahan Patrick, P Road	Hughston Hy. Perth Road	Leheup J J, " *t*
Garvin James, Loughboro	Irish John, Loughboro	Leheup John, "
Glass John J, Perth Road	Irvine Chas, "	Loekart John, "
Glidden Wm, Loughboro	Irvine John, "	Love Jos, Perth Road
Gossage Geo, "	Ivey John, "	Lyons James, Railton
Gossage John, "	Jaqueth Kenneth, "	Lyons Jas D, " *fs*
Gouge Chas, " *t*	Jaqueth Wm E, "	McCadden R, Perth R'd *t*
Graham Jos, Spaffordton	Jones Hamilton, Perth R	McCauley F D, Railton *fs*
Graham Wm G, " *fs*	Johnston David, Oates *t*	McCauley Frs, "
Granger And, Loughboro	Johnston Fr, Perth R *t*	McCauley Neil, "
Granger Francis, " *fs*	Johnston Ira, Loughbo *t*	McCauley Wm, "
Grant B, " *fs*	Johnston Jas, "	McConnell Jas, Spaffordn
Grant Jas, "	Johnston John, Perth Rd	McDonald D S, Loughbo
Green Hy, Perth Road	Johnston Lyman, "	McDonald Jas, Oates
Grooms M, Loughboro	Johnston P, Spaffordton	McDonald John, Perth R

TOWNSHIP OF LOUGHBORO.

Name	Post Office	Name	Post Office	Name	Post Office
McDonald Mich,	Oates	Perry Geo,	Wilmur	Shaw Thos,	Oates
McEwen Wm,	Loughboro	Peters Joseph,	Perth Rd'	Shea Danl,	Loughboro t
McFadden Jas,	Perth Rd'	Phillips Geo,	"	Shibley Hy,	"
McFadden Thos,	"	Pixley Edward,	Spaffordt'	Shibley Sch,	Dessert L
McGown John,	Loughboro	Pixley Ezra,	"	Sholts Wm,	Perth Road
McKeren S,	Railton	Pixley Lyman,	"	Short Ed,	Oates
McLarty Wm,	"	Pixley Miles,	"	Sigsworth Geo,	Loughbo'
McMillan A,	Loughboro	Provice Amos,	Wilmur t	Sigsworth Jas,	"
McMillan Henry,	"	Purdy D W,	Loughboro	Sigsworth John,	"
McMillan Jas,	"	Purdy E B,	"	Sigsworth Wm,	"
McMillan Jno,	"	Purdy Geo,	"	Sills Edw,	Spaffordton t
McMillan Wm,	"	Purdy J W,	"	Sills John,	Loughboro t
McQuade James,	Wilmur	Purdy K L,	"	Sills John jr,	Oates
McQuade Pat,	Spaffordto'	Purdy L W,	"	Sills Wesley,	Loughboro
McRory Jas,	Loughboro	Raymond J W,	Perth Rd	Silver John L,	Perth Rd
McRory John,	"	Raymond Wm,	" t	Silver John W,	" t
McRory W,	" t	Raymond W H,	"	Silver Sam,	Loughboro
McWilliams W,	Loughb' t	Rea Charles,	"	Simkins Bailey,	Loughbo'
Mace W D,	"	Rea Joseph,	Wilmur	Simkins Bailey B,	"
Madden Daniel,	"	Redden Jas,	Loughboro t	Simkins Harvey,	Lough'
Marks Hy,	"	Redmond Jos,	" fs	Simpson Isaac,	Kingston
Martin Charles,	"	Redmond Wm,	"	Slack Robt,	Loughboro
Martin Steph,	"	Roberts J H,	Perth Road	Slack Wm,	"
Maverty Albert,	" t	Roberts John S,	" t	Slavin John	" t
Maverty Robt,	Wilmur	Rollow Jos,	Dessert L	Smith Chas,	Railton
Merriman Chas,	Oates	Rothwell Sam,	"	Smith Henry,	Perth Road
Metcalfe J,	Dessert L t	Roushorn A,	Wilmur	Smith Norman,	Loughbo,
Middleton R,	Loughboro	Roushorn John,	Perth R t	Smith Robt,	Railton
Miles J,	Wilmur	Roushorn W,	"	Smith Thadens,	Oates
Mills Charles,	Oates	Rutledge Ar,	Spaffordton	Snider Alphens,	Perth R'
Moon Wm,	Loughboro	Rutledge Geo.	"	Snider Davis,	Loughboro
Moore Joseph,	"	Rutledge Jas,	"	Snook John A,	Dessert L'
Muclehern Jno,	Wilmur	Rutledge John,	"	Snook J N,	Dessert L
Mucklewe Geo,	Perth Rd	Rutledge Wm,	" fs	Snook Wm,	"
Murray T,	Railton	Ruttan Chas,	Loughboro	Soles Lyman,	Wilmur
Nichols Jos,	Loughboro t	Ruttan John jr,	" fs	Spafford Elijah,	Spafford'
Nichols Sidney,	"	Ruttan John,	"	Spafford Moses,	" fs
O'Brien Jas sr,	Railton	Ruttan J W,	" t	Stockwell F W,	Wilmur
O'Brien Jas jr,	"	Ruttan Miles,	Wilmur t	Stones Jabez,	Perth Road
O'Brien P,	"	Ruttan Peter,	Spafford'n t	Sullivan Michael,	Oates
O'Connor Chas,	" fs	Ruttan Wm,	Loughboro	Switzer Alf,	Loughboro
O'Connor John,	"	Ryan Ed,	Oates fs	Switzer Jno,	"
O'Connor T,	Loughboro	Ryan Mathew,	"	Switzer Norman,	" t
O'Rielly John,	" fs	Ryan Patrick, jr	"	Tett Benj,	"
O'Rielly Luke,	"	Ryan Patrick,	"	Tett John P,	" t
O'Riley Thos,	Loughboro	Ryder Thos,	Loughboro t	Thomas James,	Perth Rd
Orser Chas,	Wilmur	Sears John,	Perth Road	Thomkins Hy,	"
Page Alf,	Dessert Lake	Sears Sam,	"	Thompson Jas,	"
Page Fred,	"	Sedore Abram,	"	Thompson Robt,	"
Page Jeremiah,	"	Shales Jas,	"	Thorn Joseph,	"
Palmer Geo,	Loughboro	Shales John H,	"	Townsend A,	Loughboro
Patterson Ralph, jr,	Wil'	Shales Wm E,	"	Trousdale John,	" t
Patterson Ralph, sr,	"	Shales Wm T,	Loughboro	Trousdale J W,	"
Patterson Wm,	"	Sharp Adam,	"	Trousdale Mat jr,	" fs

TOWNSHIP OF OLDEN.

	Post Office		Post Office		Post Office
Trousdale M sr,	Loughb'	Wallace Wm,	Perth Rd	Wood Bryan,	Loughboro
Truscott Sam,	"	Walsh John,	Oates	Wood Harvey,	"
Valier Alex,	Wilmur	Walsh Lawr,	Perth Rd	Wood Jas,	"
Valier Dan,	Loughboro	Walsh Wm,	Oates	Wood John,	" *fs*
Valier Ed,	"	Walter Wallace,	Lough	Wood Sidney,	"
Valier —,	Perth Road	Wear James,	"	Woodruff Dan,	" *t*
Vankoughnet P,	Wilmur	Welstead John,	"	Woodruff Jos,	"
Vanluven Mich,	Loughbo	Whalen Chas,	Oates	Wright Abraham,	Oates
Vanluven Wesley,	"	Whalen Patrick,	"	Wright John,	Loughboro
Verrett Jas,	Desert L *t*	Whalen Wm,	"	Wright Mathew,	Oates
Votery Theo,	Perth Rd	Williams Cor,	Loughboro	Yeomans H,	Perth Road
Walker Aaron,	Desert L	Wilson Chris,	" *t*	Young Barnabas,	" *t*
Walker Chas,	"	Wilson John,	" *t*	Young Michael,	"
Walker J D,	"	Wolfe John,	Perth Rd	Young Norman,	Loughbo
Walker Stewart,	"	Wood Almon,	Loughbo' *t*	Young Wm,	Perth Road

TOWNSHIP OF OLDEN.

Acres Assessed 4,500. Population, 740.

See also the following Villages in the Township: Long Lake, Mountain Grove, Oso.

☞ The letter *t* in italics signifies tenant, *o* occupier ; all the rest are owners.

	Post Office.		Post Office		Post Office
Abbott G,	Mt Grove *o*	Campbell Chas,	Arden	Crozier W G,	Mt Grove
Abbott S,	"	Campbell John,	Oconto	Curl Edmond,	"
Allen L W,	Perth	Canning Robt,	Mt Grove	David Z,	Cataraqui
Anthony A, Sharbot Lake		Chapman Dan,	S Lake	Davy S W,	Murvale
Armstrong R,	Mt Grove	Chapman L,	"	Deroche E A,	Napanee
Armstrong Thos,	"	Charlton Wm,	Zealand	Dorey Fras,	Mtn Grove
Armstrong W J, Zealand*t*		Conboy Geo,	Mt Grove	Dorey S,	"
Asselstine M,	Oconto *o*	Conboy Jas,	Deerdock	Drew Alex,	"
Aspell Michael, Mt Grove		Conboy John	"	Drew Coffield,	"
Aspell Edw,	"	Conboy Wm,	"	Drew Geo,	Long Lake
Avery & Thompson, S L'k		Coulter Jos,	Mtn Grove	Drew Henry,	"
Babcock Har, Long Lake		Coulter Wm,	"	Droke J H,	Mtn Grove
Babcock Waldron,	" *o*	Cox David,	" *o*	Dusham John, Long Lake	
Babcock W H,	" *o*	Cox Joseph, .	". *o*	Dusham Louis,	"
Bannan Chas,	" *o*	Cox Joshua,	"	Ewart Wm,	Mtn Grove
Barr Edw,	Mt Grove	Cox Thos sr,	"	Ewens Henry,	"
Bender W H,	Long Lake	Cox Thos,	" *o*	Ewens John,	"
Bender W P,	"	Crawford Geo,	"	Ewens Wm,	"
Beverly Thos,	"	Cronk Col,	Long Lake	Flett James,	Oso Station
Bowerman Jas,	Napanee	Cronk Freeburn,	" *t*	Flynn Geo,	Mtn Grove
Bradley Geo,	Mt Grove *t*	Cronk Sylvanus,	"	Flynn Robt,	"
Brown Albert,	Parham	Cronk William,	"	Foster Aug,	Parham *t*
Burke Henry, Oso Station		Crozier A sr,	Mtn Grove	Foster Wm,	"
Burke Joseph	"	Crozier Alex,	"	Fralick H N,	Morven
Burke J K,	"	Crozier —,	"	Fraser Alex,	Mtn Grove

TOWNSHIP OF OLDEN.

Name	Post Office	Name	Post Office	Name	Post Office
Fraser Wm,	Mtn Grove	McGill Arch,	Kingston	Richey Howard,	L Lake
Gallaher Thos,	Long lake	McGinnes Alex,	Oconto	Robinson & Robinson,	Ki"
Garrett Joel,	Mtn Grove	McKeever G,	Long Lake	Robson Michael,	L Lake
Godfrey Ch,	Long Lake	McKim Nelson,	Westport	Sanderson D W,	Mt .Gro'
Godfrey E L,	Mtn Grove	McMahon Jno,	"	Sanderson H B,	Arden
Godfrey John,	"	McPherson D,	Deerdock	Sanderson J A,	Mt Grove
Green Lewis,	Long Lake t	McPherson John,	"	Sanderson James,	"
Griffith J A,	Parham	McPherson Jos,	" o	Sanperson Y,	"
Harton Jos,	Long Lake	McPherson Rich,	" o	Sanderson Wm,	"
Harton Wm,	"	Malcolm David		Scott John,	S Lake
Hawley W T,	Arden	Miller Wm,	Mt Grove	See William,	Arden
Hickey John,	Kingston	Mills Geo,	Mt Grove	Shibley H T,	Kingston
Irvine Robert,	"	Mills Jas, sen,	"	Shibley Schuyler,	"
Jack Robt,	Deseronto	Mills Jas,	Portsmouth	Smith John,	Parham
Johnston Jno,		Mills John	"	Soles Alph,	Mtn Grove
Johnston J,	Mtn Grove	Mills W B,	Arden	Soles Thos,	"
Johnston J,	Deerdock o	Montgomery Chas,	S Lake	Stinchcombe J,	"
Johnston R,	Oso Station	Motherwell Jno,	Perth	Stinchcombe R,	Long Lake
Johnston Wm,	Mtn Grove	Newman Almon,	S Lake	Store Baptist,	"
Johnston W G,	Long Lake	Parker Chas,	Mt Grove	Thompson G C,	Arden
Jordan Wm,	Wilton	Parker Jas,	"	Thompson G,	Long Lake
Keating Edw,	Long Lake	Parker Jas, jr,	"	Tryon Wm,	Sharbot Lake
Kelar Geo,	Kingston o	Parker Nelson,	S Lake	Tuttle Isaac,	"
Kenyon Thos,	"	Peters John,	"	Vanvalkenburg G,	Parh'm
Lake Moses,	Arden	Peters Val,	"	Velvey Geo,	Oconto o
Laidley Alf,	Mtn Grove	Preston Jas,	"	Velvey Ira	" o
Laidley R,	Maberly	Price C V,	Kingston	Velvey John,	Parham
Laurie Jno,	Oso Station	Price D W,	Mt Grove	Wagar Clay,	Long Lake
Lennon Jas,	Long Lake	Price J E,	Arden	Walker Hiram,	Westport
Lennon Sam,	Wilton	Price J G,	"	Warren Edw,	Deerdock
Lewis Geo,	Mtn Grove	Price L L,	"	Watson N B,	Mt Grove o
Lewis Henry,	"	Price M W,	"	Watson W J,	" o
Lewis Oliver,	"	Price Nicholas,	"	Watson Wm,	"
Love James,	Long Lake	Ruin Bernard,	Long Lake	Webster W J,	Kingston
Loyst Harvey,	Arden	Ruin John,	"	Wilson James,	S Lake o
Loyst W N,	"	Rathbun H B,	Deseronto	Worsted H,	Long Lake
McCharles M,	Deerdock	Raycroft Jno,	Long Lake	Worsted Pat,	"
McConnell W,	Portsm'th	Reiley Gerald,	"	York Martin,	" o
McDonald A,	Mtn Grove	Reiley Paul	"		
McDonald A jr,	"	Reynolds George	"		

TOWNSHIP OF OSO.

Acres assessed 3,906. Population 767.

Post offices: Clarendon Station, Oso Station, Deerdock, Oconto, Sharbot Lake, Zealand.

☞ The letter *t* in italics signifies tenants, fs., farmers' sons and o. occupiers; all the rest are owners.

Name	Post Office		Name	Post Office		Name	Post Office	
Adams Abrah,	Maberly		Burke Robt,	Oso Station		Donnelly Jno,	Zealand	
Adams Jas,	Kingston		Burke Robt, jr,	"	*fs*	Doran Wm,	Sharbot Lake	
Amey All,	Sharbot Lake		Burke Wm,	"		Duffy Isaac,	Maberly	
Armstrong John,	Maberly		Butler Geo,	"		Duffy William,	"	
Armstrong J,	"		Butler P,	"		Ellsworth Jno,	Shar Lake	
Armstrong J jr,	Zealand		Calvert Geo,	Zealand		England Alex,	"	
Armstrong R G,	Maberly		Cameron Jno,	Shar Lake		England John,	"	
Armstrong S,	Sharbot L		Campbell John,	Perth		England Wm,	"	
Armstrong Thos,	Maberly		Campbell Jno,	Oconto		Estes George,	"	
Armstrong Wm,	Zealand		Cavelry James,	"		Ferguson Dun,	Oso Stati'	
Babcock J,	Sharbot Lake		Chambers Henry,	S Lake		Fleming Robt,	S Lake	
Bamnon Chs,	"	*t*	Chambers J,	Zealand		Flett Jas,	Clareudon	
Bishop C,	Zealand		Charlton J,	Maberly		Folger Ben,	Sharbot Lake	
Bishop Joshua,	"		Charlton Jos,	"		Francis Wm,	Oso Station	
Bishop Was,	"		Charlton R,	"		Garrett Geo,	Zealand	
Bodar Simon,	Bellbrook		Coates O,	Bolingbrook		Garrett Thos,	"	
Boles Jno,	Oso Station		Cobb Thos,	Zealand		Garrett Wm,	"	
Botting Edw,	Sharbot L		Cohen Laz,	Maberly		Gould Geo,	"	
Bradshaw G,	Sharbot L		Culvert Wm,	Zealand		Grady Jno,	Shar' Lake	
Bragg John,	"		Cook I P,	Clarendon		Graham D V,	Oso Station	
Brian John,	Maberly		Conboy Dan,	Zealand		Gray Arch,	Maberly	
Briggs Geo,	Sharbot Lake		Conboy Jno,	Oso Station		Gray John,	"	
Buchanan Dan,	Maberly		Conroy Edw,	Clarendon		Gray Peter,	"	
Buchanan Geo,	"		Costello J,	S Lake		Griffith Jno,	Parham	
Buchanan Hugh,	"		Costello S,	"		Green Adolp,	Sh Lake	*t*
Burke Elijah,	Oso Station		Crain J,	Clarendon		Greer Jno,	Zealand	
Burke Henry,	"		Crain W,	Zealand		Greer Thos,	"	
Burke John,	"		Crawford F,	S Lake		Greer Wm,	Maberly	
Burke John, jr,	"	*fs*	Crawford Geo,	Oso Stati'		Hanna W R,	Bolgbrke	
Burke Joseph,	"		Davidson H,	Forfar		Harrison Piere,	Zealand	
Burke Joseph, jr,	"	*fs*	Dukson Wm,	Sharb Lake		Harrison Wm jr,	"	
Burke Jos R,	"		Dodds David,	Zealand		Harrison W sr,	Sh Lake	
Burke Rich,	"		Dodds Rich,	Sharb Lake		Henderson W,	Oso Station	
Burke Solomon,	"		Donnelly Ed,	Zealand		Holley Wm,	"	

124   TOWNSHIP OF PALMERSTON.

	Post Office		Post Office		Post Office
Hughes Jas,	Zealand	McGinnis Alex,	Oconto	Sargent Henry,	Zealand
Hughes Robt,	Maberly	McGinnis Jas,	"	Scott Cashel,	"
Irvine Robt,	Kingston	McGinnis Wm.	"	Sharbot Jos,	Sharbot L
Irwin Jas.	Oso Station	McIntyre Dan,	Shar Lake	Shaw Wm,	"
Johnson Jos,	"	McKay Ar.	Oso Station	Shibley Sch,	"
Johnson Robt.	"	McKeever Geo,	Bolingbro'	Shults John,	"
Johnson Thos,	Maberly	McLaren Pet,	Perth	Simpson I,	Kingston
Johnson Wm,	Bishops M	McPherson H,	Deerdock	Sliter H,	Bolingbroke
Joiner Chas,	Sharbot lake	McPherson H,	"	Sliter W L,	
Jones John,	Bolnigbroke	McPherson J,	"	Switzer Calvin,	Sh Lake t
Jones Step,	"	McVeigh Hy,	Shar Lake	Tharrett Wm,	"
Judge Wm.	Sharbot Lake	McVeigh Jas,	Zealand	Thompson & Avery,	"
Kelly Jas,	"	Meighan Jas.	"	Tombleson Jno,	Deerdock
Kennedy Jno,	"	Moss Jas,	Oso Station	Tysick John,	Maverly
Kennedy Sam,	Oconto	Motherwell Jno.	Perth	Tysick Jos,	Zealand
Kirkham Thos,	Maverly	Noble Isaac,	Kingston	Vanwincle D,	Shar Lake
Kirknam Wm,	"	Palmer Jas,	Maverly	Veil Ira,	Oconto
Kirkpatrick Geo,	Kingston	Palmer Jos,	"	Warren D,	Sharbot Lake
Knapp Chas,	Bolingbroke	Pappa Jos,	"	Warren Edw,	Deerdock
Knapp John W,	"	Parks John,	Elphin	Warren Jno,	"
Knapp John,	"	Paterson Jas.	Maberly	Watkins B,	Clarendon
Lees Wm,	Fallbrooke	Peters Jno,	Oso Station	Watkins P J,	"
Livingstone J,	Maberly	Ritchie Jno,	Bolingbroke	Watkins W,	"
Lomie Jno,	Perth	Robinson Jas,	Oso Station	Webster Thos,	Deerdock
Lorman Jas,	Zealand	Robinson W H,	Sh Lake	Weir Wm J,	Oso Station
Luch James,	Maberly	Robinson W,	"	Wesley Henry,	Maverly
Lyle Jas,	"	Rutledge Jas,	Maberly	Young Chas,	Zealand
McCharles A,	Zealand	Samuels Chs,	Oso Station	Young Henry,	Kingston
McEwen Thos,	Maberly	Sargent Geo,	Zealand	Young Jas,	Zealand

TOWNSHIP OF PALMERSTON.

Number of acres assessed, 2,600; population 783.

See also the following Villages in the Township: Mississippi Station, Ompah.

☞ The letter *t* in italics signifies tenant; all the rest are owners.

	Post Office		Post Office		Post Office
Adams Geo,	Ottawa	Beaupre Joseph,	Ompah	Campbell Neil,	Ompah
Agnew John,	Kingston	Beaupre Sorel,	"	Campbell Thos,	"
Allen I,	Mississippi	Boner Joel,	"	Campbell W N,	"
Allen John,	"	Booth R J,	Ottawa	Chapman C,	Seeley's Bay
Allen Robt,	"	Briscoe Thos,	Ompah	Chappel Jas,	Ompah
Allen Samuel,	"	Burnosh Moscin,	"	Clark Wm,	Mississippi
Anderson John,	Ompah	Caldwell Wm,	Ompah	Clemo Peter,	Mississippi
Andrews B J,	"	Cameron Hugh,	"	Clemo Simon,	"
Arkle Peter,	"	Cameron James	"	Collop H G,	Ompah
Avery Joseph,	"	Cameron John,	"	Compton Jas,	"
Bailey John,	High Falls *t*	Campbell Jas,	"	Coughlin Thos.	Mississip'
Hawden Jos,	Kingston	Campbell John,	"	Crawford Alex,	"

TOWNSHIP OF PALMERSTON.

Name	Post Office	Name	Post Office	Name	Post Office
Crouse C E,	Ompah t	Johnston Henry,	Ompah	Ostler Fred,	Ompah
Davis Wm,	Mississippi	Johnston H G,	"	Pepper Jas,	"
Daw Anthony,	Ompah	Johnston Jas,	"	Peters Joshua,	Mississippi
Dawson John,	"	Johnston R C,	Clarendon	Peters Sam,	"
Deaves Robt,	"	Jones J E,	Mississippi	Pierce W J,	Seeley's Bay
Denny Henry,	Mississippi	Kelly John,	"	Playfair Wm,	Elphin
Dickinson Sam,	Ompah	Kennedy Pat,	"	Porteous Arch,	Ompah
Dishaw T,	Ompah	Kennedy Thos,	"	Potter Noble,	"
Dishaw Uzeb,	"	Kirkwood Jas,	"	Pratt Robt,	Ompah
Donaldson Allen,	"	Leadbeater N J,	Ompah	Rasberry Antoine,	"
Donaldson Jas,	"	Lennox John,	"	Rasberry Jer'h,	Ompah
Donaldson Sam,	"	Linton Wm,	"	Rice Nat,	Mississippi
Donaldson S sr,	Kingston	Lownsberry Geo,	"	Robertson & Co,	"
Donaldson W J,	Ompah	Luker Rich,	"	Robinson Jas,	Clarendon
Doran Wm,	Mississippi	McDonald Dan,	Miss'pi	Robinson Jno,	Ompah
Dunham H,	Ompah	McDonald John,	"	Robinson Wm,	"
Durkin Pat,	"	McDougal Allan,	"	Ryder Jno,	"
Elkington John,	"	McDougal Duncan,	"	St Pierre Aug,	"
Elliott Geo,	"	McDougal Jas,	Ompah	St Pierre Frank,	"
Elliott Hy,	"	McDougal John,	Miss'pi	Shevlin J P,	"
Elliott John,	"	McDougal Robt,	"	Shelley B J,	Mississippi
Evans Wm,	"	McCoy R,	Mississippi	Skead James,	Ottawa
Ferguson Arch,	"	McGregor Robt,	Ottawa	Slyter P W,	Ompah
Ferguson Wm,	"	McKenzie John, jr,	Ompa'	Smith Robt,	Mississippi
Flett Jas,	Mississippi	McKinnon Hugh,	Mississ'	Stewart Chas,	Ompah
Foot Peter,	"	McLaren David,	"	Stewart Wm,	"
Garrow Joseph	Ompah	Malloch E G,	Perth	Tennant Jas,	"
Geary Arch,	"	Mann Jas,	Mississippi	Tennant John,	" t
Geddes Robt,	Mississippi	Mann Wm,	Elphin	Tennant Wm,	"
Gilchrist Jas,	"	Massey Geo, jr,	Ompah	Thomas Wm,	"
Gilchrist Jas jr,	"	Massey Geo,	"	Thompkins Thos,	Miss'pi
Goslaw Oliver,	Ompah	Matheson R J,	Perth	Turcotte Bru,	Ompah
Grant Chas A,	Clarendon	Meek Hy,	Mississippi	Vann C W,	Mississippi
Gregory M,	Ottawa	Miller John,	Ompah	Watson Alex,	Ompah
Hamel Gilbert,	Ompah	Miller Joseph,	Mississippi	Watson Andrew,	"
Hannah Al,	Mississippi	Miller Thos,	"	Watson Jas,	"
Hannah J E,	"	Miller Wm,	"	Wait Wm,	Mississippi
Hannah John,	"	Moore Anthony,	Ompah	Watt Jas,	Ompah
Hannah William,	"	Moore Baptiste,	"	Watt Jno,	"
Hitchcock John,	Ompah	Moore Sam,	"	Webb Wm,	Mississippi
Holly Wm,	High Falls	Moore Wm,	"	White Peter,	"
Hughes Dan,	Mississippi	Morrow Louis,	"	Wilson Geo,	Elphin
Hyde Joseph	Ompan	Morrow Louis jr,	"	Wilson Robt,	"
Irwin W,	Seeley's Bay	Moors Jas,	" t	Woods Robt,	Ompah
James A H,	Ompah	Moors Thos,	Seeley's Bay	Woods Thos,	"
Jamieson R D,	" t	Mundell Wm,	Ompah	Wright Adam,	Elphin
Jarb Joseph,	Ompah	O'Neil John,	Mississippi	Wright John,	Ompah
Jarbo Ad,	"	Olmstead Geo,	"		
Jarbo Fabien	"	Olmstead Geo, Jr,	"		

TOWNSHIP OF PITTSBURG.

This township is connected with the city by a bridge which was rebuilt in 1845. The land is of varied quality, some of it very rich and fertile; other parts rocky and unproductive. The Rideau Canal forms the Western boundary of this township. Acres assessed 48,276; population 2,653.

See also the following Villages in the township: Ballantyne Station, Barriefield, Birmingham, Brewer's Mills, Kingston Mills, Pitts' Ferry, Washburn, Willetsholme.

☞ The letter *t* in italics signifies tenants, fs., farmers' sons; all the rest are owners.

Name	Post Office	Name	Post Office	Name	Post Office
Abbott Wm,	Birming'm	Barnes Hy,	Kingston *t*	Brebner Jno,	Ballentyne
Abrams John jr,	Willetsh	Barnes Jas,	"	Breden Wm,	Pittsferry
Abrams John sr,	"	Barnes J R,	" *fs*	Brewer Jas,	Gananoque
Acton Robt,	Birming'm	Barrett Hy,	Barriefield	Brewster Wm,	Ballentyne
Agnew Ed,	"	Barrett Jas,	" *fs*	Britton D F,	Gananoque
Agnew Robt,	"	Barrigan Tim,	Birming'm	Brooks And,	Kingston
Allen Sam,	Brewer's Mls *t*	Bawden Hy,	Kingston	Brooks F G,	" *fs*
Allen Wm,	Barriefield *t*	Baxter Geo,	Barriefield	Brown Alf,	"
Anderson Jas,	Kingston	Baxter J D,	"	Brown And,	Willetsholme
Anglin John,	Brew' Mills	Beaton Wm,	Kingston	Brown Dan,	Washburne
Anglin Sam,	Kingston	Beaton Wm F,	" *fs*	Brown Hy,	Ballentyne
Anglin Walter,	Brewers'	Beattie Jno,	South Lake	Brown Robt,	Willetsh'me
Anglin Wm,	"	Bell John,	Willetsholme	Brown Wm,	Ballentyne
Anglin Wm B,	Kingston	Bell Thos,	"	Bryant Dan,	Kingston *fs*
Armstrong Fran,	Birming'	Bell Walter,	"	Bryant Duncan,	" *fs*
Ashley Geo,	Pittsburg	Bennett Jno,	" *fs*	Bryant Jas,	"
Ashley Jno,	"	Bennett Robt,	"	Bryant Wm,	"
Ashley Wm,	"	Birmingham Jno,	Birmin'	Bucknell Jas,	Barriefield *t*
Atkinson Hiram,	Willets'	Blake Pat,	"	Bulch John,	Kingston *t*
Atkinson Jas,	Birmingha'	Blake Thos,	"	Bullock Jno,	Kingston
Atkinson Thos,	"	Blaney W jr,	Kingston *fs*	Burnash Frs,	Brew Mills
Atkinson Wm,	"	Blaney W sr,	"	Burnash Jos,	"
Baillie M G,	Barriefield *fs*	Boner Wm,	Ballentyne	Burns John,	Birming'm
Baillie Reginald	"	Boswell Walt,	Barriefield	Burns Mat.	Barriefield
Baillie Thos,	"	Bower J P,	Seeley's Bay	Burns Wm,	Birming'm *fs*
Baillie Wm,	"	Bowles Ed,	Ballentyne	Burns Wm,	Kingston *t*
Baker Thos,	Pittsferry	Bowman Chas,	Barriefield	Burton Thos,	"
Ballentyne And,	Ballenty'	Braddon Ed jr,	King' Mls	Byrne Ed,	Barriefield
Ballentyne Jno,	Kingston	Braddon Ed sr,	Kingston	Byrne Jas,	Barriefield
Ballentyne Robt,	Ballent'	Braddon Jas,	King' Mills	Cairns Ed,	Birmingham
Barker Ed J,	Barriefield	Brash Robt,	Pittsferry *t*	Callaghan Dan,	Barriefie'

TOWNSHIP OF PITTSBURG.

	Post Office		Post Office		Post Office
Callery Pat,	Willetsholm	Donoghue T,	Kingston Ml	Germain Ar,	Birmingh'm
Carey Rich,	Birmingham	Doyle Jas,	Barriefield *fs*	Germain Wm,	"
Carey Thos,	"	Doyle Jas, sr	"	Gesner rev O,	Kingston
Cartwright R J,	Kingston	Doyle Jno, sr	"	Gillespie Hugh,	Brewers'
Case John,	"	Doyle J W,	" *fs*	Gillespie John,	Kingston *fs*
Chambly Peter,	"	Doyle Thos,	Barriefield *fs*	Gillespie J W,	"
Chapman Jno,	Willetshol'	Doyle Wm,	" *fs*	Gillespie Thos,	Brewers'
Cherry Wm,	Barriefield	Draper Ed,	" *fs*	Glenn Wm,	Washburn
Church Hiram,	Pittsferry	Draper Geo,	" *fs*	Gordon Jas,	Kingston
Clark Mat,	Kingston	Draper Thos,	"	Gordon Thos,	Willetsh'm
Clark Wm,	Kingston *t*	Duffey Francis,	Kingston	Gough Edw,	Kingston
Colquhoun H,	Washburn	Duffey Jas,	"	Gough Patrick,	"
Colquhoun John,	"	Duffey John,	"	Gough Rich jr,	"
Colquhoun R,	Willetshom	Duffey Sam,	"	Gough Rich sr,	"
Connell Robert,	Kingston	Duggan Geo,	"	Gough Robert,	"
Connell Thomas,	"	Duggan John,	" *fs*	Gould And,	Birmingham
Connor H,	South Lake *fs*	Dunden Jno,	South Lake	Grange Wm,	Barriefield
Connor T, jr "	" *fs*	Dunlop Robt,	Barriefield	Grant Alex,	Kingston
Connor T, sr "	"	Dunlop R jr,	Birmin'm *fs*	Graves Chas,	" *fs*
Consgreen John,	Brewer's	Dunlop R sr,	"	Graves Geo,	" *fs*
Conway Jas,	Barriefield *t*	Dunlop R J,	Kingston *t*	Graves Geo H,	" *fs*
Corkill Samuel,	Kingston	Edgar Jer,	Ballentyne	Graves Hy,	"
Cowan A B,	Pittsferry	Edgar Joseph,	Kingston	Graves Michael,	"
Cowan A J,	"	Edwards John,	"	Green Sam,	"
Cowan Hugh,	"	Elder James,	"	Green Wm,	Birming'm
Cowan James,	"	Elliott Jas,	Willetsholme	Greenison Jno,	Willesh'm
Cummings Jas,	Willetsh'	Elliott R J,	"	Greer John,	Kingston
Cummings Jos,	"	Elliott Thos,	"	Greer S J,	" *fs*
Cunningham E jr,	K Mills	English James,	Kingston	Grice Ab,	Willetsh'm *t*
Curtis Jas,	Washburn	English William,	"	Grice Robt,	Pittsferry
Darling Chas,	Willetsh'	Esford Henry,	Barriefield	Grice Wm,	" *fs*
Darling Noble,	"	Esford John,	" *t*	Grimshaw D,	Kingston *t*
Darragh Alex,	Kingston	Fairman A,	Gananoque *fs*	Hamilton Jas,	"
Darragh Hugh,	"	Fairman Warren,	"	Hamilton Thos,	"
Darragh Jas,	King' Mills	Fairman Wm,	"	Harding Geo,	Kingston
David Isaac,	Willetsh'me	Farrelly B,	Kingston	Harding Wm,	Willetsh'm
David Israel,	"	Ferguson Jas,	Ballentyne	Harding James,	Kingston
Davis John jr,	Pittsf'ry *fs*	Finigan Hugh,	Kingston *t*	Harding John,	"
Davis John sr,	"	Fisher Wm,	Brewers'	Harding Jno,	Willetsh'm
Deane Pat,	Kingston Mls	Forrester C jr,	S'ly Bay *fs*	Harding Wm,	"
Dick Geo,	Barriefield *t*	Forrester C sr,	"	Harrison C,	Kingston Ml
Dillon Frank,	Brewers'	Forrester Mich,	" *fs*	Hartnett Wm,	" "
Dillon Jno,	"	Franklin Chas,	Kingston	Hay Alex,	Kingston
Dillon Wm,	Willetsholme	Franklin Jos,	"	Hay Donald,	"
Dockrill Jno,	Brewer's Ml	Franklin W H,	Birmg'm	Halferty Jas,	Washburn
Dolan Wm,	Kingston Ml	Free Sam,	Ballentyne	Henderson J,	Willetsh'm
Donaldson A,	Kingston *fs*	Gambell D,	King' Mills	Henderson R,	Pittsferry
Donaldson J,	Birming'm	Garrett John,	Washburn	Henry David,	Kingston
Donaldson Jos,	"	Garrett Wm,	Barriefield	Hill Alex,	Pittsferry
Donaldson J. W.	"	Gates Abel,	Kingston	Hill D J,	Brewers'
Donaldson S,	Kingston *t*	Gates Geo,	"	Hora Arthur,	Kingston
Donaldson W,	Birming'm	Gates Jos,	" *fs*	Hora Wm,	"
Donaldson W J,	"	Gates Wm,	"	Hudson Jno,	Seeleys Bay
Donnelly J,	Seeley's Bay	George Freel,	Barriefield	Hunt H W,	Birming'm

TOWNSHIP OF PITTSBURG.

Name	Post Office	Name	Post Office	Name	Post Office
Hunter Geo.	Willetsh'me	Lyons John,	Seeley's Bay	Madden Pat'k,	Washburn
Hunter Nelson,	"	Lyons Levi,	Willetsholm	Maitland Geo,	"
Hunter Rich,	South Lake	McAdoo John,	Kingston	Maitlann Wm P,	"
Hunter Robt,	Kingston	McAdoo Wm jr,	Kingston	Major Wm,	Kingston
Hunter Wm,	"	McAdoo Wm sr,	"	Mangan Mich,	Washburn
Hutton Frs,	Birming'm	McAlpin Arch,	South Lk	Mangan Pat,	"
Hutton Jas,	"	McAlpin Robt,	" "	Mangan Rich,	"
Hutton Thos,	Birming'm	McBroom Hy,	Washburn	Martin A jr,	Kingston
Hutton Wm,	"	McCallum Alex,	Kingston	Martin A sr,	"
Hyland Wm,	Kingston	McCallum John,	Barrie'd	Martin Chas,	"
Hysop Chas jr,	Pittsferry	McCallum Pat,	Kingston	Martin Jas,	Birmingham
Hysop Chas sr,	"	McCallum Peter,	Brewers'	Martin Wm,	Brewers'
Hysop John,	Ballentyne	McCaugherty D,	Ptsfry fs	Maxwell T jr,	Gananoque
Irvine Wm,	Barriefield t	McCaugherty H,	"	Maxwell Thos sr,	"
Irvin Edward,	Kingston fs	McCaugherty J jr,	" fs	Mead Jesse,	Barrie'd t
Irwin Francis,	Kingston t	McCaugherty J sr,	"	Medley Arch,	" fs
Jackson A E,	Pittsferry	McCormack Geo,	"	Medley Jno,	"
Jackson Alex,	Willetsh'm	McDonnell —,	King' Mills	Miller Wm,	Brewers' t
Jackson Dan'l,	Pittsferry	McFarlane Jno,	Birming'	Milne Chas,	"
Jackson E B,	"	McGillivray Jno,	Washb'	Milne Jas,	"
Jackson Francis,	" fs	McGregor Wm,	Barrie'd	Milton Dan,	Kingston
Jackson Hy,	Pittsferry fs	McGuire Jas,	Kingston	Milton Ed,	King' Mills
Johnston Hy,	Washburn	McKane Sam,	Birming'm	Milton H C,	Kingston
Johnston Jas,	Willesh'me	McKanna Jno,	Brewers'	Milton J A,	Kingston
Johnston Wm,	"	McKanna Pat jr,	" fs	Milton Jno,	Barrie'd fs
Johnston Wm,	Washburn	McKanna Pat sr,	"	Milton R J,	Kingston
Johnston Wm J,	" fs	McKee Jos,	"	Milton Wm,	King' Mills
Joyce Dan,	Birmingham	McKendry David,	"	Moore Joseph,	Brewers'
Joyce David,	"	McKendry Jas,	Birming'm	Moran Benj sr,	Kingston
Joyce John,	"	McKendry Jos,	Brewers'	Mudie —,	Kingston Mills
Joyce Luke,	"	McKenty Pat,	Birming'm	Mullen Ber'd,	Kingston
Joyce Mathew,	"	McKenzie Jno,	Kingston	Mullen Mich,	Birming'm
Joyce Mat jr,	"	McLaughlin Ant,	"	Muller G F,	Barriefield
Joyce Michael,	"	McLaughlin Rt,	Barrie'd t	Mulvaney Jas,	Kingston
Joyce Pat,	"	McLean Dan,	Kingston	Mundell Jos,	Birming'm
Kane John	Brewers'	McLean Hy,	" fs	Murphy Conway,	Brewers'
Kane Sam,	"	McLean Jno,	Willetsh'me	Murphy Ed,	"
Keegan Pat,	"	McLean John jr,	Kingston	Murphy Mich,	Birming'm
Kendall J E,	Washburn	McLean John sr,	"	Murphy Rich,	Brewers'
Kilduff Jno,	Ballentyne	McLean Robt,	"	Murphy Thos,	Kingston
Kilduff Pat,	Birming'h m	McLelland D,	Pittsferry	Murphy Wm,	Brewers' t
Kilduff Thos,	Willatsh'm	McLelland Jas jr,	"	Murphy Wm G,	"
Kirkpatrick Geo,	Kingston	McLelland Jas sr,	"	Murray Jno,	"
Kirkwood John,	Washburn	McLiment D,	Pittsferry	Murray Wm,	"
Lackey Robt,	Willetsh'm	McMaster Ed,	"	Nagle Pat,	Ballentyne
Lafferty Jas,	"	McMaster Jno,	" fs	Neilon Pat,	Birmingham
Lane Chas,	Pittsferry	McMullen J E,	Seeley's	Nelson Geo,	Kingston
Lawles John,	Kingston	McMullen J jr,	"	Nelson Wm H,	Barrie'd t
Lawless Mich'l,	Kingston	McMullen M,	"	Nelson W H,	Kingston fs
Ledbeater Wm,	Brewer's	McRorey John,	Kingston	Norris Wm T,	Barrie'd t
LeHeup Harry,	Barriefield	McNabb Francis	"	O'Gorman M,	"
Lucy Geo,	Willetsholme	McNeice Jas,	Barriefield	O'Neil Patrick,	Kingston
Lucy William,	"	Madden Jas,	Washburn fs	Orr James,	Washburn t
Lunman A,	Kingston Ml	Madden Jno,	Brewer's Ml	Park John,	Willetsholm

TOWNSHIP OF PITTSBURG.

Name	Post Office	Name	Post Office	Name	Post Office
Patterson Jas,	Kingston	Seale Chas,	Kingston	Trotter R jr,	Birmingham
Patterson Jno,	Kingston	Seale John,	"	Trotter Robt sr,	"
Patterson R S,	Barriefield	Seale Wm,	"	Vanhorn Alex,	Kingston
Patterson R,	"	See David jr,	Brewer's	Vanhorn Chas,	"
Patterson Robt,	Kingston	See Robt,	"	Vanhorn Geo.	"
Payne A,	Willetsholme	Shortell Jas,	Washburn	Vanhorn Wm,	"
Peck Geo,	Birmingham	Shortell John,	"	Vanhorn Wm A,	"
Peters Freeman,	Wash'n	Shortell Patrick,	"	Vallancourt O,	Barriefield
Peters Robt,	" fs	Shortell Thos,	" fs	Vanalstine C,	Brewer's fs
Peters Samuel,	"	Shortell Wm,	"	Vanalstine D,	Kingston
Potter A,	Willetsh'm fs	Sibbett Ed,	Kingston	Vanalstine J,	Birmingham
Potter David,	Willetsholm	Smith Arch,	Washburn	Vanalstine M,	Brewer's
Potter John,	Willetsh'me	Smith Caleb,	Brewer's	Vanalstine W,	Brewers fs
Purcell Geo,	Kingston	Smith Wm,	"	Vance Chris,	Barrie'd t
Purcell Nicholas,	"	Smythe John,	King' Mills	Wafer John,	Kingston
Purcell Patrick,	"	Smythe Robt,	"	Wager W A,	Ballentyne t
Quinn Jas,	Kingston fs	Solley Jos,	Kingston t	Walker Geo,	Kingston
Quinn Owen,	"	Spafforn F K,	Willetsh'm	Walker Joseph,	" t
Quinn Terrance,	"	Sparks Sam jr,	Birming'	Waller J,	"
Ray David,	Willetshome	Sparks Sam sr,	"	Ward Geo,	Ballentyne t
Ray Thos,	Kingston	Spence Robt,	Washburn	Wartman Allen,	Washb'n
Ray William,	"	Spence T W,	South Lake	Webb Jas,	Seeley's Bay
Redfern Ed,	Birmingham	Spence Walter,	"	Webb Jno,	Brewer's
Redfern Jas,	"	Stanton Nath,	Barriefield	Webb Mich,	Seeley's Bay
Redmond J,	Brewers'	Stark Thos,	Gananoque	Weir Thos,	Brewer's
Reynolds Jno,	Willetsh'm	Stark Wm,	"	Whalen Luke jr,	Washb'n
Roach Mark,	Brewers'	Stoliker I,	South Lake	Whalen Luke sr,	"
Rogers David,	Kingston	Stratton Dav,	Kingston fs	Whitney Albert,	Pittsferry
Rogers D D,	"	Stratton Wm,	"	Whitney Fred,	"
Rogers Jas,	" fs	Stuart Geo,	" fs	Whitney T,	Kingston
Ronden Frank,	Birming'm	Stuart J,	" t	Whyte Alex,	South Lake
Rooney Henry,	Kingston	Stuart John,	"	Willett Arthur,	Birming'm
Root Albert,	Pittsferry	Stuart Wm,	"	Williams M,	Kingston t
Root Gilbert,	"	Terthewey R,	"	Wilmot Edward,	Kingston
Root Thos,	Brewer's Ml	Thomas Hy,	Willetsh'me	Wilmot Henry,	"
Rudd T G,	Kingston	Thompson Arch,	Brewers'	Wilmot John,	"
Ruttan J C,	Barriefield	Thompson Jno,	Birming'	Wilmot John A,	"
Ruttan Walter,	" fs	Thompson W,	Washburn	Wilmot John J,	"
Rutter C,	Pittsferry t	Tierney John,	Seeleys'	Wilmot P G,	Pittsferry
Ryan John,	Barriefield	Tighe Jas,	Kingston	Wilson Jas,	Willetsholm
Ryder Ira,	Birmingham	Tighe John,	"	Wilson John,	"
Ryder John,	" t	Tobin Jas,	Birmingham	Wilson Rich,	Barrie'd t
Ryder Wm,	" fs	Todd Sam,	"	Winbourne Robt,	Pittsf'y
Saybrook Jas,	Brewer's	Todd Thos,	"	Woods Geo,	Birming'm fs
Saybrook Richard,	"	Toner Geo,	"	Woods Jno,	Brewers
Saybrook Wm,	"	Toner Jas,	"	Woods Sam,	Birming'm fs
Schoales Jas,	Willetsh'm	Toner Wm,	"	Woods Walt jr,	" fs
Scott Jas,	Kingston Mills	Trotter Chas,	Birming'm	Wobds Walt sr,	"
Scott James,	Seeleys'	Trotter David,	"	Woods Wm,	" fs
Scott Wm,	Birmingham	Trotter Jas,	"	Young Wm,	Kingston
Seale Alex,	Kingston	Trotter Jno,	Brewer's Ml		

TOWNSHIP OF PORTLAND.

This Township is for the most part well settled, and there are a great number of well cultivated farms. The Kingston & Pembroke Railroad runs through this Township. Number of acres assessed, 52,284; population, 2,303.

See also the following Villages in the Township: Bellrock, Harrowsmith, Hartington, Murvale, Petworth, Verona.

☞ The letter *t* in italics signifies tenant, *fs* farmer's son; all the rest are owners.

Name	Post Office	Name	Post Office	Name	Post Office
Abrams J E,	Verona *t*	Baker Leander,	Harrow' *fs*	Buttimer Rich,	Harrow'
Abrams Jos,	Murvale	Ball Adney,	Verona *fs*	Byrne Allen,	Bellrock
Abrams J W,	Verona	Ball Chas,	" *fs*	Byrne Miles,	" *fs*
Abrams Wm,	Verona	Ball Eli P,	"	Campbell Jas,	"
Aikin Geo,	Murvale	Ball George,	"	Card Jas,	"
Alberton Thos,	Verona	Ball John,	Bellrock	Carlton Jas,	Hartington
Alberton Wm, jr,	" *t*	Bander George,	Verona *t*	Carr Alex,	Harrowsmith
Alberton Wm,	" *t*	Bander Ira,	"	Carr John,	"
Alton Geo, jr,	Loughboro	Bander J D,	"	Carr Wm,	Petworth
Alton Geo,		Bander John N,	"	Carriff John,	Bellrock
Alton Thos,	Hartington	Bander Nelson,	"	Carrigg Michael,	Bellrock
Amey D L,	Bellrock	Barston Geo,	Harrow' *t*	Carscallen Ed,	Harting'n
Ashley Geo,	Harrowsmith	Bauder Hy,	Verona	Carscallen E L,	Petworth
Ashley Nelson,	Verona	Benjamin E W,	Bellrock	Carscallen l M,	Harting'
Asselstine Cyrus,	Murvale	Blackhurst Jas,	Harrows'h	Carscallen Wm,	Petworth
Asselstine Isaac,	Petworth	Blackhurst J sr,	Harting'n	Chalice Jas,	Hartingdon
Asselstine Peter,	Murvale *t*	Blackhurst John,	" *fs*	Chalice Wm J,	" *fs*
Asselstine Syl,	Ballrock	Botting Peter,	"	Charlton Alex,	Harrow'h
Asselstine W W,	Petwor'	Boyce David,	Petworth	Charlton James,	Verona
Babcock Benj,	Hartington	Bowman Geo,	Bellrock *t*	Charlton John,	Harrow'h *t*
Babcock Damon,	Wilton	Boyce H M,	Verona	Charlton Wm A,	" *t*
Babcock Dan,	Wilton	Boyce James,	Petworth *t*	Clare Edward jr,	Bellrock
Babcock Cor,	Verona	Boyce L W,	Bellrock	Clare Edward sr,	"
Babcock Geo T,	Harting	Boyce N R,	Bellrock	Clare Martin,	" *fs*
Babcock Hy,	Harrow	Bradford Jas,	Petworth	Clare Michael,	" *fs*
Babcock Jas,	Verona	Bradford Thos,	"	Clark Alex,	Longhboro
Botting John,	Hartington	Bradshaw Chas,	Yarker	Clark Chas,	"
Babcock John M,	"	Brady John A,	Harrow'	Clark J,	Murvale
Babcock Sam,	Harrow'h	Burley John H,	"	Clark Jas,	"
Babcock W B,	Harting	Burley John R,	"	Clark John,	Petworth *fs*
Bailie Jas jr,	Wilton *fs*	Burley Syl,	"	Clark Lestor,	Harrow'h
Bailie Jas sr,	"	Burley Wesley,	Verona	Clark Sidney,	Petworth
Baker Ira,	Harrowsmith	Burtch D,	" *t*	Clark Walter,	"

TOWNSHIP OF PORTLAND. 131

Name	Post Office	Name	Post Office	Name	Post Office
Cloakey M,	Hartington	Dowker John,	Hartington	Hamilton Alex,	Murvale
Cloakey Wm,	"	Dixon Jabiz,	Verona	Hamilton Jas,	" fs
Close John,	Verona	Donnelly John,	Horrow'h	Hamilton John,	"
Clow Isaac,	Hartington	Donnelly Patrick	"	Hamilton Robt,	Harrow'
Clow John,	Harrow'h	Dool Wm E,	Hartingdon	Hamilton Wm,	Bellrock
Clow Matth's,	Harting' fs	Dowker James,	"	Hanigan B,	Loughboro fs
Clow Thos,	"	Dowker Wm S,	"	Hanigan James,	"
Clow Wm H,	"	Downey Joseph,	Lough'o	Hart John,	Harrowsmith
Coe Noah,	Harrowsmith	Doyle Michael,	Bellrock	Hawkesbury Geo,	Verona
Cole Harvey,	Murvale fs	Duggan John,	Harrow'h	Herchmer Jas,	Harrow'h
Cole Henry,	"	Dunn Lawr,	Harting' fs	Herchmer John,	"
Cole Joseph,	" fs	Dunn Mich,	"	Hicks C T,	" fs
Cole Wm,	Verona t	Ellerbeck Hy,	Harrow' fs	Hicks Henry,	Verona t
Cole W H,	"	Ellerbeck Rich,	"	Hicks Norman,	Harting' h
Collins Jas,	Loughboro	Emberly Hiram,	"	Hicks S S,	Harrow'h h
Conners John,	Bellrock t	Embury Jas,	Bellrock	Hicks Thos D,	"
Connolly Joseph,	Bellrock	Embury M E,	" fs	Hicks Wm C,	Verona t
Conway Jacob,	Harting' t	Ferguson Alex,	Harrow' t	Hill John,	Petworth t
Conway Thos,	Bellrock t	Ferguson Cor,	" t	Hobbs Wm,	Loughboro t
Cook Jas,	Harrowsmith	Ferguson Thos,	" t	Holt Hy,	Verona t
Cowdy J G,	"	Forrester Jas.		Hooper Douglas,	Bellrock
Cowdy John,	"	Foster Ed,	" t	Hornbeck Benj,	Murvale
Cowdy Sam'l,	"	Foster Jas,	"	Hornbeck Geo,	" fs
Cox David S,	" t	Freeman F C,	Verona	Hernbeck G W,	"
Craig Wm G,	Verona fs	Freeman Jno,	Hartington	Houston Sam,	"
Craig Wm sr,	"	Freeman Peter,	Lough'o	Huffman C W,	Petworth
Crawford Phil,	Bellrock t	Freeman Philip,	Yarker	Huffman H G,	" v
Cronson Hy,	Petworth t	Freeman Sam'l,	Harting'n	Huffman Levi,	" fs
Crozier Thos,	Harrow'h	Genge Thos J,	Bellrock	Huffman Meloe,	Verona
Cuepah John,	Bellrock t	Geraldi Jno Y,	Verona t	Huffman Philip,	Petworh
Cunningham Hy,	Verona	Geraldi Louis,	" t	Huffman P W,	Petworth fs
Cunningham M,	" fs	Goodberry L,	"	Huffman Wilford,	" fs
Curl James,	"	Gosling Jno jr,	Hartington	Hughes Anson,	Harrow'h
Curl John,	"	Gosling John sr,	Lough' h	Hughes Edgar,	" fs
Curran D P,	Yarker	Gowdy John,	Verona t	Hughes Jas A,	"
Curran John,	"	Graham And,	"	Hughes Jno jr,	" fs
Darling Chas,	Petworth h	Graham John,	"	Hughes Jno sr,	"
Davey Benj,	Bellrock t	Grant Jas,	Harrowsmith	Hunter John,	Verona
Davy Benj,	Verona t	Grant John,	" t	Hunter Wm J,	"
Davy Chester,	Harrow'h	Grant Thos,	Verona t	Husband Ezra,	Harrow'h
Davy Jas,	Wilton	Grant Wm B,	"	Husband John	"
Davy Michael,	Murvale	Grant A,	"	Husband Robt,	"
Davy S,	Kingston t	Grant Anson,	"	Hutchens Hy,	Murvale t
Davy S W,	Murvale t	Grant Alfred,	Bellrock t	Irish E,	Verona
Day C W,	Harrowsmith	Grant Geo,	"	Irish Jediah jr,	Hartingt'n
Day G E,	"	Griffith J A,	Verona	Irish Jediah sr,	Loughboro
Day John A,	Loughboro	Griffith Robt,	Harrow'h	Irish John A,	Hartington
Day Peter W,	Kingston	Grundell Ed,	Verona	Irish John E,	Verona
Deline Hiram,	Petworth t	Guess Joel,	Loughboro	Irish Joseph,	Bellrock
Deline Jno,	Verona	Guess Well,	Hartington	Jackson Ed,	Harrow'h t
Delyne Lester,	Petworth t	Gunn Alex,	Kingston	Jackson H,	Hartington h
Dennison David,	Harting'	Hagerman Jno,	Harrow'	Jackson Moses,	Harrow' t
Dennison Geo,	Harting'u	Hailey Morris,	Yarker t	Jackson Sperry,	"
Dennison Thos,	"	Hamilton Abe,	Verona	Jamieson Jas,	"

TOWNSHIP OF PORTLAND.

Name	Post Office
Jeffrey Ed,	Verona
Jeffrey Geo,	Hartington
Joyner Chas,	Loughboro
Joyner D L,	"
Joyner E,	Kingston
Joyner S,	Loughboro
Joyner S,	Kingston fs
Kates Jeremiah,	Verona
Kelly Arthur,	Yarker
Kelly Jas,	Bellrock
Kelly John,	"
Kelly Philip,	Yarker
Kenney Jas,	Bellrock
Kenney Mich,	"
Kingston Sam,	Hartingt'n
Kingston Thos,	Harrow'h
Kirkwood Wm,	Verona
Kish W,	Harrowsmith t
Kitson George,	Verona
Knapp M W,	Harrow'h
Knight Alfred,	Petworth t
Knowlton F R,	Verona
Lake Buckley,	Murvale
Lake Damon,	" t
Lake William,	"
Lakins E,	Petworth
Lakins John,	"
Lale Coleman,	Yarker t
Lampkins Geo,	Petworth
Laveque Thos,	Bellrock t
Lawrence Wm J,	Murvale
Lee George,	" t
Lee Israel,	"
Lee Jesse,	" t
Leonard Chas,	Harrow'h
Leonard Edg,	Harting' o
Leonard Jos,	"
Leonard Thos,	" o
Lillie George,	Petworth
Lillie Richard,	"
Lillie William	"
Lochead M,	"
Long William,	Murvale t
Loveless Jacob,	Verona
Lucas D W,	Petworth
Lucas John,	"
Ludbrook A A,	Verona
McColl Pat'k,	Harrow'h
McConnell A,	Yarker fs
McConnell Edgar,	" fs
McConnell Ed sr,	"
McConnell Jas,	" fs
McConnell John,	" fs
McConnell John	"
McCuen Mich,	Bellrock t
McCullough John,	"
McCullough Rt,	Harrow' t
McDonald Duncan,	"
McDonald Wm,	Yarker
McKenzie J T D,	Verona
McKim H H,	Murvale
McKim Oscar,	"
McKim W,	"
McLean J W,	Harrow' h
McLean Wm,	"
McMahon Alex,	Verona
McMahon John,	Parham
McMullen Hy,	Verona
Madden Rich,	"
Manson Alex,	Petworth
Manson Geo,	"
Martin Amos,	"
Martin Anson,	Verona
Martin Geo,	Loughboro
Martin John E,	Verona
Martin John O,	Bellrock
Martin Silas,	Verona
Matthews Geo,	Harrow'h
Meeks Jas,	Bellrock fs
Meeks Lycurgus,	"
Meeks Mortimer,	"
Mehen John,	"
Mehen Owen,	"
Metcalfe Jno D,	Harting'
Miller Robt,	Murvale
Moir Geo,	Bellrock
Mooey Sidney,	Kingston
Moore C A,	Hartington fs
Moore John S,	"
Moore John S,	" fs
Moran Wm,	"
Morrison Wm,	" t
Mucklewee Geo,	Harrow'
Mullen Wm,	Verona t
Murton D J,	Murvale fs
Murton George	"
Murton James	"
Myer P,	Harrowsmith
Myers Alex,	Harrow'h t
Neugen Aaron,	Petworth t
Nolan Jas,	Bellrock
O'Donnell John,	Longhb'
O'Neil Chas,	Verona
O'Neil John,	Murvale t
O'Reilly John,	Loughboro
O'Reilly Luke,	"
O'Reilly Thos,	"
Orr Joseph,	Harrow'h
Parrott Ab,	Harrow'h t
Patterson J W,	Harting'n
Patterson Robt,	Harrow'
Patterson S,	"
Patterson Wm,	Harting'n
Pennell Henry,	Murvale t
Perey John,	Verona
Perey Joseph,	" t
Perey William,	Bellrock
Pero Henry,	Verona
Perrault Adol's,	Bellrock
Perrault Francis	"
Perrault George,	" fs
Peters George,	Murvale t
Peters Hugh,	"
Peters Jacob,	Loughboro t
Peters Wm,	Murvale t
Phillips Jas,	Harrow'h
Pixley Hy,	"
Pomeroy Wm,	Bellrock
Pomeroy Wm F,	"
Porter Jas,	"
Purdy C W,	Harrow'h
Purdy Geo,	Loughboro
Purdy Gilbert,	Murvale
Purdy J F,	" fs
Quamadore W H,	Verona
Quinn William,	Verona
Randell Geo F,	Harrow'h
Redden Nelson,	Murvale
Redden Reuben	"
Redmond Jno,	Hartington
Redmond Wm,	"
Revell Ed jr,	" h
Revell, Ed sr,	"
Revell Mat jr,	" h
Revell Mat sr,	"
Revell Thomas	" t
Reynolds E,	Verona t
Reynolds Ed,	" t
Reynolds Silas,	"
Reynolds Wm,	" t
Riley Francis,	"
Rush Mich,	Petworth
Ruttan Lorenzo,	Bellrock
Ruttan Wm,	Verona t
Ryan Martin,	Murvale
Sagriff Jas,	Bellrock
Sagriff Thos,	" t
Salisbury Wm,	Verona t
Scales Benj jr,	" t
Scales Benj sr,	"
Scales Chas W,	" t
Scales George,	"

TOWNSHIP OF PORTLAND. 133

Name	Post Office	Name	Post Office	Name	Post Office
Scales Thos,	Verona	Snider Wesley,	Verona	Walker Samuel,	Verona *t*
Selze Alfred,	Murvale	Spike Aaron,	Harrow'h	Walker William,	Bellrock
Shane James,	Bellrock	Spike Wm B,	"	Wallace And,	Harrow'h
Shane Thos,	"	Spooner Laz,	Harting'n *t*	Wallace David,	"
Shaugraw Jas.	Harrow'h	Stafford Wm,	Murvale	Wallace James,	Petworth
Shaugraw Wm,	"	Stafford Zye,	"	Wallace John,	Harrow'h
Shibley B,	Murvale	Stephens Jef,	Hartington	Wallace T G,	" *t*
Shibley Chas,	"	Stephenson Jno,	Napanee	Wallace Wm,	"
Shibley H T,	Verona	Sterritt Jno,	Harrow'h	Walroth Jacob,	Verona
Shibley Jacob,	Harrow'h *h*	Stewart Chas,	" .	Walsworth G sr,	Harrow'
Shibley James,	" *h*	Stewart Sam,	"	Walsworth G jr,	" *fs*
Shibley John,	Murvale	Stewart S F,	Harrow'h	Walsworth Henry	" *t*
Shibley Sperry,	"	Storey Peter,	Verona	Walsworth J C,	"
Shibley Schuyler,	Harrow'	Storms Levi,	"	Ward Arthur,	"
Shultz John,	Murvale *t*	Storms Orange,	Wilton	Ward Nich,	Loughboro
Sigsworth E,	Hartington	Storms Secord,	Verona *t*	Warney Sidney,	Wilton
Sigsworth Jno,	Harrow's	Storms Thos,	"	Wartman Chas,	Harrow' *h*
Sigsworth T B,	Harting'n	Storring M,	Harrow'h *t*	Wartman Jacob,	Loughb'
Sigsworth T E,	"	Summer Jer,	Bellrock	Wartman John,	Harrow'h
Silver John L,	Murvale	Summers Wilmot,	" *t*	Wartman R,	Verona
Silver Niles,	" *fs*	Switzer Cephas,	"	Watson Abra,	Harrow'h
Simmons Benj.	Verona *t*	Switzer John W,	" *fs*	Watson J E,	"
Simmons M,	"	Tallen Ed,	"	Watson T H H,	"
Simmons Will,	Bellrock	Tallen Peter,	"	Watson Thos A,	"
Simpkins Hy,	Harrow'h	Timmons Denis,	" *fs*	Wattam John,	" *fs*
Simpkins M,	"	Timmons John,	" *fs*	Wattam Robt,	" *fs*
Simpkins M W,	"	Timmons Peter,	"	Wattam Wm,	"
Slack Robt,	Loughboro	Toggart Well,	Murvale *t*	Weldon S B,	Verona
Sly Henry,	Verona	Toggart Wm,	"	Wells Joseph,	" *t*
Smith Aaron,	" *t*	Townsend Alf,	Harrow' *t*	Wheeler I B,	Bellrock
Smith And,	Murvale *t*	Townsend T B jr,	" *t*	Whitty Ed,	Harrow'h
Smith Geo,	"	Townsend T B sr,	"	Whitty Hy,	Loughboro *fs*
Smith Hugh,	"	Tricky John,	" *t*	Whitty Nich,	"
Smith Joseph,	Hartington	Trousdale M,	Loughboro	Wilkins Joseph,	Verona
Smith Michael,	Murvale	Trousdale Thos,	Harrow'	Williams Cor,	Loughboro
Smythe E H,	Kingston	Trousdale Wm,	Verona	Williams J E,	" *fs*
Snider Abe,	Verona	Truscott Chas,	Harrow' *fs*	Williams Peter,	Verona
Snider Alexander,	"	Truscott John jr,	"	Williamson Jno,	Harrow'
Snider Caleb,	"	Truscott John sr,	"	Wilson Peter,	Bellrock
Snider Daniel,	"	Tryan Tobias,	Verona	Wilson Thos,	Verona
Snider Douglas,	"	Vanluven G W,	Harrow'h	Wood Dan,	Loughboro
Snider Elenson,	"	Walker Charles,	Verona	Wood Hy,	"
Snider Everet,	"	Walker, David	"	Woodruff Dan,	Verona *t*
Snider Harvey,	" *fs*	Walker Francis,	"	Woolsey Thos,	Murvale *t*
Snider J B,	"	Walker George,	"	Yeomans D,	Petworth
Snider M A,	"	Walker Hiram,	Yarker	Yeomans Jas,	"
Snider Miles,	" *fs*	Walker Jas,	Loughboro	Yeomans P,	"
Snider Nelson,	Harrow'h	Walker John,	Yarker		
Snider Robert,	Verona *fs*	Walker Miles,	"		

TOWNSHIP OF STORRINGTON.

This Township is divided off from portions of Pittsburg, Kingston and Loughboro.

Number of acres assessed, 54,179; population 2,111.

See also the following Villages in the Township: Battersea, Inverary, Lake Opinicon, Latimer.

☞ The letter *t* in italics signifies tenant; all the rest are owners.

Name	Post Office.		Name	Post Office.		Name	Post Office.
Abernethy H,	Battersea		Campbell Cal,	Inverary		Curson Wm,	Battersea
Abernethy R,	"		Campbell F M,	Latimer		Daby Just,	Latimer
Abbott Jno,	"		Campbell Hugh,	Battersea		Davidson B,	Opinion
Abbott Thos,	" *t*		Campbell Henry,	"		Dean Ptk,	Brewer's Mills
Adams Jas,	" *t*		Campbell Jas,	"		Dennie F,	Inverary
Ahern John,	Inverary		Campbell Jn,	Sunbury		Dewolfe Squ,	Battersea
Anderson G sr,	Washburn		Campbell Thos,	"		Dixon Alex,	"
Anderson G jr,	"		Card Sid,	Battersea		Dixon Geo,	"
Arthur John,	Battersea		Caverly Wm,	Latimer		Dixon Robt,	"
Arthur Samuel,	"		Chapman J,	Kingston		Dixon Thos,	"
Austin Robert,	Sunbury		Chown Arth,	"		Dixon Wm,	"
Baker William,	Latimer *t*		Chrisley Pk,	Inverary		Dochrill Jno,	"
Balls Thomas sr,	Sunbury		Christopher W,	Latimer		Dolan Alvin,	"
Balls Thomas jr,	"		Clark Edwin,	Battersea		Dolan J E,	Inverary
Balls William,	" *t*		Clark Geo,	"		Donald Jno,	Perth
Barclay J,	Inverary		Clark Jas,	"		Dougherty Jas,	Elginburg
Barnes R,	Elginburg		Clark Jno,	Sunbury		Dougherty P,	Brewer's M
Barr Adam,	Inverary		Clark Thos,	Battersea		Dowlin Dan,	Sunbury
Bennett James,	Battersea		Clark Wm,	"		Dowlin Jas,	"
Boal Robert,	" *t*		Claxton Jno,	Latimer		Dowlin Wm,	"
Bond Allan,	Inverary *t*		Clough F,	Perth		Duff Chas,	Battersea
Bond William,	Opinicon *t*		Cochrane J,	Sunbury		Duff Wm,	Inverary
Bower William,	Battersea		Cochrane J jr,	"		Edwards B,	Sunbury
Bradden James,	"		Connell R,	"		Edwards Geo,	Inverary
Brady Charles,	Latimer		Convery Dv,	Battersea		Edwards Jno,	"
Brady Edw,	Seeley's Bay		Convery Hugh,	"		Edwards Thos,	Elginburg
Brady James,	Latimer		Convery Wm,	"		Elder And,	Washburn *t*
Brewer Wall,	Battersea		Conville Thos,	Sunbury		Elder Geo,	" *t*
Britton B,	Kingston		Cooper Edw,	"		Elder Jas,	" *t*
Brown Jab,	Battersea		Cooper Wm,	Seeley's Bay		Elder Wm,	" *t*
Buck Fred,	"		Craig Robt,	Sunbury		Elliot Jno,	Kingston
Cameron P,	"		Cranston Wa,	Elginburg		Empey J,	Latimer *t*
Cairns Samuel,	Opinicon		Cuddy R,	Sunbury		Ennis Silas,	Perth
Calvin & Son,	Kingston		Curran Jas,	Latimer		Ennis Thomas,	Battersea *t*

TOWNSHIP OF STORRINGTON. 135

Name	Post Office	Name	Post Office	Name	Post Office
Eptygrove Alb,	Battersea	Holmes Jno,	Inverary	Lake Richard,	Inverary
Farrel Chas,	Seeley's B t	Hogan Thos,	Battersea	Lake William,	"
Ferguson Alex,	Battersea	Hoppins A,	Kingston	Longwith Chas,	Sunbury
Ferguson Jas,	Inverary	Hoppins Har,	Battersea	Lindsay Sam'l,	Opinicon
Ferguson Thos,	"	Horning Arn,	Elginburg	Linton Dv,	Washburn t
Ferguson Wm,	"	Horning Geo,	"	Liston Pat'k,	Latimer t
Ferris Enoch,	"	Horning Rich,	"	Loucks George,	Battersea
Fisher Jas,	Washburn	Hughes Henry,	Battersea	Lucy Anthony	"
Fisher Thos,	"	Hughes Jas,	"	Lynn James,	"
Fisher Wm,	"	Hughes Jno,	"	Lyon Charles,	Latimer
Forrester Chas,	Seeley's B	Hughes Thos,	"	Lyon Henry,	"
Foster Sim,	Washburn	Hughson Geo,	Inverary	Lyon Hor,	"
Fowler M,	Mt Chesney	Hughson J H,	"	Lyon Syl,	"
Freeman Thos,	Battersea	Hurley Jno,	Kingston	Lyon Sym,	"
George Jas,	Sunbury	Hurley Jos,	Battersea	Lyon William,	"
Gibson Jno,	Inverary	Hutchinson W,	"	McCallum And,	Sunbury
Gibson Thos,	Sunbury	Jackson And,	Sunbury	McCallum D,	"
Gibson Wm,	"	Jackson And jr,	Battersea	McCallum Jas,	Kingston
Gilmore T,	Battersea	Jackson Hir,	"	McCallum T,	Sunbury
Gorman Jas,	Seeley's Bay	Jackson Jno,	Sunbury	McCarey Ber,	Washburn t
Gorman Mth,	"	Jackson Ph	"	McConnell H,	Battersea
Gordon Jas,	Sunbury	Jamieson R,	Battersea	McConnell Wm,	Sunbury
Gordon Jos,	"	Jerrells Hy,	Seeley's bay t	McCormick M,	Seeley's t
Gordon Wm,	"	Jerrells Jas,	"	McCormick T,	Battersea
Greenie Robt,	"	Jardine And,	Battersea	McClymont Thos,	" t
Gray Jas,	Perth	Jardine F,	"	McDonald Jno,	" t
Guild And,	Washburn	Jardine Jno,	"	McFarlane Jno,	"
Gummer Jas,	Inverary	Johnston W,	Inverary	McGarvey J,	Mt Chesney
Guthrie Walter,	Perth	Jones John,	" t	McGarvey Jno,	"
Guthrie Wm,	"	Joynes Dan,	Latimer t	McGarvey Thos,	"
Hagerty Sam,	Battersea	Keeler Daniel,	Battersea	McGrath Jno,	Sunbury
Halliday J,	Opinicon	Keeler John,	"	McIlroy Jas,	Battersea
Hanley Chris,	Battersea	Keeler Wes,	" t	McIlroy Jno,	Seeley's bay
Hanley Geo,	"	Keeler William,	"	McKendry Dv,	Washburn
Hanley John,	"	Keeler William,	"	McKenna, Ptk,	Seeley's
Hanley Wm,	Sunbury	Kells Robert,	Sunbury	McMullin Jno,	"
Harpell Wm,	Inverary	Kelly Henry,	"	McNamara Har,	Inv'ry t
Harris Chris,	Battersea	Kelly John,	"	McWaters Sam,	Sunbury
Hart Arthur,	Inverary	Kennedy John,	"	Mallon Jas,	Battersea
Hartly Thos,	Battersea	Kennedy Michael	"	Mallon M,	Seeley's Bay
Hawkey Rob,	Sunbury	Knapp Andrew,	"	Mallon Ptk,	Battersea
Hawkins J,	Jones' Falls	Knapp Charles	"	Martin J,	Elginburg t
Healey Jos,	Elginburg	Knapp Henry,	"	Martin Wm,	Latimer t
Henderson Jno,	Inverary	Knapp Josh,	Elginburg	Mathers Jno,	Inverary
Henry D,	Seeley's bay	Knapp J sr,	Battersea	Maynard Geo,	Battersea
Hepburn H,	Battersea	Knapp J jr,	"	Marcue Fred,	"
Hingey E,	Perth	Knight Robert,	Inverary	Merriman Chs,	Latimer
Hitchcock Jno,	Washburn	Knight W,	"	Miller Jno,	Battersea
Hodgson Edwin,	Sunbury	Lake Chris,	Battersea	Millis Geo,	Inverary t
Hodgson J M,	"	Lake Isa,	"	Moore Chs,	Battersea
Holder Isaac,	Battersea	Lake Isa,	Inverary	Moore Dan,	"
Holder Wm,	Battersea	Lake James,	"	Moore Dan,	Inverary
Holland Jno,	Inverary	Lake John,	Battersea	Moore Wm,	"
Holmes Geo,	Battersea	Lake Robert,	"	Moorland James,	Sunbury

TOWNSHIP OF STORRINGTON.

Name	Post Office	Name	Post Office	Name	Post Office
Moorland Th,	Sunbury	Rykerk Wm,	Sunbury	Stewart S,	Jones's Falls
Morow Alex,	Battersea	Sands Geo,	Seeley's Bay	Sutherland A,	Br Mills
Morow Geo,	Inverary	Sands Thos,	Battersea	Sutherland W,	"
Morow Wm,	Sunbury	Sands William,	" t	Tait Jos,	Inverary
Morrison R A,	Inverary	Scott Henry,	" t	Teachout Jas,	Battersea
Morrison Wm,	"	Scott Hugh,	Inverary	Teeple Elias,	"
Muir Wm,	Sunbury	Scott James,	Kingston	Teeple Jas,	"
Mullin Ber,	Latimer	Scullion Henry,	Br Mills	Teeple Jno,	Opinicon
Murphy Dan,	Brewer's M	Sears John,	Inverary t	Teeple Nath,	Inverary
Murphy Jno,	"	Sears J,	Elginburg	Thomas, Chas,	Battersea
Murphy Jno,	Latimer	Sears William,	Battersea	Thompson Jas,	Perth
Murphy Mich,	Battersea t	Shannon John,	Sunbury t	Thorn Jno,	Elginburg
Murphy Ths,	Brewer's M	Shannon Robt,	"	Tierney Jno,	Seeley's bay
Neil Geo,	Sunbury	Shannon Thos,	"	Toland D H,	Sunbury
Nichol Jos,	Battersea	Shannon Wm,	"	Toland Jno,	"
Nicholson Jn,	Inverary t	Shannon Wm,	Jones' Ml	Toland Jos,	Washburn
Ormsby Wm,	Battersea	Sharp Alex,	Sunbury	Tolls Edg,	Inverary
Orr Jas,	Washburn	Sheppard Edw,	Latimer t	Tolls Levi,	"
Orr R T,	Sunbury	Sheppard Jno,	" t	Toner Jas,	Washburn t
Patterson G,	Mt Chesney	Sheppard Jno sr,	Inverary	Tuttle Jno,	Delta
Patterson J,	Latimer	Sheppard Jno jr,	"	Vanalstine A,	Battersea
Patterson Jno,	Sunbury	Sherbano James,	Kingston	Vanluven Chs,	Delta
Patterson Thos,	Sunbury	Shibley H T,	"	Vanluven Sid,	"
Patterson Wm,	"	Shibley Sch,	"	Vanvolkinburg W,	"
Patterson Wm,	Latimer	Sills Levi,	Kingston	Wakeford G S,	Sunbury
Payne Robt,	Battersea t	Simpkins Vin,	Perth t	Waldron Gor,	"
Perry George,	Inverary	Simpson Jno,	Battersea	Waldron Jno,	"
Perry Sheldon,	"	Simpson Rt,	"	Walker D J,	Inverary
Pixley Lyman,	Battersea	Sleeth Dv,	Seeley's Bay	Walker D J jr,	"
Potter Henry,	Inverary	Sleeth Geo,	Battersea	Walker Mar,	Battersea
Purdy Marshal,	Latimer	Sleeth Jno,	"	Wart Miles,	"
Purdy Robert,	"	Sleeth Sm,	"	Wartman B,	Latimer
Purvis Wm,	Sunbury	Sleeth W W,	Elginburg	Webb Ptk,	Sunbury
Quail John,	Inverary	Sleeth Wm,	"	Webb Rich,	"
Quail William,	"	Slean Sam,	Sunbury	Webb Wm,	"
Quinn Pat'k,	Kingston	Smith Adam,	"	Weir H,	"
Reynolds Wm,	Opinicon t	Smith Chs,	"	White Hy,	Battersea
Reynolds Wm,	Inverary	Smith Hugh,	"	Whalen Wm,	Seeley's bay
Richards Wm,	"	Smith Jas sr,	"	Williams Cor,	Sunbury
Ritchie Adam,	Battersea	Smith Jas,	"	Williams Sam,	Battersea
Ritchie Alex,	Inverary	Smith Lewis,	"	Wood Miles D,	Latimer
Ritchie Robt,	Battersea	Smith Wm,	Elginburg	Woolf John V,	"
Ritchie Wm,	"	Snook Mart,	Inverary	Yateman Geo,	Battersea
Robb James,	Kingston	Spooner Frs,	Latimer	Yateman Jas,	"
Robinson Thos,	Sunbury	Spooner Hiram,	"	Yateman Rich,	"
Rowan George,	Battersea	Spooner Hiram,	Sunbury t	Yateman Wm,	"
Rousehorn, J,	Elginburg	Spooner Jno,	Elginburg	Young Jas,	Sunbury
Rutledge James,	Perth	Spooner Ths,	Sunbury	Young Tobi,	Battersea
Ryder Hkory,	Washburn	Steuburg Anson,	Battersea	Young Wm,	"

TOWNSHIP OF WOLFE ISLAND.

This Township consists of an island about 27 miles long opposite Kingston and the adjacent islands. Population about

See also Wolfe Island village.

☞ The letter *t* in italics signifies tenant, *fs* farmer's son; all the rest are owners.

The Post Office is Wolfe Island unless otherwise stated.

	Post Office		Post Office		Post Office
Abbott Edward,		Briceland James,	*fs*	Crane Jno. Smith's F'ls	*t*
Abbott James sr,	*t*	Briceland John,		Crawford Samuel,	
Abbott John,	*t*	Briceland Thomas jr,		Cuff Edward,	
Abbott Samuel,		Burnham Ira,		Cuff James,	
Abbott Thos,		Burnsides Well,	*t*	Cummings Charles,	*t*
Anderson Walter		Busch George,		Cummings Spencer,	*t*
Andrews Thomas,	*t*	Busch Thomas,	*t*	Daws Arthur H,	
Baker Daniel		Bustard Adam,		Dawson Isadore,	*fs*
Baker James,		Bustard Arthur,		Dawson John,	
Baker John,		Briceland Thomas sr,		Dawson Patrick,	
Baker Michael,	*fs*	Briceland William,	*fs*	Dawson Thomas,	
Baker Thos,	*fs*	Buckley John,	*t*	Dawson Victor G,	*fs*
Bamford Wells W,	*t*	Buggee Edward,	*fs*	Dean Nelson,	
Barry Charles A,		Buggee Michael,	*fs*	Dee Daniel,	
Bennett T S,		Buggee Patrick,	*t*	Dee John,	
Berow Peter,	*t*	Bulger James,	*t*	Dee Thomas,	
Berry Archibald,	*t*	Bullis John R,		Derush William,	
Berry James,		Bullis John sr,		Devlynn Patrick,	
Berry Richard,	*t*	Bullis Robert,		Docktwer Alexander,	*t*
Berry Robert,	*t*	Bullis William,		Donnelly David,	
Bolton Richard,		Cadotte Leo,	*t*	Donnelly James,	
Bolton William,		Cadotte Thomas,	*t*	Doolan John,	
Bowman Patrick	*t*	Card William,		Dow Xavier,	
Boyd John,	*t*	Charles John,		Doyle Michael,	
Boyd Robert,		Charles Samuel,		Duire Patrick,	
Breakey John D,		Connelly James,		Durant Robert,	*t*
Breakey John R,		Connelly Thomas sr,		Eccles George,	
Bredon Wm, Kingston		Connelly Thomas jr,		Eccles John,	
Briggs George,		Connelly Patrick,		Eves John,	
Briggs Theodore,	*fs*	Cook Daniel,		Fayoe John,	
Brill Wesley,	*t*	Coyle James sr,		Fawcett Alexander,	
Briceland Edward jr,		Coyle James jr,		Fawcett William,	*t*
Briceland Edward sr,		Crammond David,		Ferguson George,	*t*

TOWNSHIP OF WOLFE ISLAND.

	Post Office		Post Office		Post Office	
Flynn John,		Horn Henderson,		Lyons Peter,	
Flynn Mathew,		Horn James,		Lyons Thomas,	
Flynn Michael,		Horn John,		McAllister George	
Flynn Thomas,		Horn Randolph		McAllister James,	
Forbes Charles,		Horn Robert,		McCarthy Edward	
Forbes Samuel,		Horn Thomas,		McCarthy James,	t
Friend George,		Horn William W,		McCarthy John,	
Friend John,		Hutchison George,		McCullough Alexander,	
Furlong Michael,	t	Irvine Richard,	t	McDonald Alexander,	
Furner George,		Irwin Chamber, Kingston		McDonald Angus,	
Gange Richard,		Johnston John,	t	McDonald Donald,	
Garner James,		Johnston James,		McDonald Donald,	
Garner Samuel,		Johnston Michael,		McDonald Duncan L,	
George John,		Jones Joseph,		McDonald James R,	
Gibson David,	t	Joslyn Almond,		McDonald James B,	t
Gillespie George,	t	Joslyn Ebener,	t	McDonald Patrick,	
Gillespie William,		Joy Spafford,		McDonald William,	t
Going Shirly,	t	Kane Edward,	t	McEvoy Patrick,	
Grant Alexander,		Kane John sr,		McFadden Reuben,	
Grant Archibald,		Kane John jr,	t	McFadden William	
Grant Donald,		Kane William,		McGlynn Edward,	
Grant John,		Keegan Michael,		McGlynn James,	
Grant Peter,		Keeley David,		McGlynn John,	
Green Fenton,		Keill Julian		McGlynn Patrick,	
Greenwood Charles,		Keill Louis,		McGrath Peter,	
Greenwood Francis,		Keill Peter,		McGrath William,	
Greenwood George,		Kelly Patrick,	t	McGregor Alexander,	
Greenwood Joseph,		Kelly Pierce,	t	McGregor Donald,	
Grey John sr,		Kemp Amos,		McGregor John,	
Griffin Michael,		Kemp James,		McGregor Peter,	
Griffin Patrick,		Kemp John,		McKenna Bernard,	
Grimshaw James,		Keyes George,		McKenna James,	t
Grimshaw Miles,		Keyes John,		McLaren Hugh,	
Grimshaw William,		Keyes Thomas sr,		McRae Alexander,	
Hackett Archibald,	t	Keyes Thomas jr,		McRae James,	
Halliday Charles,		Keyes William,		McRae John,	
Halliday John,		Kinsloe John		McRae Weir,	
Hanlon Benjamin,		Kinsloe William,		Mackey John,	t
Hanlan Michael,		Kirpatrick George,		Macready Thomas,	
Harris Luther,		Kirpatrick William,	t	Manning John,	
Hatfield Thos A,		Kayle James,		Marlow William,	
Healey David,		Kayle Joseph,		Marsh George,	
Healey Eugene,		Laird James,		Martin George,	t
Helmer Gordon,	t	Lalonde Francis,		Matheson John,	
Henderson William sr,		Larkins Henry,		Michie Joseph,	
Henderson William jr,		Laughlin Arthur,		Mitchell Franklin,	
Hennessy Patrick,		Laughlin John,		Montgomery John,	
Hennessy William,		Ledford John,		Moran James,	
Hinckley Dexter,	t	Lefleur Peter,		Moran John,	
Hinckley Henry,		Lefleur Peter sr,	t	Moran Patrick,	
Hogan James,		Leush Anthony,	t	Mosier John,	
Hogan John,		Lyons James sr,		Mosier Nicholas,	
Hogan Peter,		Lyons James jr,		Mosier Romain,	t
Hogan Thomas,		Lyons Patrick,		Mucane Henry,	

TOWNSHIP OF WOLFE ISLAND. 139

	Post Office		Post Office		Post Office
Mulhall William,	t	Pyke George,	t	Tarrant John,	
Mullin William,	t	Pyke Thomas,	t	Tarrant Robert,	
Murphy Jeremiah,	t	Quigley John,		Todd George,	t
Murphy Patrick,		Quigley Patrick,		Todd John,	t
Murphy Terrance,		Quirck Patrick,		Troy John,	
Murphy Thomas,	t	Quirck Thomas,	t	Troy Michael,	
Murphy William,		Radford I H,		Turcotte L,	t
Newell William,		Ranons George,	t	Vanness Philip,	
Niles John,		Rattray William,		Vanerder Mathew,	
Nisbitt John,	t	Rawley William,		Walsh Patrick,	
O'Brien Bernard,		Rees & Dennis,		Watkins, Charles,	t
O'Brien John,		Roberts James,		Watts Constamer,	
O'Brien Martin,	t	Ross Henry,	t	Watts Job,	
O'Brien Michael,		Sammons Uriah,		Watts Samuel,	
O'Brien Thomas,		Sims F H, Deseronto		White Edward,	
O'Connell Michael,		Smith Edward,		White John,	
O'Connell Thomas,		Smith John,		White Michael,	
O'Reilly Edward,		Snow John,	t	Whitemarsh Yered,	
O'Reilly John,		Spoor Morly,		Wills George,	
O'Reilly Patrick,		Staley Archibald,		Wills Morris,	
O'Reilly Thomas,		Staley Charles,		Wills William	
Orr Nathaniel,		Staley Daniel,	t	Winborne William,	
Payne Robert,		Staley William,		Woodman George,	
Phair James,		Stevenson Andrew,		Woodman Samuel,	
Percival Henry,		Stevenson William,		Woodman William,	
Potvine Michael.		Sullivan Francis,		Woodman William H,	
Preddie Oliver,	t	Sullivan James,		Yott Lewis,	
Purdy Samuel,	t	Taggart Daniel,		Yott Oliver,	
Pyke Cornelius,		Taggart Hugh,			
Pyke David,		Taggart William,			

W. H. IRWIN & CO.,
Directory Publishers & Publishers' Agents,
HAMILTON, ONTARIO.

City of Hamilton, published every February..........,......$2.50
City of Kingston, published every two years.................. 2.00
City of Brantford and County of Brant...................... 2.00
County of York.. 2.00
County of Perth.. 2.00
County of Waterloo... 2.00
County of Simcoe... 2.00
County of Halton.. 1.50
County of Wentworth... 2.00

Directories of Montreal, $3; Toronto, 3; Quebec, $2.50; City of Guelph and County Wellington, $3; London (Ont.) $3. Sent on receipt of Price.

VILLAGES AND POST OFFICES

IN THE

COUNTY OF FRONTENAC.

☞ **See also the Townships in which the several places are located.**

Arden.—A Village in the Township of Kennebec; distant from Oso, a station of the Kingston and Pembroke Railway, 16 miles. Population about 100.

Clark rev J T, Methodist
Edwards rev Robert, Methodist
Fletcher Wm, shoemaker
Hayes Wm R, merchant
Helm John, M D
Lyman John W, shoemaker
Mills Wm B, P M, merchant
Monds George R, merchant
Osborne David, hotel
Patterson Wm, township clerk
Price M W, township clerk
Scott Norman, blacksmith
Tallon James, miller
Williams James, miller
Wormouth Nathaniel, blacksmith
Yeomans Thomas, cabinetmaker

Ardoch.—A Village on the Mississippi River in the Township of Clarendon; 16 miles from Clarendon station on the Kingston and Pembroke Railway. Population about 100.

Cheetham George, blacksmith
Godkins James, shoemaker
Henderson John, tanner
Howell John T, carpenter
Martin Garrett, carpenter
Munroe Alex, P M, merchant
Schwager Alois, carpenter
Schwager Joseph, carpenter
Watkins Bramwell, sawmiller
Whiteduck Joseph, shoemaker

Ballantyne Station.—A Village and station of the G. T. R., in the Township of Pittsburg; 8 miles from Kingston. Population about 100.

Edward Alex, agent G T R | Hysop John, postmaster.

Barriefield.—A Village in the Township of Pittsburg, on the east side of the Cataraqui River ; 1½ miles from Kingston, with which it is connected by a bridge. Here are situated Fort Henry and Point Frederick, on which is the Royal Military College. Population of the village about 300.

Allen George, student
Anderson William, carpenter
Batten George, mariner
Batten George sr.
BELWA CHARLES, T'p Clerk
Bowman, Charles & John, boat builders
Burk William, laborer
Burns John, laborer
Butland Charles, laborer
Byrns Miles, hotel & grocer
Cherry John, laborer
Chesnut Mrs.
Colson James, laborer
Donnelly John, engineer
Dowler Richard
Forbes Robert, grocer
Garrett Mrs. R.
GEORGE FRED J, dept'y city registrar
Gorman Miss Mary
Graham John, laborer
Gunn Mrs.
Halyen Miss Rose
Hinds Mrs S.
Hume Walter, shoemaker
Hutton William, carpenter
Kennedy Timothy, laborer
Kidd Robert, laborer
Knapp H. J., boat builder
Knapp James, boat builder
Lake Mrs.
Lawles Mrs, grocer
Leader Edward, sawyer
Leader John, fisherman
McDonald Michael, laborer
McIntosh Henry, laborer
Martin John, retired
Medley George, butcher
Medley Wm, salesman
Medley William, drover
Redmond William, carpenter
Ryan John, postmaster
Ryan John, laborer
Sedford Thomas, blacksmith
Sharman Jacob, boat builder
Smith Joseph, bricklayer
STANTON REV. RICHARD, rector St. Mark's Church
Stanton Richard, cabinet maker
Stanton Mrs.
STRACHAN MARTIN, (Martin Strachan & Son)
STRACHAN MARTIN DAVID (Martin Strachan & Son)
STRACHAN MARTIN, (Martin & Martin D.,) saw, planing, sash & door mills
Tisdale Alexander, carpenter
Tisdale John, laborer
Watts Mrs.

Battersea.—A Village at the south end of Loughboro Lake, in the Township of Storrington; 14 miles from Kingston, connected by stage. Population 200.

Anglin W J, P M, merchant
Arthur Wm, stage driver
Ferguson Wm, stage driver
Gascoine James, blacksmith
Hudson John, cheese manfr
Knapp C, carriagemaker
Lake Wm, merchant
Lawson rev Jas, Methodist
Lennon Joseph, merchant
Navalstin —, hotelkeeper
Thorne John, sawmiller
Vanluven Chris, miller
Williams N, blacksmith

Bedford Mills.—A Village in the Township of Bedford, 14 concession, 12th lot; 28 miles from Kingston, on the Rideau Canal; 18 miles from Iron Ore Junction, K. & P. R.R. Population about 70.

Barker R. C., clerk
Barker Robert, millwright
Breens Jeremiah, lumber inspector
Croskery W., sawyer
Goslin O., sawyer
Green D., miner
Green H., miner
Green John, miner
Green William, miner
Kerr George, engineer
Lashaw Luke, mariner
Lea Daniel, miner
Moriarty Daniel, engineer
Moulton E., sawyer
Moulton James, sawyer
Pritchard D. P., mariner
Scott William, mariner
Spicer Joel, sawyer
Steenbury George, miller
Stenens A., engineer
TETT, J. P. & BRO., merchants, millers, lumbermen
Tobin P., laborer
Turner E., sawyer
Wyatt William, carpenter

Bellrock—A Village in the Township of Portland, 20 miles from Napanee.

Coffey Mrs. Mary, P.M., merchant
Garinger Francis, carpenter
Hooper Samuel, miller
Percy John, blacksmith

Birmingham (Joyceville)—A Village in the Township of Pittsburgh, 12 miles from Kingston.

Birmingham Mrs E., Postmistress
Joyce L., carriage maker
Murphy J., hotel
Nimmo Rev. J. H., Church Eng.

Brewer's Mills—A Village in the Township of Pittsburg 17 miles from Kingston.

Anglin Robert, P M, merchant
Brewer James, machinist
Dean Patrick, laborer
D'Saunhac rev Paul, R C
Keys Charles, wagonmaker
Keyes James, merchant
McKeever Francis, blacksmith

Cataraqui—A Village in the Township of Kingston, on the Kingston and Napanee road, 3 miles from the city. Here is located the Cataraqui Cemetery, containing 100 acres. The village has two churches, English and Methodist. Population about 200.

Alderd Owen, porter K & P R
Berry Henry, carpenter
Bigham John, M D
Brown M J, M D
Day Johnson, brickmaker
Ely Samuel, tailor
Harrigan John, blacksmith
Haycock Fred, pedler
Haycock Joseph, gardener
Hennessey Mrs Catharine, boarding
Leeman Sandford, tollgate keeper
McKim John, pedler
McKim P, clerk 2nd Div Court
McMichael Osborne, gardener
Martin W D, potter
Nicol David, gardener
Nicol Joseph, gardener
Northmore Joseph, P M, merchant
Purdy W J, merchant
Riley Edward, brickmaker
Shorey rev E, Methodist
Simpson John, township clerk
Walker Charles, fanning mills
Walker James, carpenter

Clarendon Station—A Post Office in the Township of Oso. Bramwell Watkins, postmaster.

Cole Lake—A Post Office in the Township of Hinchinbrook. Robert Killins, postmaster.

Collins Bay—A Village and station of the G. T. R., in the Township of Kingston, in the 2nd concession; 7 miles from Kingston. Population 150.

Dougal Fred, carpenter
Ferguson John, station agent
Garrett Wm, blacksmith
Leslie Wm, manager Collins Bay Rafting Co
LOSIE J J, P M, merchant
McDonald Wm K, blacksmith
McGuire A, miller
Marsh George, hotelkeeper
Meachem Thos, engineer
Moffatt James, engineer
Rankin D, customhouse officer
Riley —, section foreman

D'Arcy—A Post Office in the Township of Howe Island. W. J. Sugrue, Postmaster.

Deerdock—A Post Office in the Township of Oso. John Warren, Postmaster.

Desert Lake—A Post Office in the Township of Loughboro.

Smith & Co., merchants | Snook William, Postmaster

Elginburg—A Village in the Township of Kingston on the 5th and 6th Concession and 17th and 18th Lots. 7 miles from Kingston. Population about 200.

Baker Rev. George, Methodist
Chant Rev. Joseph H., Methodist
Edwards John W., teacher
Elginburg John P., blacksmith
Guess Thomas, cheese maker
Jackson Simon, wagon maker
Lawson William, wagon maker
McBride James, blacksmith
MEECHAM MRS. E., postmist'ss
Parkin George, cheese maker

Fermoy—A Village in the Township of Bedford, 40 miles from Kingston

Botting Benjamin, merchant
Cook R., township clerk
Crozier Wm., hotel keeper
Hansen Henry, merchant
Kish John, carpenter
McLene John, grocer
Peters Elias, blacksmith
Rogers Joseph, shoemaker
Truelove James, saw mills
Watt Mrs. Ellen, Postmistress

Garden Island—An Island in the St. Lawrence, directly opposite Kingston, being 1¾ miles distant. A station of the Great North Western Telegraph Co. Here are located the extensive shipyards of Messrs Calvin & Son, who own nearly all the Island. Connected in summer by ferry boat four times a day, and in winter by stage twice a day. Population about 600.

COUNCIL :—D. D. Calvin, Reeve ; Anthony Malone, Hiram Calvin, Wm. Martin, Luke O'Reilly, Councillors ; George Malone, Clerk; Richard Raymond, Treasurer.

A'Brien George, master mariner
A'Brien Thomas, shipwright
A'Brien Wm, teamster
Achee Joseph, raftsman
Adset Samuel, teamster
Andre Peter, shipwright
Allen Fred, raftsman
Allen James F. foreman
Blackwell H, raftsman
Blanchett H, raftsman
Boyd Isaac, engineer
Brebant Augustus, shipwright

GARDEN ISLAND, ETC.

CALVIN & SON, (D D & Hiram A,) merchants, shipowners, etc
Clement Joseph, raftsman
Compeau Felix, raftsman
Compeau, Joseph, raftsman
Compeau Melia, raftsman
Cottenden Charles, raftsman
Cottenden George, raftsman
Cumming Mrs,
Cunningham Daniel, shipwright
Cushen John, teamster
Crosby Wm, sailor
Davey Albert, raftsman
Davey Benjamin, shipwright
Decaire Antoine, raftsman
Decare Baptiste, raftsman
Delzelle James, carpenter
Derocher Henry, raftsman
Desforges Baptiste, raftsman
Dignem Thomas, shipwright
Dix James, master sailor
Dix John, sailmaker
Dix Joseph, coroner, sailmaker
Doyle Patrick, shipwright
Dugdale Alfred, customs officer
Emond Moses jr., blacksmith
Emond Moses sr, blacksmith
Ferguson Thomas, shipwright
Garand John, raftsman
Glenn Andrew, blacksmith
Gobiel Edward, shipwright
Gray Thomas, engineer
Harper Harvey, sailor
Hickey James, engineer
Jones Peter, machinist
Kennedy David sr, carpenter
Kennedy James, raftsman
Kenosh Joseph, raftsman
Lafavre David, boatman
Lalonde Paul, raftsman
Lamber George, raftsman
Lapper Thomas, carpenter
LaRiche Hugh S, carpenter
Laurance Joseph, raftsman
Lawrence Francis, sailor
Lewers David, farmer
McCready William, engineer
McGarretty George, teamster
McMasters Andrew, raftsman
McNab Narcisse, cook
Malone Abraham, master mariner
MALONE ANTHONY, P M, J P, agent G N W Telegraph Co, bookkeeper
Marshall William, J P
Martin Ephriam, carpenter
Martin William, sawyer
Membery Henry, raftsman
Mulligan Alexander, sailor
Mullen John, engineer
O'Reilly Luke, carpenter
Philips John, sailor
Raymond Richard, raftsman
Rice Thomas, boilermaker
Rodrigue Ephraim, raftsman
Rogey William, boilermaker
Roney Fred, shipwright
Roney Henry, foreman shipwright
Sauve George, blacksmith
Sauve Joseph, blacksmith
Smith Thomas, engineer
Snell John, sailor
Symons John, engineer
Symons Robert, engineer
Theriault Francis, engineer
Watson Alex, raftsman
Wilkinson Charles, harnessmaker

Glenburnie—A Post Office in the Township of Kingston. George Hunter, postmaster.

Glenvale—A Post Office in the Township of Kingston. Robert Gibson, postmaster.

Godfrey—A Post Office in the Township of Hinchinbrook, 28 miles from Kingston. Wm J Lake, postmaster.

Hardinge—A Post Office in the Township of Barrie, 52 miles from Napanee. Thomas Tapping, postmaster.

Harlowe—A Post Office in the Township of Barrie. Thomas Neale, postmaster.

Harrowsmith—A Village and Station on the Kingston & Pembroke Railway in the Township of Portland, 19 miles from Kingston. Population about 300.

Asselstine George, painter
Baker Ira, undertaker
Bertram Bros., carriage makers
Blackhurst James, blacksmith
Buck Danford, blacksmith
Cook Thomas, hotel keeper
Day C. P., station master
Day Horatio, saw miller
Day W. D. P., M.D.
Donnelly James, township clerk
Dunham George, shoemaker
Griffith Wm., merchant
Martin Charles, saw miller
Mills Samuel, butcher
Parkin Richard, tailor
Peck Rev. William, methodist
Roberts William, carpenter
Smith J. R., M.D.
Stewart Samuel F., postmaster
Stone Charles, harness maker
Thompson & Clark, grocers
Thompson Wm., wheelwright
Vanluvan G. W., harness maker
Walsworth Jefferson, hotel keeper

Hartington—A Village and Station on the Kingston & Pembroke Railway in the Township of Portland, 22 miles from Kingston.

Campbell Benj., postm'r, saw m'l
Patterson William, merchant
Cannon Wm., carriage maker
Taylor Josiah, carpenter

Howe Island—A Post Office in the Township of Howe Island.

Melville M., township clerk | O'Brien James, postmaster

Inverary—A Village on Lot 20, in the 2nd Concession of the Township of Storrington, 12 miles from Kingston. Population about 100.

Barclay J., laborer
Bass Rev. W. A., Methodist
CAVERLY N, P M, general merchant (*see adv.*)
Dennis B, laborer
Dennis F, harnessmaker
Ferguson John, laborer
Harrison & Knight, carriagemakers
Harrison H P, woodworker
Hurd J, trader
Kellan A, laborer
Lovey J, butcher
McNamara H, bailiff
Marsh G, blacksmith
Patterson R, hotelkeeper,
Richards J. mason
Richards S, builder
RITCHIE A, township clerk
Tapper A, laborer
Walker D J, clerk 5th Div court

Kingston Mills—A Village in the Township of Pittsburg, 2nd concession, 36 lot, quarter mile from G. T. R. station called Rideau; 6 miles from Kingston; population about 150. This village is situated on the Rideau Canal, and has first-class water power and a large mill running the year round.

Blake Thomas, financial agent
Bradden Edward jr, drover
Bradden Edw sr, real estate dealer
Bradden James, lumber dealer
Butler John, carpenter
Byrne James, capt 47th regiment
Conners Morris, laborer
Connor P O'Connell, miller
Cunningham Edward sr, V S
Deane Joseph, lockmaster and collector
DEANE JOSEPH J, postmaster
Doyle James, butcher
Doyle James K, barber
Doyle John, J P
Doyle John jr., carpenter
Graham Donald, laborer
Green Thomas, hide dealer
Harrison Charles, builder
Harrison Henry, stock dealer
Hartnell William, mariner
Henderson John, foreman G.T.R.
Higgins Bernard, Roman Catholic
Hogan John jr, cheesemaker
Hogan John sr, dairyman
Hughes Thomas, miller
Hutchins Edward, agent G.T.R.
Keenan Felix, notary public
Lemon Wm, painter
Lundman Albert, butcher
McAdoo Samuel jr, butcher
McAdoo Samuel sr, drover
McAdoo Wm, butcher
McGraghan John, blacksmith
Marteg John, cheesemaker
Moran Bernard sr, drover
Murdock Martin, pawnbroker
O'Callaghan Daniel, teacher
Redmond John, laborer
Redmond Mrs John, midwife
Reid Joseph, mariner
Sargent Robt, lumber merchant
Smith John, wines and liquors
Thompson James S, miller
Tighe Michael, blacksmith
Waldon John, laborer

LAKE OPINICON, LATIMER, ETC.

Lake Opinicon—A Village on the Rideau Canal in the Township of Storrington, 14th Con., 16th Lot, 29 miles from Kingston. The nearest railway station is Harrowsmith, K.P.R., 20 miles. This Village was settled in 1834. Bryce J. Davidson, J.P., was appointed the first postmaster on the 1st March, 1871, and still occupies the position. Population about 250.

Bolton John, miner
Cameron Miss F., teacher
Cameron Peter jr, miner
Cameron Peter sr, lumberman
Chapman Howard, miner
Corkey Michael, miner
DAVIDSON BRYCE J, J.P., postmaster.
Davidson Wm, miner
Dennison Mrs. Catharine
Fluke David, miner
Harris Joseph, miner
Hattan Arch, miner
Hattan Peter, miner
Hughson Seth, miner
Hughson Wesley, miner
Hunter James, miner
Keith Mrs. Rachel
Laffonier Isaac, miner
Lindsay John, shoemaker
Linklater John, miner
Nicols Mrs, Wilbur
O'Brien James, miner
Poole John, sawyer
Poole Mrs, Matilda
Randall John jr, laborer
Randall John sr, laborer
Randall Wm, lumberman
Randall Wm N, miner
Robinson Samuel, miner
Sidney William, laborer
Singleton Charles W, constable
Stokes Robert, laborer
Stokes William, laborer
Williams Cornelius, lumberman
Young James, carpenter
Young Thomas, miner
Young William, miner

Latimer—A Post Office in the Township of Storrington.

Long Lake—A Post Office in the Township of Olden. James Bender, postmaster.

Loughboro (Sydenham)—A Post Office in the Township of Loughboro.

Dunlop Neil, M D
McQuade rev H, Methodist
Madden Hugh, postmaster
Poole rev M G, Church of Engl'd
Ruttan Chas, clerk 3rd Div court
Wilson J, township clerk

Mississippi Station—A Village and Station on the Kingston & Pembroke Railway, in the Township of Palmerston, 70 miles from Kingston.

Clark Norman, P.M., agt. K.P.R
Jones D. F., hotel keeper
McLaren Peter, saw mills
Mace Wm. D., merchant

Mountain Grove—A Post Office in the Township of Olden, 48 miles from Kingston. Alexander McDonald, Postmaster.

Murvale—A Post Office in the Township of Portland. Michael Dovey, Postmaster.

Oates—A Post Office in the Township of Loughboro. James Cosgrove, Postmaster.

Oconto—A Post Office in the Township of Oso. Alexander McGinnis, Postmaster

Ompah—A Post Office in the Township of Palmerston.
Briscoe J. R., postmaster | ELKINGTON J., M.D., tp. clerk

Oso Station—A Post Office in the Township of Oso. Solomon Bourke, Postmaster.

Ossa—A Post Office in the Township of Olden. · James A. Anderson, Postmaster.

Parham—A Village and Station on the Kingston and Pembroke Railway, in the Township of Hinchinbrooke 39 miles from Kingston.

Benjamin J. W., merchant | House Richard, merchant
Farrar Rev. H., Church of Eng. | Orser Rev. E. A., Methodist
Griffith J. A., P.M., merchant | Simpkins Wm. H., carriagemaker
Hartman N., carpenter | Siverbrick Albert, blacksmith
Hampton T. J., agent K. & P.R. | Siverbrick Wm., hotel keeper

Perth Road—A Post Office in the Township of Loughboro. James Stoness, Postmaster.

Petworth—A Post Office in the Township of Portland, at the head of the Napanee River, 18 miles from Napanee.

Brown Sylvester, grocer | Vannest James, carpenter
Peters Gideon, blacksmith | Vannest John, postmaster
Smith Ira, blacksmith | Vannest Lewis, merchant

Pittsferry—A Post Office in the Township of Pittsburg.
Gallagher rev J, BA, Presbyterian | Root Lewis, postmaster

Plevna—A Village in the Township of Clarendon, 4 miles from Gemley, on the T. & O.RR. Population about 100.

Card Jethro, saw mills
Dawson Geo. W., P.M., merchant
Hicks Bros, (Lorn Guy & Geo. A.) furniture
Hicks Norman A., pedlar
Holden Chas., wagon maker
McMullen Wm., shoemaker
McPherson Angus, merchant
Meeks Andrew, cooper
Muldoon Jonathan, hotel keeper
Ohlmann Leobald, trapper
Playfair Elisha, township clerk, hotel keeper
Plotz Wm. C. P., carpenter
Proudfoot James, hotel
Tucker James, miller
Wood Miller, blacksmith

Portsmouth—An incorporated Village adjoining the city on its western boundary, connected with it by the street railway. Here is located the Kingston Penitentiary, a very handsome building, situated at the eastern end of the village, on the river's banks. At the western end is the Kingston Asylum for the Insane; the building is a very fine and handsome structure of cut stone; the grounds are most beautiful and are tastily laid out. Among the other principal buildings are the Warden's residence, a most beautiful structure, surrounded by ornamental grounds well laid out; and the Episcopal and Methodist churches, Town Hall and a number of private residences. Population, exclusive of the Asylum and Penitentiary, about 900.

COUNCIL—James Adams, reeve; James Halliday, Joseph Fisher, John Gleeson, Alex McLeod, councillors; Thos Kelly, clerk; Thomas McCammon, treasurer; Edward Beaupre, collector; William Graham, street inspector; John R Brown, constable.

CHURCHES—Church of England, rev F W Dobbs; Methodist, rev T C Buchanan.

Adams James, architect
Aikins Alex, hospital steward, K P
Aikins Wm H L, baker
Aitken Mary, matron, Asylum for the Insane
Allen Joseph A,
Allen William R,
ANGLIN WM, bursar, Asylum for the Insane
Appleton Robert, gardener
Arundell Wm, laborer
Arthurs Robert, laborer
ASYLUM FOR THE INSANE,
Baker Wm, manager A Gunn & Co
Baiden Eli, gardener
Baiden Richard, gardener
Bannister John, carpenter
Baugh Francis, carpenter
Beaupre Edward sr, carpenter
Beaupre Isaiah, carpenter
Beaupre Peter, hotelkeeper
Belanger Maxime, carpenter
Betts Henry A,
Blakely Robert, sailor

PORTSMOUTH.

Brown John R, constable
Buchanan rev T C, Methodist
Buck Mathew, carpenter
Burk Edward F, butcher
Burke Henry, laborer
Cameron Alex, contractor
CAMPBELL JAMES, grocer
Carlton John, carpenter
CARTWRIGHT REV C E, Protestant chaplain, K P
CLARKE C K, M D, asst medical supt, Asylum for the Insane
Collins Alfred, laborer
Convery James, carpenter
Craig Thomas, sailor
Crawford Wm, keeper, K P
CREIGHTON JOHN, Warden Kingston Penitentiary
CREIGHTON ROBERT R, clerk, K P
Crimmons Pat'k, keeper, Asylum
Culcheth John, baker
Dearing Wm, laborer
Dillon Jeremiah,
Dobbs Rev. F. W., Eng. Church
Dodds James H., blacksmith
Dodds Robert, blacksmith
Donnelly John, keeper K.P.
Dooley Wm., laborer
Doyle James, keeper K.P.
Driscoll Jeremiah, keeper K.P.
Elliott Charles, keeper Asylum
Evans Edward, printer
Evans Thos., keeper Asylum
Fisher John, clerk
Fisher Joseph & Wm., brewers
Fitzgibbon Daniel, keeper K.P.
Fitzgerald Patrick, carpenter
Flynn John, laborer
Ford George, gardener
Forsythe Joseph,
Friendship John, gardener
Gillespie James, keeper, K P
Gleeson John, ice dealer

Graham Richard, bookkeeper
Graham Wm, carpenter
Gunn A & Co, tanners
Halliday James,
Henstridge Josephus, teacher
Hogan Wm, blacksmith
Holland George, keeper, K P
Holland James, laborer
Holland Wm., laborer
Howard Thomas, carpenter
Hurst William
Johnson Edward, keeper Asylum
KELLY THOS., village clerk
Kennedy John
Kennedy Patrick, laborer
Kennedy Thos. C., clerk
Kennedy Wm., grocer
Kerr Hugh, keeper Asylum
KINGSTON PENITENTIARY, John Creighton, warden
Leahy Edward, watchmaker
Leahy Mary, matron K.P.
Leahy Michael, keeper K.P.
Leahy Thos, bookkeeper
Lindsay Hugh P, laborer
Lindsay Robert, carpenter
Little Joseph, keeper, K P
Lowe Samuel, grocer
McDonald Thos, operator
Macdonell Arch, keeper, Asylum
McCammon Robert, baker
McCammon Thomas, keeper, K P
McCarthy James, postmaster
McCauley George, keeper, K P
McCauley Robert, keeper, K P
McConnell Wm. keeper, K P
McCorville Charles, keeper, K P
McConville Wm., grocer
McGein Bernard, keeper K.P.
McLeon Allan, steward Asylum
McLeod Alexander,
McLeod John, (Chatterton & McLeod)
McManus Hugh

McManus John
McNulty Wm. J.
McWaters Alexander, laborer
McWater Thomas, laborer
Marks John, carpenter
Mathewson James, B. keeper K.P.
Mathewson John P., carpenter
Metcalfe William
METCALF W G, M D, medical supt, Asylum for the Insane
Mills James, carpenter
Mills John, keeper, K P
Milne Alex, engineer
Mooney Edward, keeper, K P
Mooney John, laborer
Moore James W, laborer
Nicholson John, carpenter
Norris Robert, carpenter
O'Donnell P, store keeper, K P
O'Neil Richard, keeper, K P
Paine John, mason
Paine Thomas, keeper, K P
Porter Andrew, laborer
Porter Wm. laborer
Potter Joseph, gardener
Priestly Robert, keeper, K P
Rugh Thomas, tinsmith
Quinn Patrick, hotelkeeper
Redmond Patrick, keeper, K P
Roach John, laborer
Seally John, guard, K P
Schroder James, J P
Scobell S W, accountant, K P
Sexton George,
Seymour Isaiah, carpenter
Shine Henry, carpenter
Short James, hotelkeeper
Smith Thomas, keeper K.P.
Stewart James B., engineer
Stewart John, carpenter.
SULLIVAN WM., deputy warden Kingston Penitentiary
Swift John, messenger K.P.
Tait Adam, laborer
WALKEM JOSEPH, (Walkem & Walkem,) barrister
Weir James, steward K.P.
Welch Lawrence, keeper K.P.
Wishart John sr, carpenter
Woodhouse Henry, keeper K.P.
Woods William, laborer

Railton—A Village in the Township of Loughboro ; 18 miles from Kingston.

Carey Patrick, cheesemaker
Dwyer Mrs John, P M
Healey James D, cheesemaker
Keys Michael, weaver
McWilliams rev C A, R C
Maverty Alex, teacher
Mullen Arthur, carpenter
O'Brien Martin, teacher
O'Connor Thomas, cheesemaker
O'Donnell Daniel, blacksmith
O'Reilly James, hotelkeeper

St. Lawrence—A Post Office in the Township of Wolfe Island. S D Woodman, postmaster.

Sangster P. O.—(See Township of Bedford.) James Young, postmaster.

Sharbot Lake—A Village and station of Kingston & Pembroke Railway in the Township of Oso, 48 miles from Kingston.

Charlton Mrs J, P M
Perry Joseph, hotelkeeper
Raycroft James, butcher
Ryan J & Co,
Shibley & Warner, merchants
Stewart Bros, general merchants
Thomson & Avery, sawmillers
Vigneaux Thomas, shoemaker

Sharpton—A Post Office in the Township of Kingston, 12 miles from Kingston.

Spaffordton—A Post Office in the Township of Loughboro, 8 miles from Harrowsmith.

Counter Henry, postmaster
Fillion Edward, painter
Haley Morris, blacksmith
Wood Miles, carpenter

Sunbury—A Village in the Township of Storrington, 12 miles from Kingston. Population about 100.

Gay Robert, merchant and carriage maker
Hall Thomas
Mc Bride John, P.M., merchant
McNeily John, township treasurer
Nobbs George, blacksmith

Tichborne—A Post Office in the Township of Bedford.

Verona—A Village and Station on the Kingston & Pembroke RR, in the Township of Portland, 22 miles from Kingston. Population about 300.

Abrams Howard, hotel
Billmore Peter, cooper
Bradshaw Samuel, merchant
Brown Rev. Daniel
Buchanan George, shoemaker
Campbell John G., miller
Claxton William, M.D.
Drader Nelson, cabinet maker
Grant Alexander, P.M., agent K. & P.RR, and clerk Div. Court
Jeraldine Louis, hotel keeper
Kirkwood Alex., saw mills
Lampson Alvan, merchant
McMullen Joseph, merchant
Smith James, blacksmith
Snyder Jacob, baker
Stedman Wm., merchant
Wager Rev. P., Methodist
Walker Steward, saw mills

Washburn—A Village in the Township of Pittsburgh.

Foster J, miller
McGillivray John, postmaster

Westbrook—A Village in the Township of Kingston in the 3rd Concession, and 3rd and 4th Lots, 2 miles from Collinsby, a station on the G.T.R. Population 100.

Ashley George, hotel keeper
Benjamin George, butcher
Bridge Amos, carpenter
BRIDGE ANDREW, P.M., churn manufacturer and apiarest
Cook John, merchant
Howard Russell, speculator
Jackson William, mason
Knight Henry, horse dealer
Leonard Nathaniel, wagon maker
McDonald Malcolm, blacksmith
McEwen George, blacksmith
Marshall Frank, apiarist

Willetsholme—A Post Office in the Township of Pittsburg. Josiah Abrams, postmaster.

Wilmur P. O.—(See Township of Loughboro.) J K Freeman, postmaster.

Wolfe Island (Marysville).—A Village in the Township of Wolfe Island, 3 miles from Kingston; connected by steamboat in summer and stage in winter. Population 400.

BAKER E J, P M, merchant
Baker Miss, grocer
Bray Henry, fisherman
Brown James, fisherman
Brueland William,
Card Wm B, livery
Cattanach Daniel, wheelwright
Clench James, wheelwright
Connelly Michael, mariner
Crawford Ezra, mariner
Crawford James, blacksmith
Crawford Thomas, mariner
Dickson C. R., M.D.
Doran William, teamster
Davis Gilbert, blacksmith
Davis J. Y., joiner
Davis John, mariner
Davis Richard, butcher
Fitzgerald John
Godfrey Rev. J., Church England
Grace —, shoemaker
Grant O. G., carpenter
Griffin & Taylor, (Edward & Wilson,) blacksmiths
Hatfield T. A., merchant, tp clerk
Hennessy James, fisherman
Hitchcock H O, hotelkeeper
Horne C L, fisherman
Horne George, mariner
Horne W W, mariner
Kelly R J, harnessmaker
Keys & Going (Thos and Shirley), grain dealers
Knapp Jas., laborer
Lanagan Daniel, mariner
Larkin John, fisherman
Lawson D. J., miller
McCaui John, laborer
McClement Miss Edith, teacher
McConville Miss B., teacher
McCormack John, mariner
McCrea Bros., merchants
McCrea George, laborer

McDonald D. L, mariner
McLaren Alex., boarding
Mackey John, hotel keeper
Mackey Thos., mariner
Murphy Miss, grocer
Newell William, mariner
O'Shay Michael, mariner
Oser William, laborer
Pyke David, fisherman
Regan Patrick, laborer
Robertson Charles O., laborer
Rogers James, laborer
Roger Andrew, mariner
Rousseaux Edward, blacksmith
Saunderson Henry, tailor
Shaver Simon
Sluman Gilbert, merchant
Spratt Rev. T. J., Roman Catholic
Trickey Peter, laborer
Troy Patrick, fisherman
Wess Rev., Methodist
Whitemarsh John, laborer

Zealand—A Post Office in the Township of Oso. Willian Armstrong, Postmaster.

W. H. IRWIN & CO.,

Directory Publishers & Publishers' Agents,

HAMILTON, ONTARIO.

City of Hamilton, published every February	$2.50
City of Kingston, published every two years	2.00
City of Brantford and County of Brant	2.00
County of York	2.00
County of Perth	2.00
County of Waterloo	2.00
County of Simcoe	2.00
County of Halton	1.50
County of Wentworth	2.00

Directories of Montreal, $3; Toronto, 3; Quebec, $2,50; City of Guelph and County Wellington, $3; London (Ont.) $3. Sent on receipt of Price.

INDEX OF
Townships, Post Offices and Villages :

	Page.		Page.
Arden	140	Loughboro Township	110
Ardoch	140	Loughboro	148
Ballantyne Station	140	Miller Township	107
Barrie Township	104	Mississippi Station	148
Barriefield	141	Mountain Grove	149
Battersea	142	Murvale	149
Bedford Township	105	Oates	149
Bedford Mills	142	Oconto	149
Bellrock	142	Olden Township	121
Birmingham	142	Ompah	149
Brewer's Mills	143	Oso Township	123
Cananto North Township	124	Oso Station	149
Cananto South Township	124	Osa	149
Cataraqui	143	Palmerston Township	124
Clarendon Township	107	Parham	149
Clarendon Station	143	Perth Road	149
Cole Lake	143	Petworth	149
Collinsby	143	Pittsburg Township	126
D'Arcy	144	Pittsferry	149
Deerdock	144	Plevna	150
Desert Lake	144	Portland Township	130
Elginburg	144	Portsmouth	150
Fermoy	144	Railton	152
Garden Island	144	St. Lawrence	152
Glenburnie	145	Sangster	152
Glenvale	146	Sharbot Lake	153
Godfrey	145	Sharpton	153
Hardinge	146	Spaffordton	153
Harlowe	146	Storrington Township	134
Harrowsmith	146	Sunbury	153
Hartington	146	Sydenham, see Loughboro	
Hinchinbrooke Township	118	Tichborne	153
Howe Island Township	110	Verona	153
Howe Island	146	Washburn	153
Inverary	147	Westbrook	154
Kennebec Township	111	Willetsholme	154
Kingston Mills	147	Wilmur	154
Kingston Township	112	Wolfe Island Township	137
Lake Opinicon	148	Wolfe Island Village	154
Latimer	148	Zealand	155
Long Lake	148		

IT KEEPS THE LEAD.
THE BRITISH WHIG

NEWSY, SPICY, ENTERPRISING.

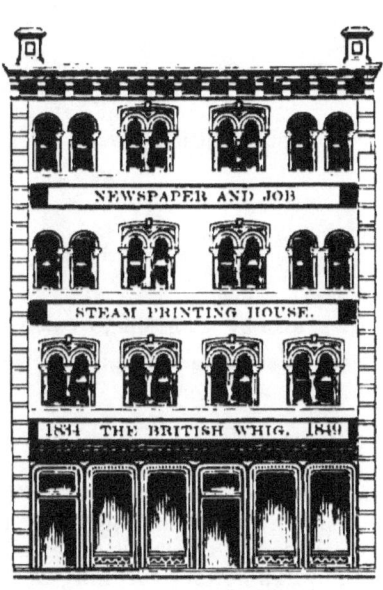

Largest Local Circulation Of both Daily and Weekly.

Handsomest Printing Office in Eastern Ontario. The Best Workmen in every Department. Eight Presses effect the Printing of every Job, from a Mammoth Poster to a Visiting Card, without delay. The largest and most stylish assortment of Type. Large stock of General Papers, Memorial Cards, Fancy Programmes, Bills of Fare, and Cards generally. Bill Heads, Letter Heads, &c., made into Pads.

E. J. B. PENSE, - PUBLISHER.

LAWS

RELATING TO

Building Societies, Loan Companies, Banks and Banking and other Monetary Institutions.

A Compilation of the Acts passed by the Dominion Parliament and the Provincial Legislature, before and since Confederation, on the above Subject.

  This book has been highly recommended by leading members of the legal profession, bankers, and managers of Building and Loan Companies as a handy book of reference, the compiler having in his possession over one hundred letters speaking of the work in terms of the highest praise.

  The volume contains 426 pages, royal octavo, is well printed and handsomely bound.

    Full Cloth $2 00
    Half Cloth (law style).......... .... 8 00

☞ **Orders will receive prompt attention.**

Address

U. S. GARLAND,
Department of Finance, Ottawa, Ont.

www.ingramcontent.com/pod-product-compliance
Lightning Source LLC
Chambersburg PA
CBHW030339170426
43202CB00010B/1170